Ekaterina Markova

Liberalization and Regulation of the Telecommunications Sector in Transition Countries

The Case of Russia

Physica-Verlag
A Springer Company

Dr. Ekaterina Markova
Europäisches Institut für Internationale
Wirtschaftsbeziehungen (EIIW)/European
Institute for International Economic Relations
Bergische Universität Wuppertal
Campus Freudenberg
Rainer-Gruenter-Straße 21
D-42119 Wuppertal
Germany
markova@eiiw.uni-wuppertal.de

ISBN 978-3-7908-2103-1 e-ISBN 978-3-7908-2104-8

DOI: 10.1007/978-3-7908-2104-8

Contributions to Economics ISSN 1431-1933

Library of Congress Control Number: 2008935639

Cover design: SPi Publishing Services

Printed on acid-free paper

9 8 7 6 5 4 3 2 1

springer.com

Table of Contents

List of Figures

List of Tables

Preface

This dissertation was written at the European Institute for International Economic Relations (EIIW) at the University of Potsdam and at the University of Wuppertal and was, at the beginning, connected with the Research Project "Integration of Russia into the World Economy." Financial support of this project by the Alfried Krupp von Bohlen and Halbach-Foundation is greatly appreciated. This dissertation was completed, thanks to the scholarship of the Friedrich-Naumann-Foundation. Many thanks for this financial support and encouragement towards a more liberal way of thinking.

I am indebted to many people for the successful completion of this research work. My first debt of gratitude must go to my supervisor, Prof. Dr. Paul J.J. Welfens. He patiently provided the vision, encouragement, and advice necessary for me to complete my dissertation. I would also like to thank Prof. Dr. Ronald Schettkat for being my second supervisor as well as Prof. Dr. Norbert Koubek, Prof. Dr. Hans Frambach, and Prof. Dr. Hans-Joachim Niessen for being members of the exam commission. I convey my sincere thanks to Prof. Dr. Justus Haucap for fruitful discussions and helpful suggestions as well as for his support during my scholarship time. Thanks go out to my colleagues from Wuppertal and Potsdam: Dr. Dora Borbely, PD Dr. Andre Jungmittag, Jens Perret, Christopher Schumann, Martin Keim, Michael Vogelsang, Dr. Ralf Wiegert, Zornitsa Kutlina, and Edeltraut Friese, who supported me with helpful ideas and discussions as well as provided their morale support. I extend special thanks to my colleague Jaroslaw Ponder, who not only encouraged me to write this dissertation in the first place, but also has been an unending source of fruitful advice and suggestion, as well as constructive criticism. I owe a debt to Prof. Dr. Gerhard Arminger as well as to Dr. Sergey Gelman for their valuable econometrics support. I thank Daniel Nies, Dagmar Cordes, and Ulrike Boller for the editing and proofreading of this book.

I am extremely grateful for the assistance, generosity, and advice I received from Reinhard Wieck and Dr. Andreas Fier during my research stay at the Deutsche Telekom. Their support strongly increased the practice orientation of my dissertation.

Finally, I thank my parents for their love, support, encouragement, and understanding in dealing with all the challenges I have faced. I am especially grateful to my dear spouse Laszlo, who strongly motivated me to finish this dissertation, especially during the last difficult years. Without their help, this dissertation would not have been written.

This dissertation is dedicated to my parents, who always made my education one of their top priorities, and who taught me to never ever give up.

Düsseldorf, July 2008 *Ekaterina Markova*

1 Introduction

"Technology is not kind...
It does not wait...
It does not say please...
It slams into existing systems...
And often destroys them...
While creating a new system"
Joseph Schumpeter

"The experience of transition from centrally planned to a market economy is an historically unprecedented process, and one that is by no means finished in many countries in Eastern Europe and the former Soviet Union."
Johannes F. Linn, World Bank

"You will not grasp her with your mind
Or cover with a common label,
For Russia is one of a kind –
Believe in her, if you are able..."
Fedor I. Tjutchev

The economic and regulatory dynamics in the telecommunications sector is the subject of this study. Telecommunications are increasingly recognized as a key component in the infrastructure of economic development (Saunders et al. 1994, p. 3). The link between telecommunications infrastructure investment and economic performance is well established empirically and is significantly positive (Röller and Wavermann 2001, p. 921).

The telecommunications market as a very dynamic market depends on both innovations and investment in technologies, products and services. A high degree of innovation is the main characteristic of the telecommunications industry and ICT sector, respectively (OECD 2007a, p. 79, 2006, p. 14). The development of new technologies is emerging at a rapid pace. As a result, a high level of investment is required to maintain a modern state of the telecommunications sector.

The two main telecommunications trends, which result from technological development, are obvious. On the one hand, due to technological innovations e.g. voice over IP (Internet telephony), the internationalization dynamics worldwide are intensifying and telecommunications as well as related digital markets are being globalized. (Welfens 2006, p. 5). On the other hand, in 2006, digital convergence, the process of historically separated markets such as voice, data, TV are becoming a single market due to digitalization, is a reality rather than an expectation, thus blurring the traditional definition of the telecommunications market.

For many years, state owned monopolies existed in the telecommunications sector (with the exception of the US, where the monopoly was privately owned).

The main reason for this was the prevailing view that the telecommunications sector, as other network sectors, is a natural monopoly. Many governments often experienced budget deficits and could not afford to cover the needed investment volumes. After privatization and liberalization examples in the USA and the UK (with emphasis on liberalization which is the opening up of the market for competition after 1984) as well as new developments in the economic theory, other countries, partly inspired by the US and the UK, started privatization and liberalization reforms in telecommunications as well. To solve the problem of transition from a monopoly to competition, a regulatory agency, mostly independent from state authority, was established. This agency was meant to carry out the sector-specific regulation of the telecommunications sector. After the establishment of competition, this sector is to be subject to the general law of competition. This was a standard view in 1998 when the telecommunications market in the EU was opened within an EU policy initiative.

Currently, two main directions of telecommunications regulation in the developed world can be observed. In 2005, the US regulator FCC took a course on deregulation in the telecommunications sector by abolishing the mandatory unbundling obligations (FCC 2005). In the FCC's view,[1] these deregulation measures will increase incentives to invest, especially in the high speed broadband infrastructure. The regulation in the European Union is still on the way of unbundling, reflecting the view that the regulatory interventions are encouraging competition, which should be the main driver of investment and innovation in the sector.

The aim of this research is to describe and analyze the strategies for the future developments of the telecommunications sector in transition countries. Rapid globalization processes worldwide force transition countries to build a strong telecommunications sector. A developed telecommunications sector is not only a factor attracting FDI into a country and telecommunications in particular but is also able to invest e.g. in the neighboring countries, increasing a country's competitiveness and welfare (OECD 2007b).

This research work is focused on the strategic developments in the three main directions: privatization, liberalization and regulation of the telecommunications sector. Privatization refers to the degree of state ownership, liberalization to the openness to and actual amount of competition and regulation to state supervision of the sector. Moreover, these processes are investigated in terms of three main telecommunications areas: fixed telecommunications, mobile telecommunications, as well as broadband infrastructure and content. Due to the convergence developments, the borders between these three fields are blurring.

The process of transition from a socialist command system to a market-based economy challenges the telecommunications industry strongly,[2] making the investigation quite interesting in many respects. In transition economies, the telecommunications sector was shaped by a state owned monopoly company, which basically

[1] "Perpetuating the application of outdated regulations on only one set of Internet access providers inhibits infrastructure investment, innovation, and competition generally". Kevin Martin, Chairman of the Federal Communications Commission, News Release, 5. August 2005.

[2] see e.g. Schenk et al. (1997); Von Hirschausen (2002).

provided services to state owned firms in the industry and the services sector, while services offered to households were quite insufficient. As a result, at the beginning of the transition process, there was an enormous excess demand in the household market. Moreover, the transition to a decentralized market economy and particularly also the creation of new firms stimulated an enormous growth of demand in the telecommunications sector. The special focus of this study is laid on Russia, the biggest country among transition countries. The other transition countries are not considered so deeply in terms of the telecommunications sectors but are taken into account in the empirical parts of this investigation.

Investigation of the Russian telecommunications sector was widely neglected in the literature.[3] Russia, as the biggest transition country, still has a strong influence in the region through economic linkages, including significant outward FDI, and old political interdependences. In terms of the macroeconomic indicators, economic development of this country is in the middle between advanced Eastern European EU-member countries and less developed CIS countries. Analysis and investigations of policy options in privatization, liberalization and regulation in Russia may serve as an example for the development of concepts in the other CIS countries.

Russia's territory extends to many thousands of kilometers. However, the biggest part of its population, about 80%, is concentrated in the European part of the country. The Eastern parts of Russia are under populated. Furthermore, Russia has a high degree of urbanization – about 80% of population live in cities. Another important characteristic of this country is its geographical location – more than half of the country lies north of 60° north latitude. This means very harsh weather conditions, for example soil which is permanently frozen to depths as far as several hundred meters. As a result, deployment of some telecommunications technologies may be more difficult. Big distances inside the country should rather increase the role of telecommunications.

The following questions are to be answered in this investigation. The results of Chaps. 2, 3, and 4 provide the basis for the answers to these questions and main conclusion are presented in Chap. 5.

1. What role do telecommunications play in the economic development of transition countries? How strong are the linkages between economic development and telecommunications infrastructure in transition countries? The hypothesis is that this relationship is significant, positive as well as causal because telecommunications are connected to other sectors of the economy through backup and forward-linkages. Moreover, at the beginning of the 1990s, the level of the telecommunications development in transition countries was significantly lower in comparison to the developed economies. This is the reason to assume that that the impact of telecommunications in such countries is much higher.
2. What are the main differences in the telecommunications sector of transition countries compared to the developed countries? The low level of fixed telecommunications and high penetration of the mobile telecommunications are

[3] as exception see e.g. OECD (2002); Dobrovolskaya and Saluena (2004), Petuhova and Vronetz (2000).

very significant factors in terms of the resulting market structures. The country specific regulatory actions have also strong influence on the structures in the Russian telecommunications market.

3. What are the main policy options for the development of the fixed, mobile as well as broadband infrastructure and Internet usage promotion in transition countries and especially in Russia? The differences in the market structures require different strategies in terms of privatization, liberalization and regulation processes. The simple copy of processes should be treated cautiously in the transition economies.

This research work is structured as following. In the second chapter, trends in the telecommunications industry worldwide, in transition countries and in particular in Russia are considered. At the beginning, the structure of the telecommunications industry and its technological developments are presented. Afterwards, the focus is directed towards the state of sector reforms worldwide and to factors influencing reforming processes. One such external factor, WTO regulation of telecommunications services as an international framework for the telecommunications development, is presented. Furthermore, some countries' examples in terms of the sector reforming processes and current states, especially in the regulatory field are considered. Then the initial situation in the transition countries after the socialist command economy is investigated. In the following section, the special focus is taken on telecommunications sector in Russia. Firstly, the development of Russian telecommunications in comparison to the advanced developed transition countries and other comparable countries based on the most recognized international rankings is investigated. Secondly, the institutional structure of Russian telecommunications is described. Then the market structure and main market players are described, following by the in depth analysis of the current state of fixed and mobile telecommunications sectors as well as broadband development, Internet dynamics and Information Society in Russia.

In the third chapter, the theoretical aspects of privatization and liberalization in telecommunications are explored. First of all, the basic definitions of the network industries such as network effects in telecommunications, links between natural monopoly and price setting as well as static and dynamic efficiency are explained. Then the attention is turned towards the concept of monopolistic bottleneck and disaggregated approach, which were and are the theoretical basis for the privatization and liberalization processes. Afterwards, privatization as an economic option to improve performance and to attract investment is considered. Privatization in this work is interpreted in the broader context; this means that all forms of private participation – e.g. management contracts, greenfield projects – is taken into consideration. After the main obstacles for privatization during the transition process are investigated, the attention is directed to timing, sequencing and staging issues in the telecommunications reforming process. Finally, the process of liberalization in telecommunications is reflected upon. Restructuring, as an element of liberalization, is described and liberalization of market entry and price liberalization including cross-subsidizing mechanisms is scrutinized.

In the fourth chapter of this research, the theory of network regulation is studied, focusing on the one hand on classical topics in the normative regulatory theory. The topics include price regulation of the retail prices through rate-of-return regulation vs. price-cap regulation, access/interconnection regulation based on backward-looking and forward-looking cost-based pricing as well as regulation of universal services and service quality. On the other hand, the positive theory of the regulation is taken into account and issues of regulatory capture and institutional design in the transition economies are discussed.

In the fifth chapter of this work, linkages between economic development and telecommunications in transition countries are investigated empirically, finding a positive and significant influence of telecommunications infrastructure stocks on countries' economic developments. Then policy options for the Russian telecommunications sector are studied based on the country-specific conditions. Modernization of the fixed telecommunications sector includes such topics as efficiency through privatization, liberalization and tariff rebalancing, increasing of teledensity and universal services program, self-selective packages and private public partnership, investment in the next generation infrastructure and regulatory positions concerning VoIP. Afterwards, the mobile telecommunications sector is examined. The claim that mobile telecommunications is bridging the digital divide in transiton economies is studied empirically. Moreover, the instruments for stimulating of mobile diffusion in Russia are investigated. Futhermore, the broadband infrastructure and broadband content are studied from the demand and supply side, providing broadband profile for Russia with its strengths and weaknesses. The international experiences are used providing the basis for policy options. Finally, the consequences of posive theory of the regulation in Russia are investigated and issues of institutional modernization are presented.

The study is concluded with a summary of the main findings and opening the horizon for further research work.

2 Trends in the Telecommunications Industry Worldwide, and in Russia in Particular

The telecommunications industry is in a state of transformation and becoming ever more complex. Fast changes in the communication landscape, resulting from technological change and the development of new services, are affecting the core business of telecommunication operators. The industry is to refocus on emerging higher value-added services, which often require significant investment in new network technologies, and balancing this against shareholders' focus on shorter-term performance (OECD 2007a, p. 18).

The following main trends are evident in the telecommunications sector:

1. Convergence of traditionally different technologies and industries resulting in the blurring of market definitions: Primarily, the word "convergence" was used to describe a wide range of phenomena from the increased interaction of complementary technologies (e.g. fixed and mobile) to the use of a single network to carry a range of media such as communications and entertainment. In 2006, one distinguishes not only technological convergence but also Industrial convergence when industries with different backgrounds are competing in new markets as a result of common platforms, networks and services with similar functionalities (EC 2006). This happens both at the horizontal level, where traditionally separated industries compete with each other, e.g. cable and telecommunications operators offering VoIP, and at the vertical level, where new partnerships emerge, bringing about the need for new business models and sometimes trends towards vertical integration e.g. application providers' or end-user device producers' move to adjacent areas. As a result, it is obvious that bundling offers should be provided by a telecommunications operator to sustain in the current competitive environment. Furthermore, for a successful telecommunications operator it is not enough to offer only bundling offers. Business expansion through M&A domestically and internationally as well as gaining entry into adjacent areas, e.g. into mobile advertising, are required to ensure competitiveness.
2. Increasingly global nature of some types of technology services: Increased penetration of broadband provides a platform for services to be sold on a global basis. This phenomenon challenges the regulatory framework, especially the need to regulate at a retail level. In Europe, industry globalization stimulates the discussion about the necessity of a single European telecommunications regulator.[1]
3. Movement towards using Internet Protocol (IP) in the transmission of all services, together with all the benefits (and problems) that it provides: Telecommunications operators around the world are replacing the multiple networks

[1] "...a symbol for the single market for telecoms is the creation of the new European Telecom Market Authority which will be an integral part of the reform package" Viviane Reding, Speech, Plenary meeting of the ERG, Athens, 11 October 2007.

based on legacy technologies with a single network based on an IP core. Market demand on converged products is accelerating this trend.

4. Strong growth in bandwidth demand and challenge of serving that demand with aged infrastructure: The utility of the Internet is currently limited by access bandwidth. The limits of the existing copper access infrastructure have already been reached at some points. Operators around the world are moving to increase the bandwidth through deployment of fiber to the customer premises. These projects are usually very expensive and require a reasonable degree of confidence that the investment will be recovered.
5. Changing structure of the industry, consolidation in some areas and fragmentation in others: Consolidation is often seen as a major force in the industry. In comparison to the US, the European operators are significantly weaker based on subscribers' numbers and revenues. The continuation of the consolidation trends are to be expected in Europe.[2] Regarding the fragmentation, market liberalization and in particular local loop unbundling obligations are a driving force in Europe to increase fragmentation of the telecoms market, which is a potential threat to investment.[3]

All of these trends have an enormous impact on the regulatory implications in the telecommunications industry. In this chapter, the general structure and technological developments in the telecommunications industry worldwide is presented. Then attention is directed to the current state of telecommunications around the world. The reforming processes and their reasons are presented. Furthermore, the WTO agreements on telecommunications, as the main international regulatory framework in this sector, are described. The most interesting examples of sector reforming around the world are explained. In Sect. 2.3, the historical development of telecommunications regulation in the centrally planned system is presented, giving an idea, where the liberalization processes in the transition countries were started. Then the focus is shifted to the Russian telecommunications sector, which is of special interest in this research, and an in depth analysis of the current state takes place.

2.1 Industry Structure and Technological Developments

Historically, telecommunications industry consists of the three following areas: technology, infrastructure/service and application (see Fig. 2.1). In this work, the middle segment "Infrastructure/service area" is of special interest. However, taking into account the rapid changes related to convergence processes described

[2] based on Portel.de, 10.09.2007, http://www.portel.de/nc/nachricht/artikel/15909-arndt-rautenberg-occ-mobilfunk-konsolidierung-in-europa-wird-kommen/12/.

[3] "…we still do not have an internal market for telecoms. The reason for this is mainly a regulatory one: the fragmentation of the internal market into 27 different regulatory systems". Viviane Reding, Speech, 20th Plenary Meeting of the ERG, Brussels, 15 February 2007.

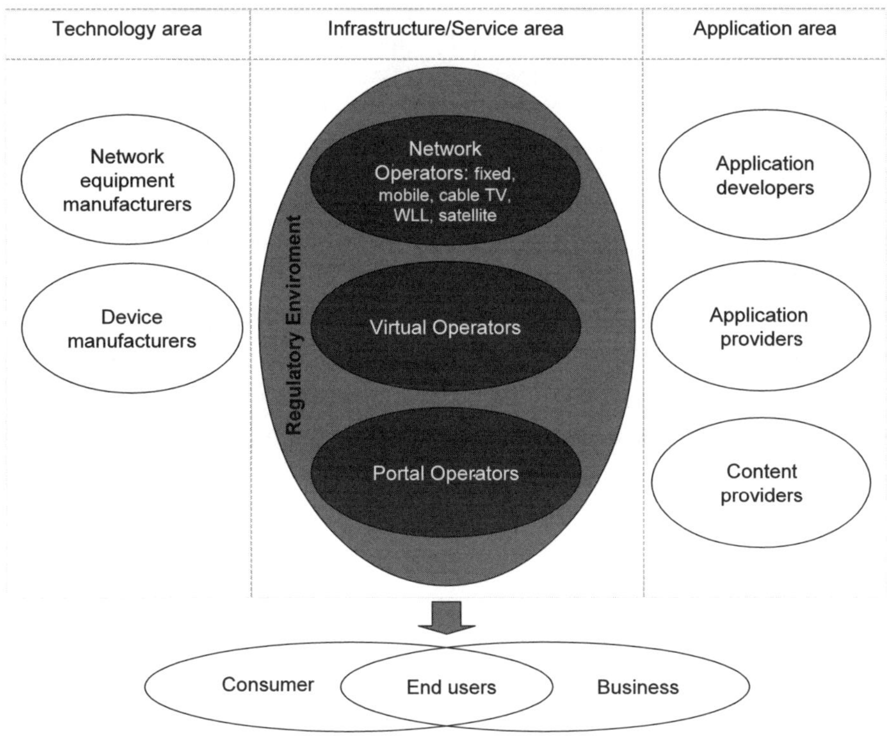

Source: Modified figure from the EITO (2002, p. 205)

Fig. 2.1. Key players of the telecommunications industry

at the beginning of this chapter and blurred boundaries of traditional telecommunications industry (e.g. Aldi, retailer chain in Germany, is at the same time MVNOs on the German market or Disney broadcasting company, which among content provider as well as a MVNO in the French market or outsourcing of mobile networks maintenance by e.g. 3 UK and 3 Italy to network equipment manufacturing Ericsson), the other areas will also be taken into consideration.

Generally, in the telecommunications sector, two levels are distinguished: infrastructure and services, which can be provided on this infrastructure. Telecommunications services differ in intermediates for the other operators and end-customers products. Intermediates are services of incumbent or other operators to operators, who offer telecommunications services to end-customers. These services are often called wholesale services. Intermediates are based on infrastructure availability. The end-customer products are e.g. local, long-distance and international calls as well as access to telecommunications services. This relationship is illustrated in Fig. 2.2 (Kruse 2001, p. 84).

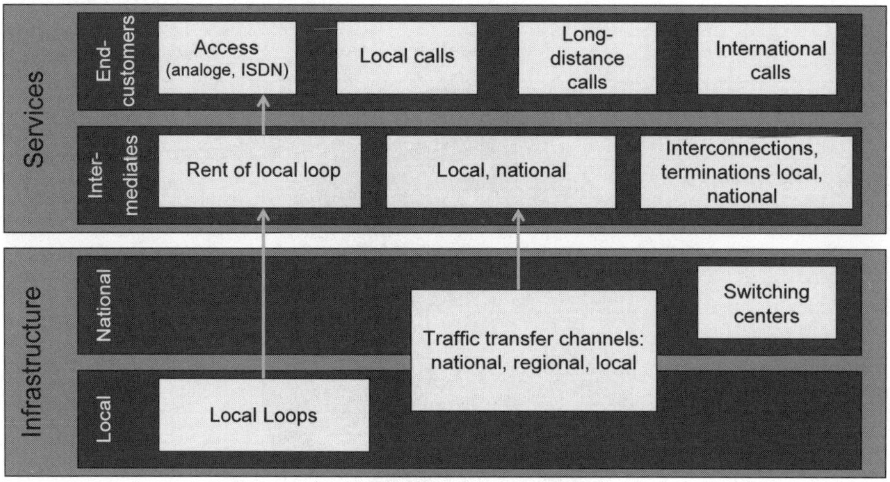

Source: Kruse (2001, p. 84)

Fig. 2.2. Services and infrastructure in the telecommunications sector

The following technological changes are distinguished in the telecommunications sector (EC 2005a, b, pp. 4–5):

1. Increasing bandwidth or data transmission speed in access technologies: The next technologies, developed over the last 15 years, are becoming available: ADSL, cable modem, fiber optic networks, power line communications (PLC), wireless LAN (WiFi, WiMAX), third generation mobile communications (3G), terrestrial radio technologies, satellite, etc. This is the reason for accelerating the migration of customers from narrowband to broadband access. The availability of greater bandwidth triggers the development of new broadband services/content.
2. Development of wireless technologies: Mobile technologies have radically changed the demand structure. The number of mobile subscriptions often exceeds the number of fixed line subscriptions. Moreover, broadband wireless technologies offer broadband access at an increasing number of locations.
3. Integration of services over packet switched transmission networks: Packet-switched networks, compared to circuit switched networks, where a permanent channel or bandwidth is dedicated to enable communication, splits data into packets or cell units for an optimized transmission. This results in the provision over the same network fixed or mobile circuit switched-voice along with packet-switched Internet, video, TV broadcasting depending on the network transmission capacity. Voice transmission is already partly based on Voice over IP (VoIP). In the future, the share of packet-switched voice will significantly increase.

4. Integration of IT and telecommunications technologies: The new generation of telecommunications terminals based on the above mentioned network platforms offer an increasing range of features to the end user. These new terminals, like mobile phones, PDA, TV-set top boxes, game stations, benefit from the important progress made in the field of microprocessors, electronic memories, miniaturization, storage and display technologies.
5. Flat rate connections and bundling offers: Packet switched technologies are associated with the availability of broadband access technologies. Increased customer retention can be achieved through the development of a flat rate connection as well as offering different bundling offers.

In the following, the main current technologies are presented. With respect to telecommunications infrastructure, telephone networks are made up of two main elements: switches and transmission. Switches allow the routing of voice, video, and data signals throughout network. Transmission can be decomposed into wireline (twisted pair of copper wires, coaxial cable, fiber optic etc.) and wireless (via satellite, cellular radio, microwave, personal communications services (PCS)). The benefit of wireless technology, compared to wireline transmission, is the mobility factor; however, wireless equipment, especially for advanced services, is quite expensive. Moreover, a wireless network is more sensitive towards interference and faces bandwidth problems.

The second important characteristic of a telecommunications network is its speed (or bandwidth), measured in bits per second. Based on this characteristic, there are narrowband and broadband networks depending on the connection speed. The border between these two networks is not well defined. Many attempt to associate broadband with a particular speed or set of services, but in reality the term "broadband" is more of a moving target. However, it is generally recognized that today's dial-up Internet speeds, topping at around 56 Kbp s^{-1}, are not broadband connections. But beyond that there are quite different views. The FCC has defined broadband as starting at 200 Kbp s^{-1}, the OECD at 256 Kbp s^{-1}, the ITU considers a network whose capacity, both up and down, sums to 256 Kbp s^{-1} or above (Best and Pehrson 2005, p. 4). Due to the fact that current debates are first of all dealing with broadband deployment, we will consider broadband technologies in detail.

- *Wireline Networks*

The basic network is the public switched telephone network (PSTN). As a rule, the competitive entry first takes place in the long-distance segment. The local loop of the PSTN still quite widely perceived as a bottleneck. Some elements of the local network, such as the link close to customer premises, require essentially fixed costs. Because these elements are crucial parts of network, lawmakers and regulators have been preoccupied with the access of all telecommunications actors to these (Laffont and Tirole 2000, p. 12).

The general representation of the local loop is given in Fig. 2.3. The individual connections from the interface at the customer premises form the distribution plant. The cost of the distribution plant is by and large non-traffic sensitive.

This means that at current usage level it does not vary much with the customer's telecommunications usage. The feeder plant gathers the lines of the distribution plant and consists of concentrated bundles of cables that terminate at the central office. The feeder plant exhibits "economies of shared plant" and it too is rather traffic insensitive. As a result, the cost of the transmission from the customer to the switch (the local loop) is non-traffic sensitive. It involves (large) fixed costs and no marginal costs.

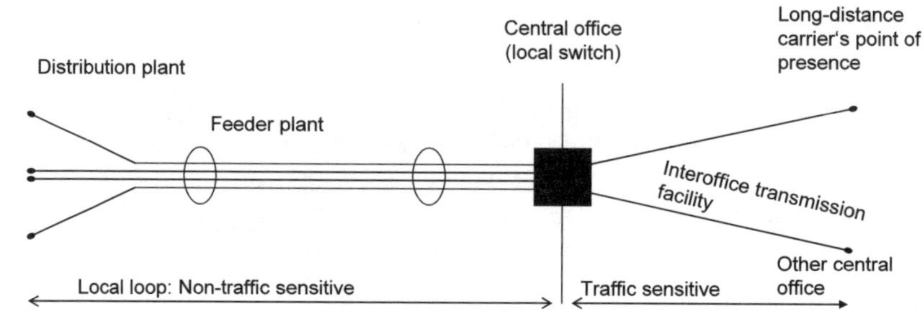

Source: Laffont and Tirole 2000, p. 13

Fig. 2.3. The old-fashioned local loop

Then the first switch follows. Part of the costs of the central office is non-traffic sensitive (e.g. existence of office, design of software); part depends on the number of connecting lines; and the third part (the switches themselves) varies with volume and is thus traffic sensitive. Then further transmission facilities take the call from the central office to a long-distance carrier or to another switch in the local area. There is a trade-off between the number of central offices and the costs of the distribution and feeder plants.

Cable, Hybrid Fiber Coaxial, and Fiber networks also present wireline networks and are considered below.

a. Upgrades to PSTN: Dial-up and ISDN

Since the 1920s, traditional wireline transmission technology has meant the twisted pair of copper wires, which still connect the customer premises to a remote terminal or a central office (first switch). Copper wire pairs are well suited to carry voice, but they have rather limited capacity. However, due to high teledensity in developed countries, PSTN has long served as a primary access network to the Internet, through dialup modems or leased telephone lines. Data rates vary between 2.4 and 56 Kbps per connection depending on the quality of the analogue copper telephone line, whether or not the network operator's central office switch is digital, whether the switches are clock synchronized, and whether the switches are connected via modern media like fiber or microwave.

Another possibility to increase capacity of PSTN network was upgrade to ISDN. This requires a digital network to the user premises, and thus investment in equipment both at the central office and at the user end. According to the cost assessment, if already installed, ISDN is still an alternative for Internet access in areas where more advanced services such as DSL, cable networks or fiber networks cannot be used. However, if ISDN is not already installed, DSL appears to be a better investment since it facilitates cheaper and higher quality broadband service. ISDN and some DSL systems are not designed to be used over the same infrastructure. Users that have upgraded from PSTN to ISDN may have to downgrade again, before upgrading to DSL. The ISDN equipment supports automatic opening of new channels as needed when the traffic increases, thereby providing from 64 to 1.5/2 Mbps connections.

Even in the best of circumstances with 56/64 Kbps maximum bandwidth per connection at voice tariffs, dialup systems or ISDN systems are not able to offer competitive broadband services.

b. Digital Subscriber Line (DSL)

DSL includes a family of technologies which provide a digital connection in an unused part of the frequency spectrum of the copper wire subscriber line in the telephone network. This technology provides a significant enhancement of the installed PSTN base and protects the value of the copper network. Usually, this is accomplished by installing a simple remote DSL unit at the subscriber's site and a DSL rack at the central office building. In this basic configuration, the system is rather simple and economical, as it is not necessary to deploy new access lines (EITO 2004, p. 100).

The bandwidth that DSL systems can provide has been increasing and there are now systems installed that can provide 256 Kbps–1.2 Mbps upstream and 512 Kbps–28 Mbps downstream. The limits are set by the attenuation of signals at higher frequencies, which depends on the quality of the copper lines and their installation. The distance between the subscriber and the exchange usually has to be in range 0.3–5 km, depending on data rates.

ADSL (Asymmetric Digital Subscriber Line) is the most widely deployed DSL technology, where the data channels use one frequency band for a low speed upstream channel (25–138 KHz) and another for a high-speed downstream channel (139 KHz–1.1 MHz). Data transmission speeds vary mainly based on the distance between the subscriber and the central office. Some users cannot be reached by ADSL due to their distance from the central office. In Denmark in 2004, for example, about 5% of households could not be reached by any ADSL services and only 70% of the population could access a 2 Mbps connection. More recent ADSL standards, such as ADSL2 and ADSL2+ promise improved capacity and coverage.

VDSL (Very high-rate Digital Subscriber Line) is similar to ADSL but optimized for shorter distances, 300–1,500 m. Existing systems offer capacities up to 52 Mbps by including more high frequency bandwidth in the copper cables and by deploying more efficient modulation. To extend the range, VDSL requires deployment of a fiber optical backbone network to the curb, block or neighborhood (street cabinet), and a power supply for the street cabinet, which is not required by PSTN. This increases deployment costs significantly. It has also other limitations, including interference from ADSL and AM radio services. VDSL2, a standard under development, promises to achieve bit rates of up to 100 Mbps.[4]

c. Cable TV Networks

Cable TV (CATV) networks use coaxial cable, initially only for distribution of TV-channels in a tree-structured network created by using passive splitters, to reach all users in a point-to-multipoint topology. Broadband communication over cable TV networks is accomplished by transferring data full duplex via unused bandwidth in the cable, similar to what DSL does over PSTN. The standard is "Data over Cable Service Interface Specification" (DOCSIS). The basic data rates are 54 Mbps downstream and 3 Mbps upstream. An Internet Service Provider (ISP) connects to the cable company central office (known as the head end by CATV operators) and uses the cable network to connect to users.

Like in the DSL case, equipment has to be installed both on the operator side and at the customer premises. On the operator side a cable modem termination system (CMTS) is installed that separates the digital communication channel from the CATV circuits, aggregates connections from different users and feeds them into the ISP network. On the user side, a splitter and a cable modem (CM) must be installed. The splitter divides the incoming signal between the TV set and the cable modem. On the other side of the modem, the user can connect a computer or a residential gateway via an Ethernet port and a USB telephone connecting to a Voice over IP service, if provided by the ISP.

From an economic point of view, broadband over cable is favorable in areas where there is already an existing cable network. The tree-structured point to multi-point technique has, however, several severe disadvantages compared to point-to-point solutions:

- For the regulator, it is less attractive since it has a lock-in effect by preventing local loop unbundling on the physical and link levels.
- For the operator, it is more complex to plan, manage and upgrade.
- For the user, the performance depends on traffic from other users due to sharing without traffic control of individual connections. Users in a neighborhood (typically, 100–2,000 homes) share the available bandwidth provided by a single coaxial cable line. Therefore, connection speed can vary between 10 Mbps and a few Kbps depending on the traffic from other users. While most networks share a fixed amount of bandwidth between users, cable networks generally spread over larger areas and require more attention to such performance issues.
- The broadcasting technique also raises concerns regarding security and privacy. To address these concerns, the DOCSIS standard includes encryption and other privacy features that are supported by most cable modems.

[4] VDSL projects are introduced by many telecom operators around the world. The driving force for implementation of this innovation is relatively long distances between customers and the first switch.

d. Hybrid Fiber Coaxial Networks

Hybrid Fiber Coaxial (HFC) is a network integrating a conventional coaxial cable network, and fiber optic cables between the head end and the curb, block or neighborhood interfaced by converters. An HFC network may carry a variety of signal types, including analogue TV, digital TV, telephone, and data. It increases the competitiveness of the cable operators industry in a similar way as the PON (Passive Optical Network) reinforces the wireline operator industry.

e. Fiber Networks

The technologies described thus far are primarily dedicated to other services and have to be modified to provide broadband Internet access. In this section, a closer look is taken at fiber technology, which is deployed primarily for broadband access. In the developed countries, where the legacy infrastructure is well developed, current debates are going about whether optical fiber should be deployed from carrier directly into the home (Fiber To The Premises also called as Fiber To The Home) or to within several hundred feet of the home or office. Here the optics are converted into electronics for delivery into the premises, typically using DSL (Fiber To The Curb or also called Fiber To The Neighborhood and Fiber To The Node). Due to the cost advantages, many developed countries decided to deploy the second group of fiber technologies.

The countries, where there is the lack of legacy infrastructure, can clearly turn this aspect into strength in the form of leapfrogging by coordinating fiber deployment with other infrastructure programmes, especially extensions of the power grid (as power and ICTs mutually boost each other's market), as well as along railways, pipelines and roads. Many developing countries have in recent years developed such strengths, including political awareness manifested in national ICT policies and National Information and Communication Infrastructure (NICI) plans. The availability of infrastructure creates new opportunities, where the regulatory environment allows those who recognize these opportunities to act.

An optical fiber is a hair-thin thread of glass that transports light waves with very low diminution over long distances. Fiber is deployed in cables. Standard cables contain 24, 40 or 96 fibers. Cables can be deployed under ground in conduits, under water as submarine cables or hanging in poles or pylons. The cost of deploying fiber is mainly associated with the extent of the civil engineering work involved. The marginal cost of adding more fiber cores in a cable is generally very low compared to the costs associated with deploying other infrastructure.

Power utility companies deploy fiber, primarily for supervision, control and data acquisition (SCADA) of the power grid, but are increasingly adding more fiber at a very low marginal cost to lease to others. These companies normally use a special ground wire with a fiber cable in the core (optical power ground wire, OPGW) in green field installations or wrap fiber around the transmission lines in brown field installations (known as SkyWrap). Thus, every power grid substation, including in rural and underserved areas, becomes a point of presence for access to fiber.

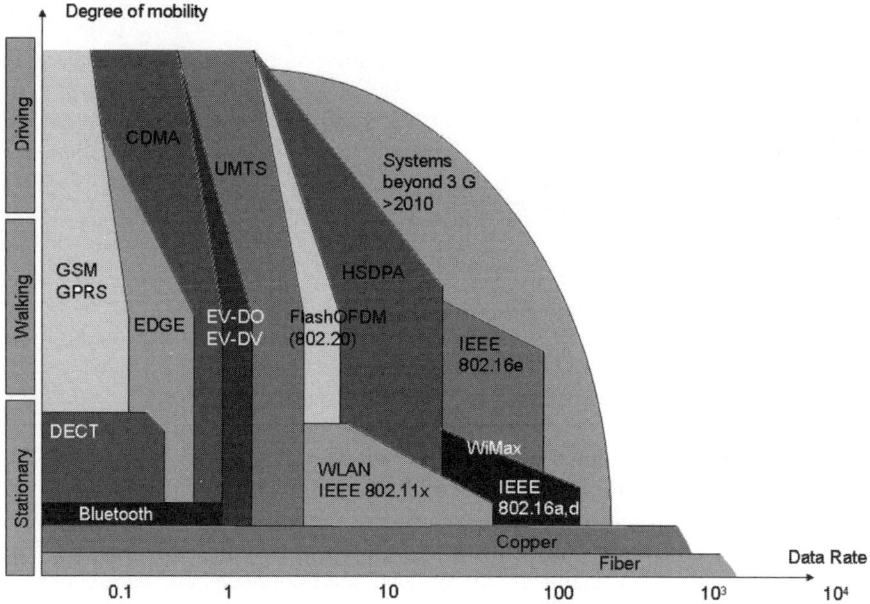

Source: Best and Pehrson (2005, p. 42)

Fig. 2.4. Degree of mobility vs. user data rates for the broadband wireless access

- *Wireless Access Networks*

Wireless access networks can be divided in two main areas: mobile networks, focusing mostly on mobility moving towards high capacity and the data networking sector, offering fixed wireless solutions moving towards mobility. Fig. 2.4 provides a picture of this current development.

a. Mobile Networks

Cellular telephone technology was a major improvement in mobile communications because it introduced the concept of reuse of the same frequencies in multiple geographical areas, called cells. The principle of frequency reuse realized through low powered mobiles and radio equipment at each cell site, permits the same radio frequencies to be reused in different cells, multiplying calling capacity without creating interference. This method is more spectrum efficient than earlier mobile systems which used a high powered, centrally located transmitter, to communicate on a small number of frequencies. As a result, channels were monopolized and not re-used over a wide area.

Complex signaling routines handle call placements, call requests, handovers, or call transfers from one cell to another as well as roaming, moving from one carrier's area to another. There are three common technologies used by the cellular radio systems for transmitting information: frequency division multiple access (FDMA), time division multiple access (TDMA), and code division multiple access (CDMA). The FDMA separates the spectrum into distinct voice channels by splitting it into uniform chunks of bandwidth and used mainly for the analogue transmission. The TDMA and the CDMA are used for the digital transmission. The former segments a single channel into time slots, carrying specific information. Rather than using a unique channel for a call, as does TDMA/GSM, CDMA instead uses all the available frequencies for a given call. This technology is somewhat similar to packet switching in which a voice call (or data) is divided into individual packets, sent over available frequencies, and then reassembled for transmission to the other party. CDMA has greater capacity potential than TDMA/GSM with an increase of about three times that over GSM. CDMA also has superior handoff capability when a user transits from one cell to the adjacent cell. When a GSM customer changes cells, the customer typically receives a new frequency channel. CDMA uses a 'soft' handoff when for a period of time the customer uses both the previous and future cells. This feature has increased importance in data transmission where file transfers can become corrupted more easily with TDMA (Hausman 2002, p. 566).

The original radio technology used in cellular was analogue technologies. There were many different mobile network systems such as NMT, AMPS, ETACS.[5] The former were used primarily in Scandinavia, some European countries, including Russia and Poland, the Middle East and Asia, in the 450 MHz frequency rage. The AMPS was used in the USA, Latin America, Australia, New Zealand and partly used in Russia, in the 800 MHz frequency rage. ETACS were used in Europe and Asia-Pacific.

In Europe, a patchwork of analogue systems ETACS (and TACS) was hitting the capacity and interoperability wall (Belk 2004, p. 5). The European wireless network operators agreed to implement the GSM, first digital technology, operating in the 900 MHz and were preparing for full commercial deployment of GSM. This cellular technology is still the most implemented in Europe. In opposite to this decision the USA did not adopt a common standard of the second generation technologies. One group of the companies adopted the TDMA standard, the other group adopted CDMA. The lack of standardization influenced the diffusion process ranking the USA in terms of penetration rates behind Europe. The last two standards were also used in Latin America, New Zealand, parts of Russia and Asia-Pacific. In Japan the PDC digital standard was implemented. All digital networks standards mentioned in this section usually belong to the second generation (2G) mobile systems technology.

The third generation (3G) mobile systems technology offers an increase in data transfer speed that it is very important considering the constantly increasing volume of data in mobile services. The ITU developed the concept for the IMT 2000 as a global standard for 3G wireless communications. IMT 2000 gives the capability of providing value added services and applications on the basis of a single standard. IMT 2000 is characterized by, first, flexibility through the supporting of a wide range of services and applications accommodating five possible radio interfaces (W-CDMA, CDMA 2000, TD-SDMA/UTRA TDD, UWC 136/EDGE, DECT) based on three

[5] Traditionally, all analogue mobile standards are called the first generation network (1G).

different access technologies, second, affordability for the consumers and operators, and third, compatibility with the existing system and modular design system for easy expansion (ITU 2003, p. 15). Figure 2.5 shows the ways of transferring the mobile system of second generation (2G) technology to the third generation (3G).

The CDMA 2000 technology can be considered to be an upgrade to the existing IS-95 (CDMAone) systems. IS-95 network operators will be able to convert existing systems from IS-95 to CDMA 2000 by installing new cards in their current base stations. They do not have to invest in totally new equipment (MASSON 2000, p. 8). The new coding format for packet data 1xDO requires one IS-95 channel and is allowed to increase data capacity even up to ten times compared to CDMA 2000 and six to ten times compared to IS-95. Future versions of this will be capable of data and voice (1xEV-DV).

The W-CDMA (or UMTS) is a system designed for use in a new spectrum, typically the new IMT-2000 band. It will require major new equipment installation by the network operators. TD-SCDMA is an alternative candidate for using unpaired spectrum allocations, which was proposed in China due to its large population.

On the evolutionary path between W-CDMA and GMS lie the mobile technologies standards of the 2.5 generation. GPRS, based on the GSM, allows information to be sent and received across a mobile telephone network standard, by using the packet switching which enhances the spectrum efficiency. GPRS allows achievement of the theoretical maximum speeds of data transfer, up to 171.2 kbps.

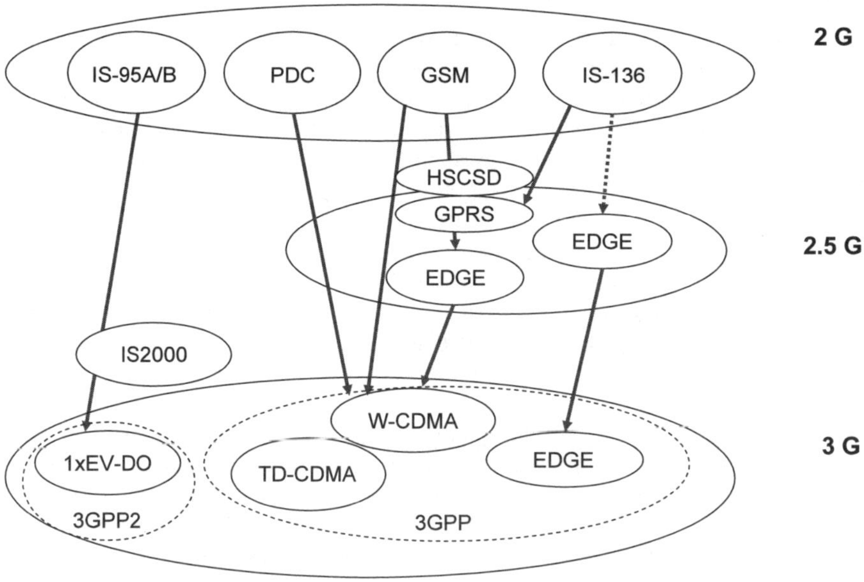

Source: Masson 2000, p. 15

Fig. 2.5. Second to third generation migration

EDGE can be deployed as well on mobile networks that are based on the TDMA access standard. EDGE is a mobile technology system that is faster than the standard GSM and GPRS, and uses a new modulation scheme to enable data transfer at speeds up to 384 kbps and uses GSM infrastructure.

At the beginning of 2006, 3G, which most notably UMTS, are the most widely deployed mobile broadband technology with a huge established presence in terms of operators, customer base, brand, deployed based station sites, and backhaul capacity. Standardized by 3 GPP in its Release 5, HSDPA[6] is a tremendous performance upgrade for UMTS packet data, enabling peak data rates up to 14.4 Mbit s^{-1}, although the initial limit is 1.8 Mbit s^{-1}. Latency is also reduced, and spectral efficiency is improved as well.

The progress of wireless communications technology is fast and there is already talk about fourth (4G) and fifth (5G) generations in mobile technology networks, which are entirely packet-switched networks with higher bandwidths to provide multimedia services and lower costs. The speeds of 4G can theoretically be promised up to 1 Gbps. In addition, the 4G networks are characterized by tight network security. There are plans are to implement the 4G network by 2010. 5G is expected to be a more intelligent technology that interconnects the entire world without limits through incredible transmission speed with no restriction for access and zone size.

b. Data Networks

Fixed broadband access has already become an urban commodity in the developed counties, but so far there have been few means of delivering these bandwidth-consuming services effectively and affordably to the significant number of rural and mobile users. Recent advances in e.g. signal processing, radio protocols, and mobile network infrastructure and now enabling the concept of mobile broadband for consumers around the world (Aarnikoivu and Winter 2006).

1b. WiMAX

The WiMAX is a range of technologies including those that comport to the emerging set of IEEE 802.16 standards. WiMAX systems promise to be very high capacity (up to 134.4 Mbp s^{-1} in a 28 MHz channel), travel long distances (50 Km or more), not require line of site, work at vehicular speeds (under the 802.16e extension), enjoy high spectral efficiency (by using OFDM, under the 802.16a/d extension), and be inexpensive (with base stations in the $10,000 range). Many experts talk about WiMAX like a broadband wireless dream-come-true but for the fact that not all of these extensions have worked yet in the real world and all of these desirable qualities cannot be enjoyed at the same time under the same network (e.g. there is not at present a cheap, efficient, high-capacity system that works at vehicular speeds). Nonetheless, WiMAX systems show great promise for

[6] An evolution of the W-CDMA standard, HSDPA achieves the increase in data transfer speeds by defining a new W-CDMA channel: a high-speed downlink shared channel (HS-DSCH) that operates in a different way from existing W-CDMA channels and is used for downlink communications to the mobile.

the provision of broadband Internet services especially in remote areas and especially when fully ubiquitous access and vehicular speeds with seamless handoff is not a high priority.

2b. IEEE 802.20

In comparison to WiMAX, which started as a fixed wireless technology, and which has since been evolving towards the support of mobility (under the .16e extension), the IEEE 802.20 standard originated explicitly as a mobile broadband technology. According to the technology experts, the original mobility design should prove beneficial to the standard (as opposed to trying to add support for mobility onto an existing fixed wireless standard). On the other hand, one significant advantage of the 802.16 family of systems is a first mover advantage and at present receives stronger industry support from major players. Through its recent acquisition of Flarion Technologies and their Flash-OFDM technology, Qualcomm, has just demonstrated its support of the emerging 802.20 standard. This system plans to comport to the 802.20 standard as it is finalized.

Orthogonal frequency-division multiplexing (OFDM) is emerging as a leading technology for providing very high bandwidth wireless connectivity. With increasing wireless service speed, more and more radio spectrum is required. This spectrum is an expensive resource, thus spectral efficiency, the number of bits that can be encoded into a single radio cycle becomes more and more important. OFDM based technologies, including WiMAX, enjoy spectral efficiencies of around 4 bps Hz^{-1} as compared to 802.11d, for instance, which is under 2 bps Hz^{-1}. OFDM works by segmenting available spectrum by frequency and carrying a portion of user data on each of these frequencies. Each of these frequencies is unique and non-overlapping, and thus orthogonal one to the next. This ensures that there is no interference between the various tones. This technique, along with other sophisticated improvements in digital signal processing, has produced an efficient and speedy network technology. Flash-OFDM can deliver to users a capacity of around 1 Mbps downstream and 0.5 Mbps upstream while motionless. While moving at vehicular speeds, available bandwidth is diminished. One significant strength of the Flash-OFDM system is its spectral efficiency at about 4 bps per Hz (similar efficiency is planned for the 802.16a OFDM extension). When spectrum is scarce and/or expensive, this is a great advantage. In some rural and underserved areas where the microwave radio bands are relatively underutilized, this advantage need not be so compelling.

To sum up, it is clear that there are a number of complementary and often-competing standards, standard setting institutions, proprietary offerings, and vendors. While considerable effort is being put into interoperability and merging of these various systems, it is still likely that many areas will have installed a heterogeneous collection of wireless networks. Ongoing research work has been studying ways to integrate across these various network technologies. For instance, the Third Generation Partnership Project (3GPP) has been studying systems to inter-network 3G systems with WiMAX or Wi-Fi networks. Issues have included handoff; authentication, authorization and accounting (AAA); and other considerations.

2.2 Current Worldwide Trends

2.2.1 Sector Reforms and their Driving Forces

In general, sector reform in telecommunications can be measured according to three variables: privatization, deregulation and liberalization. Privatization refers to the degree of state ownership, deregulation to the degree of state supervision of the sector and liberalization to the openness to and actual amount of competition (Vogelsang 2003, p. 313).

Sector reforms can be described by a variety of factors, not all of which need to be sector-specific. If reforms occur in the same sector throughout the world, then the sector-specific circumstances have to be strongly and/or closely interrelated with the non sector-specific factors. The sector-specific factors include the following prime candidates (Vogelsang 2003, p. 314):

- Technical changes in the sector, which are described above, in particular, through digitization (implying convergence of media), cellular technology, fiber optics, and progress in computer technology.
- Demand changes, such as expansion and diversification of demand, an increase in dependence of the rest of the economy on the telecommunications sector and, in particular, the globalization of telecommunications.
- Changes in governance technologies, such as new organizational setups, property rights and incentives. Some of these have been developed in the course of telecommunication reforms and may therefore not have been causes but rather facilitating factors. They include price-caps, interconnection regulation, spectrum auctions, and proxy cost models.

Against this background, the traditional monopoly became increasingly doubtful. The combination of all these developments called for competition as the preferred mode of market organization, because it presumably knows best how to adapt to technical and demand changes and because those changes themselves destroyed natural monopoly properties. The importance of economies of scale and of sunk costs was reduced by the technical and demand changes in all parts of the telecommunication network, at the moment maybe with some exception in the local loop. In the course of globalization of telecommunications, restrictive telecommunications regimes can be bypassed by channeling communication through other countries. All these changes and emerging competition further disadvantaged public enterprises over private telecommunications carriers due to their poor adaptation to competition and changing market conditions. In terms of media and technologies convergence, harmonization of conflicting regulation, liberalization and privatization policies in different parts of the telecommunications sector is required (Vogelsang 2003, p. 315).

Telecommunication reforms took place at different times and in different forms in different countries. Vogelsang (2003, p. 315) insists that the simple explanation for this is that the strength of the underlying reasons for reform differed between countries. However, the other country specific explanations related to the telecommunications sector are also important for telecommunications reforms:

1. The original state of sector governance, in particular, whether the dominant supplier was a private enterprise or public enterprise and the type of regulatory tradition that came with it
2. The state of the country's telecommunications sector reform relative to its peers; in particular, successful reforms in a comparable country (cross-country learning and herding)
3. Sector crisis
4. Change in the composition of potential winners and losers.

The original sector governance is particularly important, because certain types of governance are more conductive to change than others and any sector reforms have to overcome resistance against change from existing institutions. The forces of change have to be sufficiently powerful. This holds, in particular, for public administrations, based on constitutional privileges, public ownership, civil servant status of employees and monopoly provision of services. In competitive markets, many changes occur automatically because market forces put resisters aside. Regulated private enterprises are somewhere in between.

Furthermore, country specific but non sector-specific explanations play a significant role in the reforming process. These may include the following issues:

1. The country's institutional endowment, which includes legislative and executive institutions, judicial institutions, custom and informal norms, ruling interests and ideologies in a country and its administrative capabilities;
2. Wealth, population density, metropolitan centres, country size;
3. Economic or governmental crisis (inflation, unemployment, budget deficits);
4. Change in government with or without a change in ruling ideology.

Another important issue, which certainly has an impact on the reforming processes and was not mentioned above, are international organizations and countries unions, such as WTO, ITU, World Bank, ERBD or European Union. They influence the reforming developments with their agreements, documents, and directives. On the level of the European Union, the European Commission develops the policies on the European level. The EU members have to implement these directives. This has a significant impact on the sector development in these countries. As one historical example serves, the Greenbook on Telecommunications 1987, constituted policy input in the direction of liberalization and contained a series of proposals aimed at the gradual introduction of liberalization. This document gave a strong impulse for the reforming processes in the EU countries. ITU is a pre-eminent intergovernmental organization, where member states, sector members and associates work together to enable the growth and sustained development of telecommunications and information networks. ITU also works to facilitate universal access so that people everywhere can participate in, and benefit from, the global information economy and society – thus advancing the "right to communicat". As an example serve ITU documents in the fields of telecommunications standardization. World

Bank (worldwide) and ERBD (in transition economies) help among many sectors in the telecommunications sector as well to define the right policy objectives and in some cases to finance these plans. The WTO's regulation of telecommunications services has an especially high impact on the telecommunications reforms worldwide and is considered in the next chapter.

2.2.2 WTO Regulation of Telecommunications Services

A special impact on reforming the sector, in developing countries in particular, has been the liberalization agreement of the World Trade Organization's Group on Basic Telecommunications. The WTO Basic Telecommunications Agreement commits the signatories to liberalize basic telecommunications. Originally, 69 countries signed the agreement, but by early 1999, the number was up to 80 of the 132 WTO members. Twenty of these countries, including not only the advanced, industrialized nations but also some developing economies, e.g. Chile, Dominican Republic, El Salvador, and Guatemala, committed to completely open their markets for competition and foreign direct investment (FDI). The other developing and transition countries have embarked on less ambitious reforms. Although, there are many differences in the goals and reform processes, the main direction is unmistakable.

The background for trade in telecommunications services between the WTO member countries are the multilateral trade rules provided in the General Agreement on Trade in Services (GATS). The GATS includes the Annex on telecommunications, which focuses on the specific points pertaining to trade in telecom services, such as access to public networks. After the Uruguay Round, the members agreed to continue negotiations on basic telecommunications with a view to progressive liberalization of trade in telecommunications. Adopted in 1996 and entering into force in 1998, the Fourth Protocol of the GATS (or Agreements on Basic Telecommunications Services (ABT)) provides the legal basis for the annexation of new basic telecommunications schedules to the Uruguay Round services schedules. Signatories to the ABT, as well as countries wishing to join the WTO, must bring their regulatory and licensing practices into compliance with WTO trade rules. One of the main results of the recent negotiations is the Reference Paper, a compilation of regulatory principles considered binding in their basic telecommunications commitments.

The trade rules applicable to telecommunications primarily include the following issues: licensing process, interconnections, fair competition, universal services and the establishment of independent regulation.

Concerning the licensing process, all WTO member states are bound by the "general obligations and disciplines" of the GATS. Three of these are directly relevant to the licensing process:

- Most-Favored-Nation (MFN) Treatment (GATS Article II): a licensing regime must grant market access to operators from a WTO member country on terms "no less favorable" than terms applicable to operators from "any other country";

- Transparency (GATS Article III): all laws and rules affecting trade in services must be published. The Telecommunications Annex specially requires, among other things, publication of all notification, registration or licensing requirements, as well as any other forms of recognition and approval needed before foreign service suppliers can lawfully do business in a member country;
- Barriers to trade (GATS Article VI): licensing requirements must not "constitute unnecessary barriers to trade".

The WTO Regulation Reference Paper, which was annexed to many countries' commitments in the context of the Fourth Protocol of the GATS, binds them to adopt the following two main points, which are directly relevant to licensing:

1. Public availability of licensing criteria. Where a license is required, the following will be made publicly available:
    - All licensing criteria and the period of time normally required to reach a decision concerning an application for a license and
    - The terms and conditions of individual licenses. The reasons for the denial of a license will be made known to the applicant upon request.
2. Allocation and use of scarce resources. Any procedures for the allocation and use of scarce resources, including frequencies, numbers and rights of way, will be carried out in an objective, timely, transparent and non-discriminatory manner. The current state of allocated frequency bands will be made publicly available, but detailed identification of frequencies allocated for specific government purposes is not required.

Concerning interconnection rules, introduced in ABT, there is the informal Reference Paper focusing on this issue in detail. The paper's central principles are non-discrimination, transparency, and the availability of reasonable interconnection terms, including cost-oriented rates and unbundled access from "major suppliers". According to the Reference Paper, a major supplier is a supplier which has the ability to materially affect the terms of participation in the relevant market for basic telecommunications services as a result of (a) control over essential facilities or (b) use of its position in the market. Under the term "essential facilities", one can understand this to mean those facilities of a public telecommunications transport network or service that (a) are exclusively or predominantly provided by a single or limited number or suppliers; and (b) cannot feasibly be economically or technically substituted in order to provide a service. The Reference Paper requires the public availability of the procedures for interconnection negotiations and the transparency of interconnections arrangements.

With respect to fair competition, the WTO Agreement on Basic Telecommunications establishes prohibitions against anti-competitive practices. The WTO Reference Paper requires signatory countries to maintain appropriate measures to prevent anti-competitive practices. These should include in particular:

- Engaging in anti-competitive cross-subsidization;
- Using information obtained from competitors with anti-competitive results; and

- Not making technical information available to other services suppliers on a timely basis about essential facilities and commercially relevant information which are necessary for them to provide services.

Regarding universal services, member countries have the right to define the type of universal service obligation. Such obligations will not be regarded as anti-competitive per se, provided they are administered in a transparent, non-discriminatory and competitively neutral manner and are not more burdensome than necessary for the kind of universal service defined by the member.

Concerning the independent regulator, the regulatory body in a member country must be separate from, and not accountable to, any supplier of basic telecommunications services. The decisions of and the procedures used by regulators shall be impartial with respect to all market participants.

After the general overview of the sector reform and its driving forces including agreements on the international level, the attention will be turned to selected countries and their experiences.

2.2.3 Successful Reform Examples from Selected Countries

For the purpose of this research, two country examples USA and Germany will be considered, giving some insights on the similarities and the differences in the sector reform in the US and Western Europe. Some aspects of the historical development are described. Then the attention is directed to the current regulatory aspects.

2.2.3.1 The United States

Reform of the telecommunications sector in the USA has a long history and was discussed in many research studies.[7] The provision of telecommunications services in the US was traditionally the *de facto* monopoly of the Bell operating companies (BOCs) and was known as the Bell System. AT&T was formed in 1887 and merged with Bell Laboratories, set up by the inventor of the telephone, Alexander Graham Bell, around 1876. AT&T was able to force virtually all of the independent telephone companies to sell their networks through denying access to its network. Soon it acquired all major markets for local telephone service, controlled the interconnections between these markets, and managed the research, development, and manufacture of telecommunications equipment. Only a very limited number of independent companies provided local telephone services in specific geographic regions.

From the late 1960s until early 1980s, AT&T had lost monopoly positions in such areas as production and supply of equipment and customer premises markets. In order to exempt itself from anti-trust actions, it was obligated to provide universal services. Furthermore, in the 1970s, the next step to break the monopoly position of AT&T was to allow entry in the long-distance market. MCI and Sprint entered this market segment.

---

[7] e.g. Welfens and Graack 1996, p. 97; De Bijl and Peitz, 2003, p. 23.

At the beginning of 1984, AT&T's 22 BOCs were divested into seven regional BOCs (RBOCs). Rulings also defined the areas in which the companies were allowed to offer services, known as local access and transport areas (LATAs). The RBOCs were limited to providing intraLATA services and were excluded from providing interLATA services, information services, or manufacturing telecommunications equipment and CPE (although they were able to sell CPE). The seven RBOCs were: Ameritech, Bell Atlantic, BellSouth, NYNEX, Pacific Telesis, Southwestern Bell Communications (SBC), and US WEST. AT&T, one-fifth its original size, offered long-distance and international services and continued to manufacture telecommunications equipment.

By the end of 2006, the US telecommunications industry has seemingly come full circle. There were just three RBOCs still operating – AT&T, Verizon and Qwest – following a series of mergers and acquisitions within the industry. SBC Communications having acquired its former parent, AT&T, kept the century-old brand name for itself. Moreover, in 2006, the FCC approved the merger of AT & T and BellSouth. Verizon Communications swallowed up MCI. Qwest's merger or acquisition deal is not planned at the moment, but one is "likely" in the long term.[8]

Back to the reforming processes, in February 1996, the Telecommunications Act was passed and superseded the 1934 Communications Act. The aim was to provide more relevant regulation to reflect market and technology changes. The 1996 act was supposed to move US telecommunications regulation away from the courts and into the hands of the state regulators.

The Telecommunications Act of 1996 primarily aimed to introduce competition in the local loop, which was still a bottleneck controlled by local operators. The idea was to establish competition not only in the long-distance segment but also in the local telephony market. To encourage this competition, the *unbundling obligations* were introduced. The RBOCs had to unbundle the local loop and to lease parts of their networks to newcomers in the markets. Any services were allowed to be bought for resale at a wholesale discount.

After many court cases and broad public discussion[9] in February 2005, the FCC released a decision on new unbundling rules. The FCC eliminated the requirement to unbundle mass market local switching on a nationwide basis, with the obligation to accept new orders ending as of the effective date of the order (FCC 2005). The FCC also established a one-year transition for existing UNE switching arrangements. For high-capacity transmission facilities, the FCC established criteria for determining whether high-capacity loops, transport, or dark fiber transport must be unbundled in individual wire centres, and stated that these standards were expected to affect only a small number of wire centres. The FCC also eliminated the obligation to provide dark fiber loops and found that there was no obligation to provide UNEs exclusively for wireless or long-distance services. This development is often considered as a course on deregulation in the US telecommunications

[8] Press article "Analyst says no deal linked to CEO's exit", Jeff Smith, Rocky Mountain News, 26 June 2007.

[9] e.g. Alleman and Rappoport (2005).

industry. After this decision, main market players announced high investments in the high speed infrastructure.[10]

The Telecommunication Act of 1996 also required that competition be present in local markets before the Baby Bells were allowed *to enter the long-distance segment*. The RBOCs have been petitioning the FCC to allow them to offer in-region long-distance services since the passage of the 1996 Telecommunications Act, although it was not until December 1999 that the first approval was granted, e.g. SBC Communications received approval to offer long-distance services in selected states from June 2000 and, as of mid-October 2003, was authorised to provide such services in all of its 13 local service areas.

In respect to *universal service obligations,* the Act of 1996 states that "consumers in all regions of the nation, including low-income consumers and those in rural, insular, and high-cost areas, should have access to telecommunications and information services". Due to the structure of the industry in the US, some local operators have to be compensated for providing universal service and a complicated mechanism for the financing of universal services was implemented. One of the universal service mechanism are interstate access charges, which are the rates long-distance carriers pay for the use and availability of local exchange carriers' (LECs) facilities for the origination and termination of interstate service. Interstate access charges were many times modified by the regulator. Another universal services mechanism is support to high-cost areas served by large local exchange carriers (LECs). This funding mechanism provides additional support for local telephone services in many states.

New Telecommunications Bill

Early in November 2005, draft telecommunications legislation was released for review. This new legislation would represent the broadest reforms in the telecommunications sector since 1996 and are designed specifically to pre-empt state regulation of broadband services and – most significantly – make it easier for the RBOCs to enter the video services market. This legislation would treat broadband video as an interstate service under the FCC's authority and require municipal authorities to grant video franchises to telephone companies.

However, this controversial telecommunications bill, opening the way for phone and cable companies to compete on video services, was highly debated, especially on the net neutrality issue (some experts called this debate a civil war) and was not adopted until 2007. Net neutrality backers oppose a plan by high-speed Internet providers to create online speed lanes and give faster service to preferred content providers. They argue that innovations like Internet telephony or instant-messaging would have developed without the freedom people now have. On the other hand is net neutrality opponents' need to prioritize data in order to be profitable. Some experts believe that the potential problems of discrimination among content providers would be eliminated through more competition among broadband providers.

[10] for more details on this see Baumgarten and Markova (2006)

2.2.3.2 Germany

The roots of the German telecommunications reforms go back in the 1960s.[11] Due to some deficits in the early 1960s, the federal government established an expert commission for the German Bundespost to look for the solution. The recommendations of the commission included the following: increasing the independence of the Bundespost and separating its sovereign tasks from its commercial tasks. Only minor organizational recommendations were implemented from these recommendations. The same happened with the recommendations of the second commission report in 1970.

A first official major telecommunications reform proposal came from the German Monopoly Commission in 1981 and focused on liberalization of the telecommunications equipment market. However, little happened in this respect between the time of this proposal and the publishing of the EC Greenbook in 1987. The Postreform 1 in 1989 was implemented based on the suggestions of the Witte Commission. The infrastructure responsibility remained with the state. The universal service policy was based on a network monopoly, which provided financing and cross-subsidization. The Postreform 1 differentiated between monopoly services (telephony), mandatory services (those that Deutsche Telekom had to offer on a universal basis) and free services (that Deutsche Telekom had the freedom to discontinue). A significant reformation was the organizational separation of the post office, bank and telecom as well as the separation of entrepreneurial and regulatory functions. The legal status of the enterprises, however, was not changed. The reform in Germany in this time is in line with, but did not go beyond, the EC policy. Shortly after the Postreform 1, the mobile competition was introduced through the private new entrant, which had begun operations at the same time as Deutsche Telekom.

In 1994, the Postreform 2 followed. It allowed the privatization of the Deutsche Telekom, which was an important step in the reforming process. A special fond was created with the aim to allow the firm usage of public servants as regular employees. From this point in time, the state no longer had to provide telecommunications itself but only had to assure that it is provided adequately. The universal services were now obligated by law. Postreform 1 and Postreform 2 are the basis for the further liberalization and regulatory reforms. The reforming of institutional framework in Germany is characterized by the three following aspects: (1) the relative broad privatization of an ex-monopolist company; (2) the liberalization of the market entry; (3) the deregulation in form of decreasing state interventions.

In 1996, the partial liberalization and privatization of the Deutsche Telekom followed. However, the major further liberalization and regulatory reforms, in the form of the TKG, passed in 1996, was based on the EC liberalization package. The main goal of this EU package is an establishment of national regulators and the opening of voice markets by the beginning of 1998. On the January 1, 1998,

[11] Historical developments of reform in the telecommunications sector are presented extensively by Vogelsang (2003), Dewenter and Haucap (2004) and are summarized in this section based on these sources.

the Regulatory Authority for Telecommunications and Posts, known as Reg TP, came under the Federal Ministry of Economics and Labor (BMWA), which undertakes basic policy tasks. Reg TP had various powers, such as the authority to grant and revoke licenses, assign and supervise frequencies, impose universal service obligations, control network access and interconnection, and approve or review the tariffs and tariff-related general business terms and conditions of market-dominant operators.

The TKG 1996 had to be brought into line with the substantially revised European standards due to the European Union reform package of 2002, which covered all forms of electronic communications services. This process took longer than expected to complete, but the revised legislation, the Telecommunications Act of 2004, finally entered into force on July 1, 2004. In 2005, the Reg TP was renamed the Federal Network Agency for Electricity, Gas, Telecommunications, Post and Railway (Bundesnetzagentur für Elektrizität, Gas, Telekommunikations, Post und Eisenbahnen, known as BNetzA for short). BNetzA took on immediate responsibility for the energy sectors; responsibility for the railway infrastructure market was transferred to BNetzA on January 1, 2006.

In 2007, the TKG 2004 is still in place. It focused on such issues as abolishment of licensing requirements, market analysis and notifications of SMP operators, requirements for SMP operators to offer access to their networks as well as rate regulation for SMP operators especially in respect to access services and facilities. In the following, the main aspects of this legislation and its practical implementations are presented:

Licensing

To follow the EC's Authorisation Directive 2002, RegTP abandoned most of the license requirements of the TKG 1996. However, rights of way for the installation of telecommunications lines still must be transferred by the regulator. Commercial providers are only subject to a notification requirement. BNetzA is able to impose ex post measures in cases of breaches of duty. Such measures range from requiring a company to state its views, issuing orders, imposing financial penalties and, as a last resort, prohibiting a company from providing services.

According to the BNetzA,[12] 2,045 registered operators and providers of telecommunications services were on the German market by the end of 2005, around 2,304 at the end of 2004 and 2,184 at the end of 2003.

Market Analysis and Notifications

Based on the TKG 2004, market regulation must be preceded by market definition (to identify the relevant markets) and market analysis (to define operators with SMP in these markets). BNetzA must give interested parties, the regulatory bodies of other EU countries, and the European Commission (EC) the opportunity to comment on the markets defined and analyzed by BNetzA. The EC has a veto right in respect to identifying relevant markets and determining the presence or absence of SMP. In respect to market regulation decisions or market remedies,

---

[12] http://www.bundesnetzagentur.de/media/archive/1522.pdf.

the EC does not have a veto right. Market regulation decisions are made by the BNetzA's Ruling Chambers. Applicable remedies, resulting from the presence or absence of SMP, are determined by regulatory order rather than deriving directly from legislation.

Until February 2007, BNetzA did not submit two market notifications from the eighteen required.[13] Only in two markets, effective competition was found and in one market, partial competition was established. In other cases, SMP positions were identified and market remedies are adopted. The famous German case in respect to market analysis is the new VDSL network of the Deutsche Telekom, where the German government allowed the BNetzA's exemption of the Deutsche Telekom from unbundling obligations for VDSL fiber network. Due to the fact that the European Union does not have veto power on the national decision, the European Commission is to take the German government to the European Court of Justice (EC 2007, p. 107 in Annex 1).[14]

Rate Regulations

The TKG 1996 postulated that tariffs for the telecommunications services of market-dominant providers and their affiliates were subject to special regulatory oversight and control. The tariff rates of all service providers were subject to European and German laws.

Based on the TKG 2004, rates are primarily regulated for access services and facilities, where access and rates orders are issued together. The cost of efficient service provision must not be exceeded in such cases. The approval of the BNetzA is required to give prior (ex ante) approval to rates for access services that an SMP operator is mandated to provide. Ex post price controls are made, when the operator in question does not also have an SMP in the retail, but which control access to end users (such as alternative access providers).

Concerning retail services, ex ante approval is limited to markets in which sustainable competition is not expected to develop in the foreseeable future. If an SMP company intends to introduce or change the price for a retail service, at the same time it must submit a corresponding wholesale offer to its competitors which satisfies the requirements of anti-competitive pricing controls, to ensure that competitors are able to offer comparable services in the retail market without delay.

Any cases of anti-competitive behavior by a company in levying and agreeing rates are investigated by BNetzA for all non-regulated rates.

Access and Interconnection Rules

According to the TKG 1996, specific obligations concerning access to networks and interconnections are imposed. For example, every operator of a public telecommunications network, irrespective of the operator's market position, is obliged upon request to offer to other network operators interconnection to its networks.

[13] for more details see http://ec.europa.eu/information_society/policy/ecomm/article_7/index_en.htm.

[14] Meanwhile, the BNetzA has already issued legislation, obligating DTAG to provide access to cable tubes.

If an agreement on interconnection cannot be reached, the BNetzA orders the interconnection on other terms.

A market-dominant provider, offering telecommunications services to the public in a particular market, must allow every user access to its network or parts thereof. It must also grant to its competitors access to essential services it uses internally upon the same conditions it applies to itself, unless different conditions can be objectively justified. Agreements on special network access (including interconnection) must be immediately reported to the BNetzA for execution. The regulator publishes the terms and conditions for interconnection agreements. This publication with terms and conditions will constitute a basic offer that must be included in the general business terms and conditions of a market-dominant provider.

In 2001, Reg TP established a new interconnection tariff regime. The main difference here is that operators are charged on the basis of the network elements used (element-based charging), thus replacing the former regime of distance-based charging. In 2003, the Deutsche Telekom was explicitly obliged to allow call-by-call and pre-selection for local calls.

Based on the TKG 2004, obligations concerning access to networks are dependent on market analysis. The BNetzA must explicitly require SMP operators to offer unbundled broadband access such as bitstream access. Until June, 2008, SMP operators are obliged to provide bundled resale (i.e. wholesale line rental only in conjunction with calls). Beginning on July 1, 2008, the regulator can also order unbundled resale.

At the European level, the current Telecommunications Review is ongoing. The new legislation should be published in 2007 and after that, the EU member states have to implement the new EU legislations in their national laws. The discussions during the consultation process are very lively, especially on such issues as regulation and investment incentives, spectrum authorization and trading, market analysis and notifications and possible deregulation in this respect. At the same time, the European Commission is finishing the Audiovisual Service Directive, which will be the new legislation in respect to traditional broadcasting as well as non-linear audiovisual services such as IPTV, Video on Demand. Considering the state of increasing convergence processes, it is expected that this directive will have a strong impact on the industry. The German telecommunications sector, as a part of the European market, has taken an active part in the discussions on the European level to ensure the beneficial implementation of the legislation later on the national level.

To summarize, two country examples were considered in detail: the USA and Germany. The US telecommunications industry has a long tradition in regulation, went through vertical separation in the middle of 1980s, and experienced strong M&A developments after that. The industry consisted of three major companies at the end of 2006 and is still on the deregulation course presented through such actions as abolishment of unbundling obligations or spectrum trading. The German telecommunications industry had to be developed under the EU legislation and experienced both advantages and challenges of this approach. It did not have to follow the vertical separation approach like in the US and due to this fact had intensively dealt with asymmetric regulation. There are many other countries, which experiences are worth attention, e.g. the UK, as the country with the longest liberalization traditions in Europe and its long beliefs in duopoly as the way to industry restructuring. France as a country, which has very successfully implemented the EU unbundling policy; in the Netherlands, where the telcos are strongly challenged by cable operators, an advanced level of competition is present in the market, which keeps the level of regulatory intervention relatively low; Asian countries such as Japan and Korea show very successful developments in broadband. The broadband penetration there is the highest in the world, which success was mostly achieved through state politics and aid (see e.g. Point Topic 2007; OECD 2007a).

2.3 Telecommunications Infrastructure Policy in the Socialist Command Economy

In the socialist system, the definition and the development of infrastructure is very different than in the countries with market economies. The infrastructure development was not subordinated to the requirements of the (profit-oriented) production process for the sake of producing value-added. Its objective was to improve the functionality of the socio-economic superstructures (VNIICI 1982; Tjulpanow 1969, 303ff). The main objective of infrastructure was the reproduction of the labor force. In the Soviet-type system, the notion of infrastructure was very broad and included categories that would not belong to infrastructure in a market economy, such as rolling stock of the transportation system, trade, IT and new technology, storing services and "everyday infrastructure", e.g. shoe repair shops, hairdressers, tailors, photographers.

Generally, the Soviet-type of economy is characterized by the following main principles (von Hirschhausen 2002, p. 31): (1) abandonment of the money-commodity relationship and the "capitalist" principles of "value added"; (2) dominance of the Communist Party in important questions regarding the production of goods (plan) and their distribution (through pricing policies, direct distribution, etc.); (3) absence of a separation between the Party and economic activity; (4) absence of money as a universal equivalent of value. These principles were fully reflected in the Soviet infrastructure policy.

As a result, a telecommunications sector was built, where ownership, operation, finances and control was concentrated in the public hands like in many EU market economies but with a completely different background. The owner of telecommunications infrastructure was the state; other forms of ownership did not exist. The state introduced in the telecommunications sector the plans for the next five years on the local, regional and national levels and controlled these. The planning process was strongly politicized. The communist party used the telecommunications system for controlling and restraining information flows. The telecommunications was not oriented on profits and the cost-profit analysis was not realized in the command economy (Campbell 1995). The telecommunications infrastructure was financed by the state, because private finance activity was not allowed. The biggest part of clients of the socialist telecommunications system consisted of corporations und not of private clients. The quality of the connections was neglected; the telecommunications network used analogue equipment with an average yearly fault rate of about 40 per 100 lines in the first half of the 1990s (ITU 2006a). The average fixed line telecommunications penetration rate was about 15%, making the private ownership of a phone a luxury. According to the ITU Database (2006), at the beginning of 1990s, around 10 million people in Russia were on the waiting list to receive a phone connection. Due to these facts, the Russian telecommunications sector was a public monopoly with lower penetration rates and quite poor performance. However, one must consider the fact that it was under other circumstances as in the market economy. In the organized hierarchically socialist system, vertical communications lines in industry were provided by state telecommunications operators, but the individual horizontal communication links, which are vital for competing firms in the market economies, were quite neglected (Welfens 1996, p. 90).

2.4 Current Developments in the Russian Telecommunications Sector

Before proceeding with the details on the current developments in the Russian telecommunications sector, the attention will be directed to the performance of the Russian economy, the Russian ICT sector, and in particular the Russian telecommunications sector in international comparison. In the author's view, the international ranking studies are the best instrument to assess the Russian performance. Although there may be a certain degree of subjectivity in each ranking method, representations of results from a couple of different ranking studies will provide an adequate overview on the development trends. Investigation is started by considering the Russian performance in terms of macroeconomic developments and the political situation (based on the Index of Economic Freedom as well as partly on the Growth Competitiveness Index), and then the focus shifts to the performance of the Russian ICT and particularly the telecommunications sector (based on the Growth Competitiveness Index, Digital Opportunities Index, Network Readiness Index as well as E-Readiness Ranking of Economist Intelligence Unit). To gain an objective picture, the Russian performance rankings are compared to the performance rankings of the biggest Eastern-European EU countries such as Hungary, Czech Republic, and Poland, other big world economies such as China, India, and Brazil as well as the Ukraine as one of the CIS countries showing a relatively high GDP per capita. According to the Index of Economic Freedom 2006 (IEF 2006), which measures economic freedom worldwide, Russia is ranked 122nd out of 161 countries and categorized as "mostly unfree". Figure 2.6 presents the total score of the index and its sub-indexes in comparison between Russia and other countries.

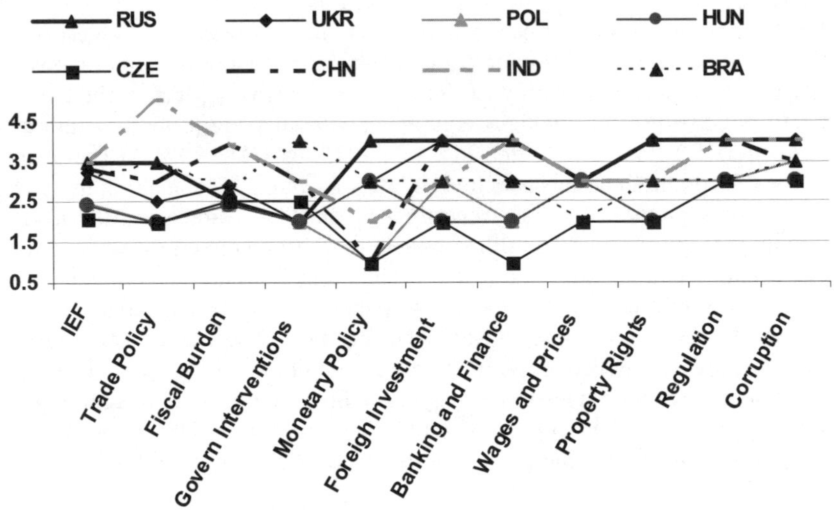

1 = the best, 5 = the worst score

Source: Index of Economic Freedom (2006)

Fig. 2.6. Index of Economic Freedom and its subindexes

In the category "Freedom from Government Interventions," measuring all government expenditures and state-owned enterprises, Russia performs better compared to 2005 and other investigated countries. However, in relation to other sub-indexes, this positive performance cannot be found very often. The most critical index components for Russia are "Monetary Freedom," "Freedom in Foreign Investment," "Freedom in Banking and Financing," "Freedom in Property Rights" as well as "Freedom from Regulation" (or "Business Freedom"), and "Freedom from Corruption" where the Russian scores are weak in relation to the peer group's.

The Growth Competitiveness Index 2005–2006 is a study conducted by the World Economic Forum, comparing 117 economies. The Russian total score and subindex scores are presented in Fig. 2.7. On the background of the relatively high "Macroeconomic" subindex score, Russia has a low score in "Technology" and "Public-institutions" subindexes. Russia ranks 90th in the "Public-institutions" subindex. Figure 2.8 presents the components of the "Technology" subindex. This indicates, on the one hand, the big potential of the Russian science, resulting in the high score of subindex component "Innovations", and on the other hand, the Russian weaknesses in terms of "ICT development" and "Technology Transfer" subindex components. Especially in the "Technology Transfer" category, Russia is lagging behind the investigated countries.

The Digital Opportunities Index from ITU measures the magnitude of the digital divide and has been applied on 40 economies. The structure and the Russian ranks are illustrated in Fig. 2.9. Russia's overall rank is 30. The scores of this index are presented in Fig. 2.10. All Russian score values are under median in

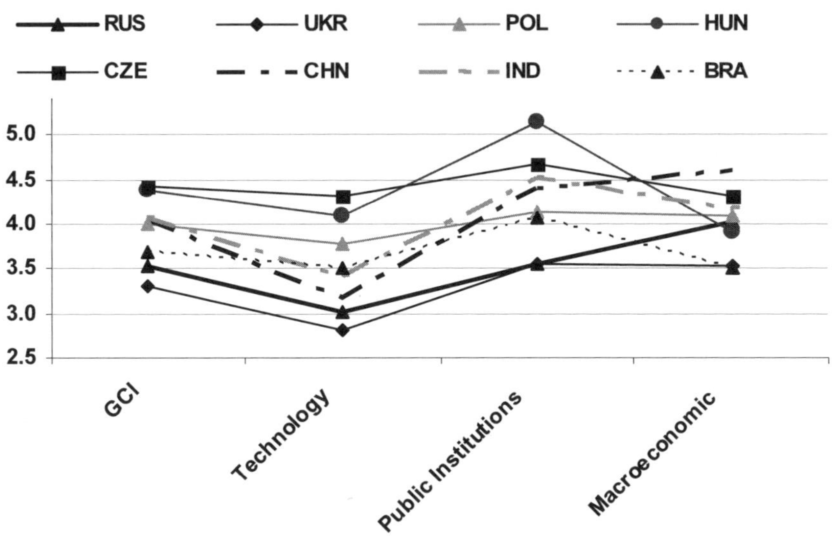

Source: The Global Competitiveness Report (2005)

Fig. 2.7. Growth Competitiveness Index and its subindexes

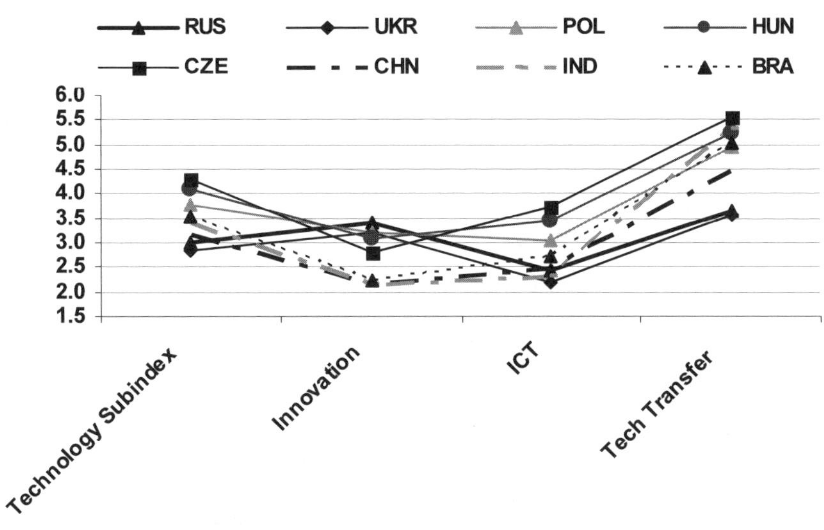

Source: The Global Competitiveness Report (2005)

Fig. 2.8. Technology subindex of the Growth Competitiveness Index and its components

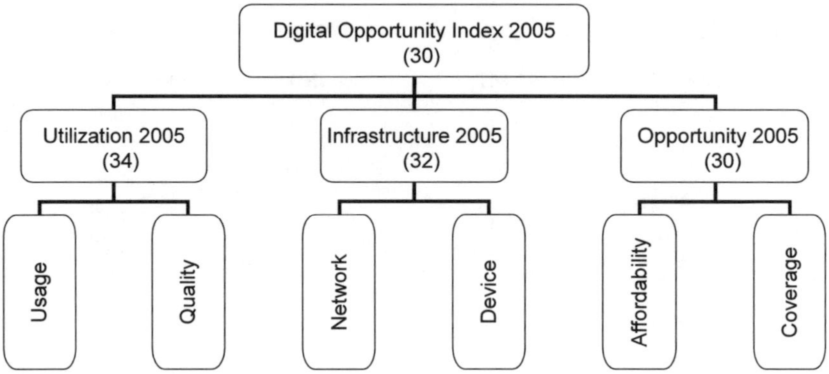

Source: ITU (2006b)

Fig. 2.9. Digital Opportunities Index 2005: structure and the Russian ranks

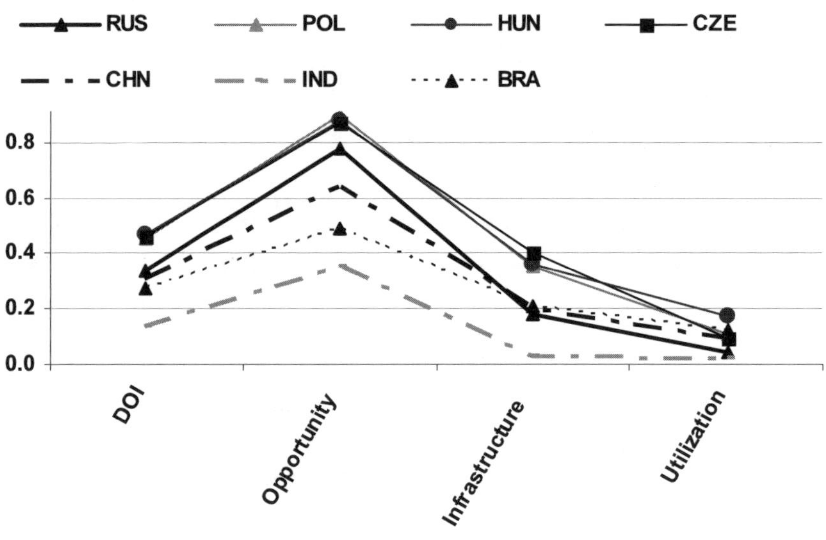

Source: ITU (2006b)

Fig. 2.10. Digital Opportunities Index 2005 and its subindexes

respect to all subcategories. In the subcategory "Opportunity", which measures basic access (reflected by mobile coverage) and affordability of networks, Russia is ranked 30th. The next subcategory "Utilization" shows the extent of ICT "Usage" and "Quality". "Quality" means a level of access, which enables higher degrees of functionality, supporting services such as video streaming. As a result, the number of desirable applications for information society such as telemedicine, e-government, and e-learning enhances, increasing their "Usage." In the subcategory "Utilization", Russia is ranked 34th. Finally, the subcategory "Infrastructure", which includes network indicators and device's availability, providing the interface between users and networks, is ranked 23rd.

The NRI index, covering a total of 104 economies in 2004–2005, measures "the degree of preparation of a nation or community to participate in and benefit from ICT developments." Based on the NRI index, the success of a country participating in and benefiting from ICT can be very well benchmarked. As illustrated in Fig. 2.11, this index is composed of three subindexes, which measure (1) the environment for ICT offered by a given country or community, (2) the readiness of the community's key stakeholders – individuals, business, and governments – as well as (3) usage of ICT among these stakeholders.

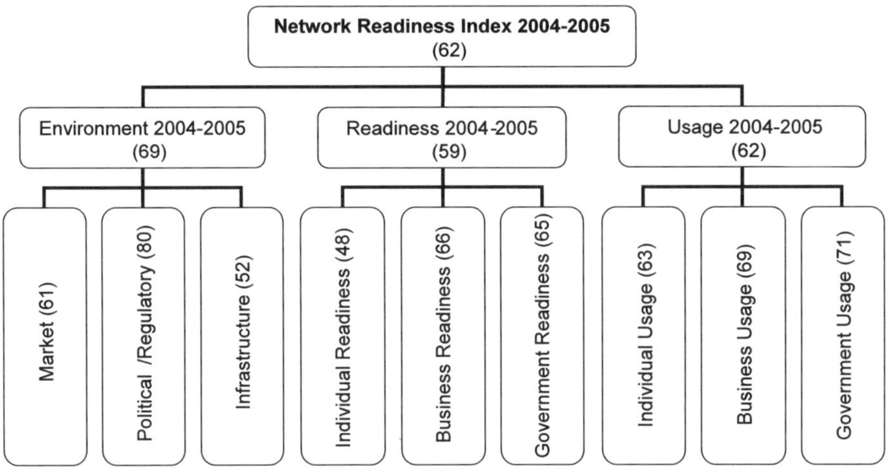

Source: The Global Information Technology Report (2005)

Fig. 2.11. Network Readiness Index (NRI) 2004–2005: structure and the Russian ranks

In order to compare the Russian performance with the performance of other countries, the regional benchmark of the NRI index is considered. As illustrated in Fig. 2.12, Russia's has the scores of the overall index as well as its components are close to the weighted average for Central and Eastern Europe. This is far below the scores of many Central- and Eastern-European countries like Hungary and the Czech Republic but higher than the score of Poland. The low Polish ranking is a controversial issue due to the fact that the other rankings do not prove this fact. The Polish NRI ranking will be presented in this analysis for information only. The most interesting finding from this index is that large countries such as, China, India, and Brazil ranked quite above Russia.

In the following, a closer look is taken at the subindex components of this NRI index. In the first subindex "Environment" (see Fig. 2.13), which measures the environment for ICT offered by a given country or community, the trend that Russia ranks lower compared to Hungary and the Czech Republic can be noticed.

A similar trend is valid in respect to the large economies China, India, and Brazil, with the exception of the component "Infrastructure", wherein these economies are relatively weak.

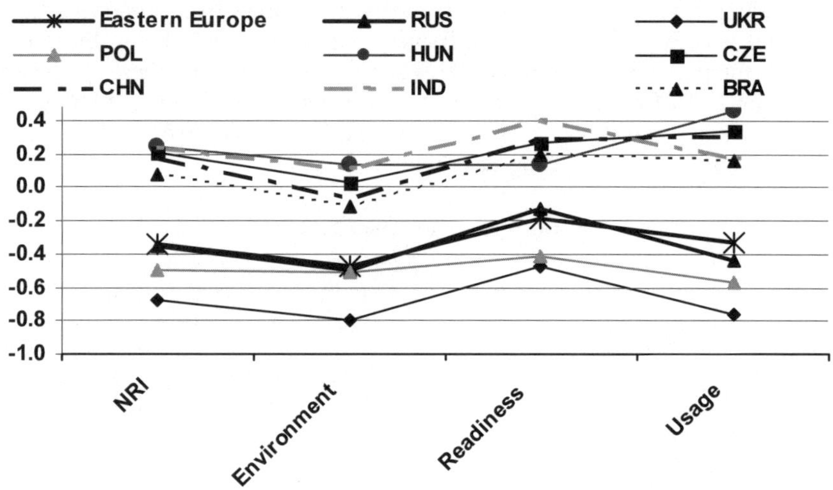

Source: The Global Information Technology Report (2005)

Fig. 2.12. Comparison of NRI 2004–2005 between Russia and other countries

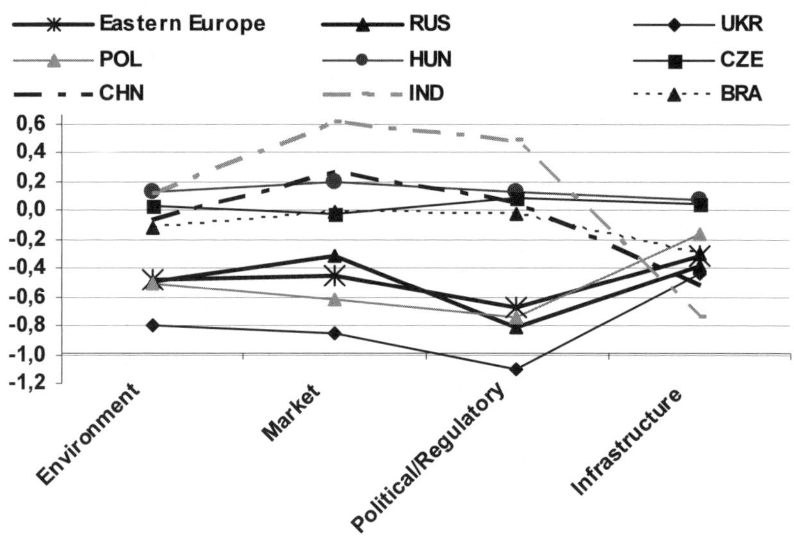

Source: The Global Information Technology Report (2005)

Fig. 2.13. Comparison of subindex "Environment" in NRI 2004–2005 between Russia and other countries

In terms of readiness of the community's key stakeholders – individuals, business, and governments – Russia performs well regarding individuals but shows disappointing results in business and governments (see Fig. 2.14). In respect to readiness and usage of the business and governments, Russia underperforms compared to Hungary and Czech Republic as well as China, India, and Brazil (see Fig. 2.14 and Fig. 2.15).

According to the 2005 e-readiness rankings from Economist Intelligence Unit, which rank the ability of 65 countries to promote and support digital business and ICT technologies, Russia ranks 52nd. This is a higher rank than in 2004, but it still shows the relatively low level of the Russian e-readiness compared to that of other world nations. In "Connectivity" as well as in "Social and Cultural Environment", Russia ranks relatively high, whereas in "Legal Policy Environment" as well as in "Consumer and Business Adoptions", it ranks particularly low (see Fig. 2.16).

To sum up, according to the ranking studies, Russia enjoins high economic growth and relatively stable macroeconomics indicators, however, it has a low quality of political institutions. In the field of ICTs, Russia has a quite developed infrastructure and a higher quality of human capital, which is often reflected by the individual readiness and usage. This is certainly the strength of Russia. On the other hand, policy issues and readiness/usage of the government are insufficient. Based on the fact that Russia is very often lagging behind large world economies like China, India, and Brazil regarding IKT policy issues, special attention should be directed to this weakness to avoid Russia further falling behind in these issues.

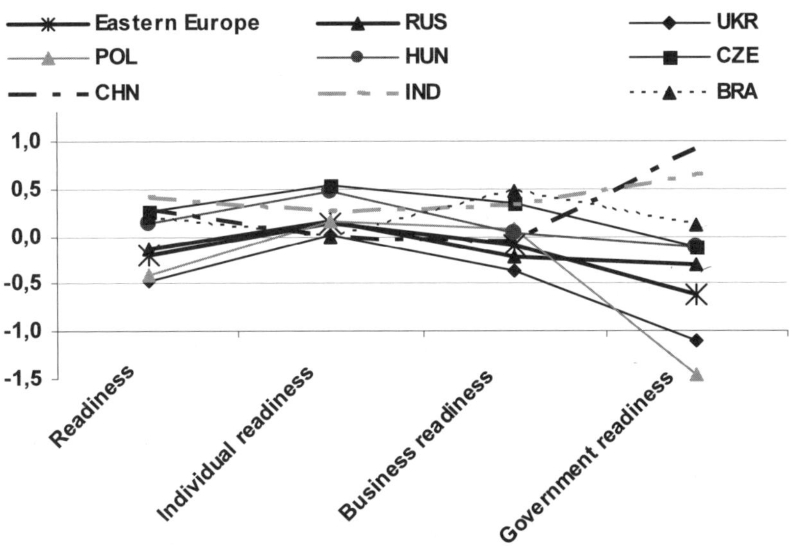

Source: The Global Information Technology Report (2005)

Fig. 2.14. Comparison of subindex "Readiness" in NRI 2004–2005 between Russia and other countries

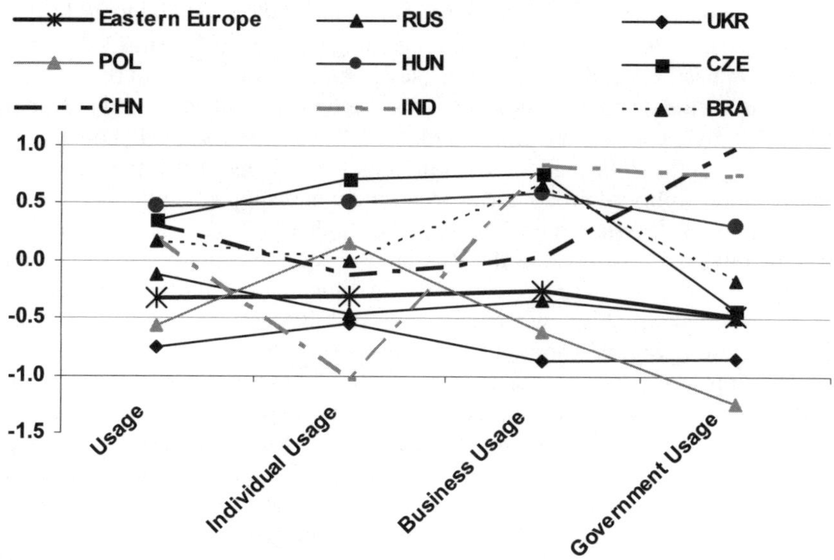

Source: The Global Information Technology Report (2005)

Fig. 2.15. Comparison of subindex "Usage" in NRI 2004–2005 between Russia and other countries

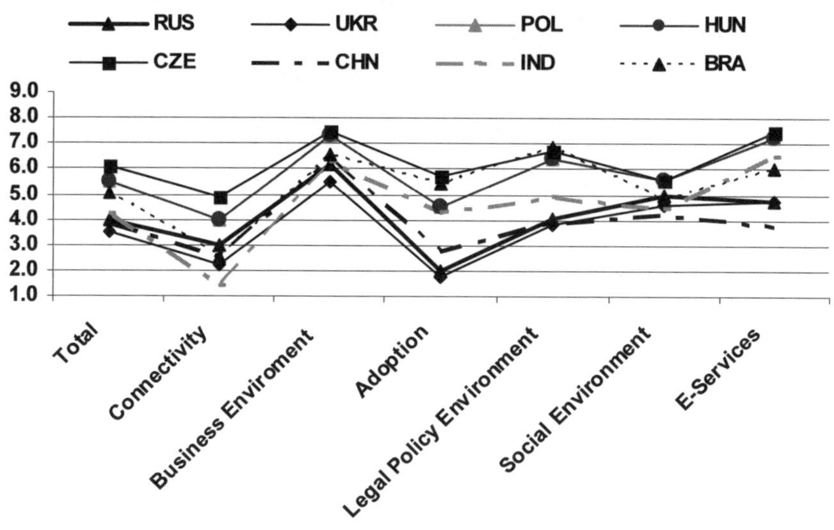

Source: Economist Intelligence Unit (2005)

Fig. 2.16. The 2005 E-Readiness Ranking

2.4.1 General Sector Trends

From 2000 to 2005, the Russian telecommunications market has demonstrated strong growth and in 2005, its overall revenues volume exceeded $21.9 billion. This accounts for 2.86% of GDP and is considerably higher compared to $4.7 billion in 2000. The CAGRs from 2000 to 2005 account 36% per year. For comparison, the CAGRs from 1994 to 1999 account only 10% per year, showing the impact of the Russian crises in 1998–1999. The telecommunications revenues as a percentage of GDP and telecommunications revenues per capita in comparison to other countries are illustrated in Fig. 2.17. This percentage of GDP is close to the average level of developed countries and is lower than in most transition countries. The reasons may lie in the fact that in the developed countries, low prices and high access rates ensure a revenue level which is comparable with the revenue level in the Russian monopoly situation with the access deficit of telecommunications services and high monopoly prices. Moreover, another reason explaining this phenomenon may be some distortions when calculating a ratio to the Russian GDP, which has a high share of oil production. As presented in Fig. 2.17, the Russian population spends less than average on telecommunications. Based on the fact that Russia has a low population density geographically and often harsh climate conditions, it is more logical to suggest high usage and willingness to pay for telecommunications services.

As illustrated in Fig. 2.18, the Russian revenues of mobile telecommunications and Internet services account for more than half of the telecommunications revenues. This trend is similar to the trends in other transition countries and is accelerating over time.

The quality of telecommunications networks in Russia is improving; however, it is still lagging behind especially in rural areas. Figure 2.19 presents the share of

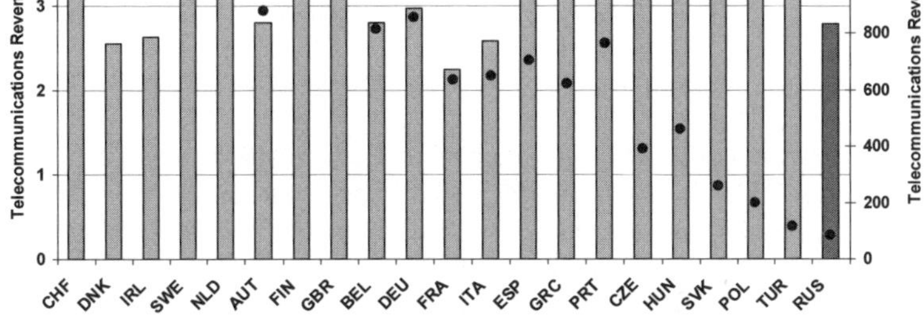

Source: OECD (2005a), Minsvyaz (2006) and own calculations

Fig. 2.17. Telecommunications revenues 2003

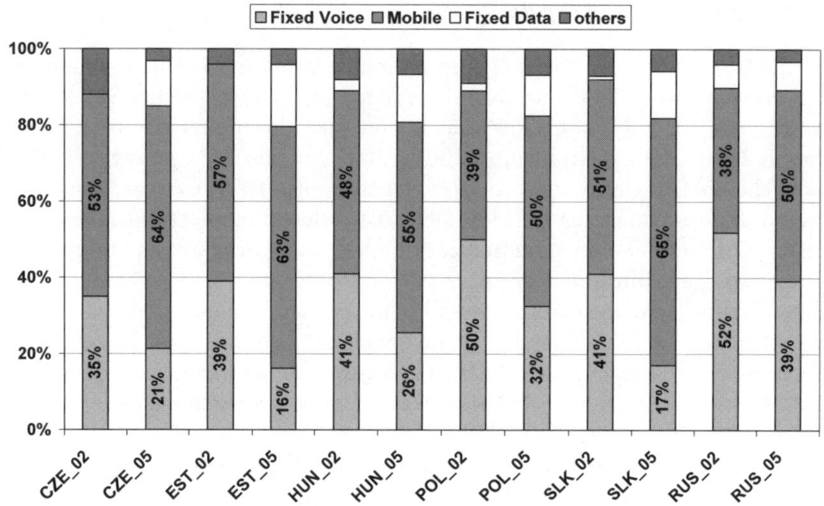

Source: IBM (2003), EITO (2006), Minsvyaz (2006) and own calculations

Fig. 2.18. Components of telecommunications revenues in 2002 and 2005

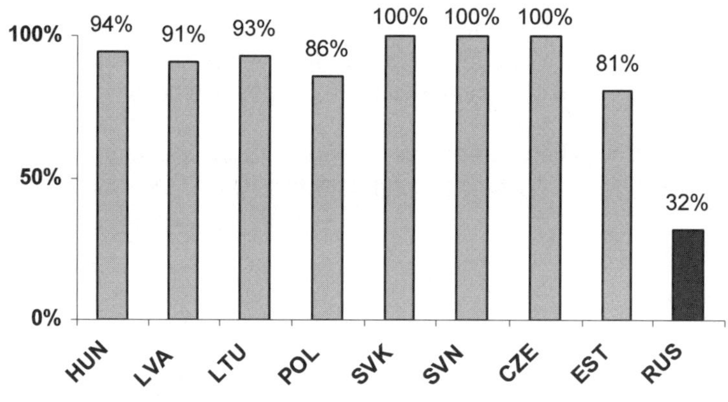

Note: for POL and RUS the data are available only in 2002

Source: ITU (2006a)

Fig. 2.19. Digitalization level of telecommunications networks 2004

digital main lines in comparison to other advanced transition economies. According to Minsvyaz, in 2004 the share of digital lines as a percentage of automatic lines (up to 2003 all lines are automatic according to ITU) in Russia in rural areas accounts for only 28% and in residential areas 59.1%. The Russian telecommunications sector shows a significantly low quality of telecommunications services for users. The level of telephone faults per 100 main lines was 35 in 1999. This is relatively high in comparison to other countries in the same time period, for example Czech Republic with 20 and Finland with 8 (ITU 2006a).

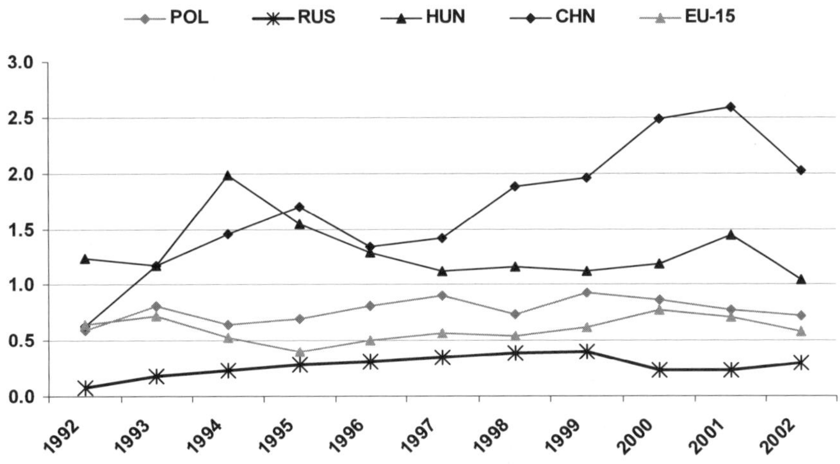

Source: ITU (2005) and own calculations

Fig. 2.20. Share of telecommunications investment as percentage of GDP

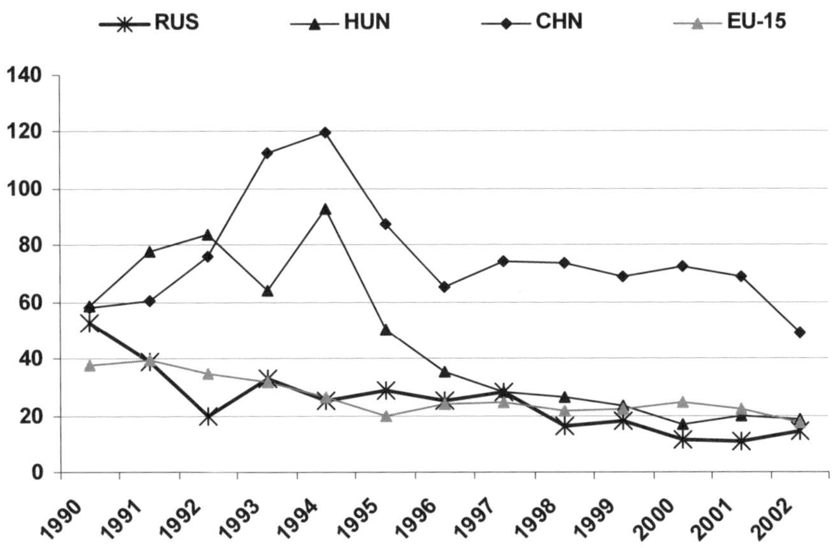

Source: ITU (2005) and own calculations

Fig. 2.21. Share of telecommunications investment as percentage of telecommunications revenues

The needs of Russia with respect to telecommunications investment are huge, with rather different estimates abounding. As illustrated in Fig. 2.20, in the period from 1992 to 2002, the share of telecommunications investment as a percentage of GDP in Russia is low in comparison to the shares of other transition countries, China and the EU-15. The share of telecommunications investment as a percentage to sector revenues is presented in Fig. 2.21 and confirms the weak Russian performance. The backwardness of Russia is quite remarkable compared to advanced transition countries and China.

The share of private participation in infrastructure serves as one of the most important indicators of infrastructure development. Comparing amounts of private participation in telecommunications, it is obvious that private participation in the Russian telecommunications sector in relation to GDP or per capita is lower compared to other transition countries and is only higher than in China (see Fig. 2.22).

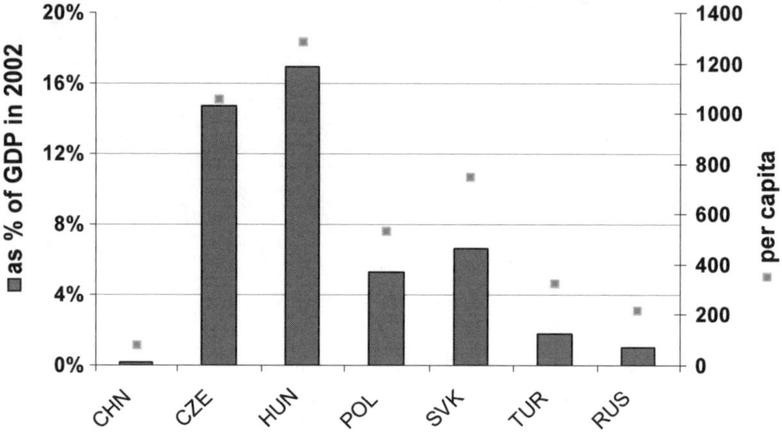

Source: PPI Database of The World Bank[15]

Fig. 2.22. Cumulated infrastructure investments in telecommunications projects with private participation in comparison 1990–2003

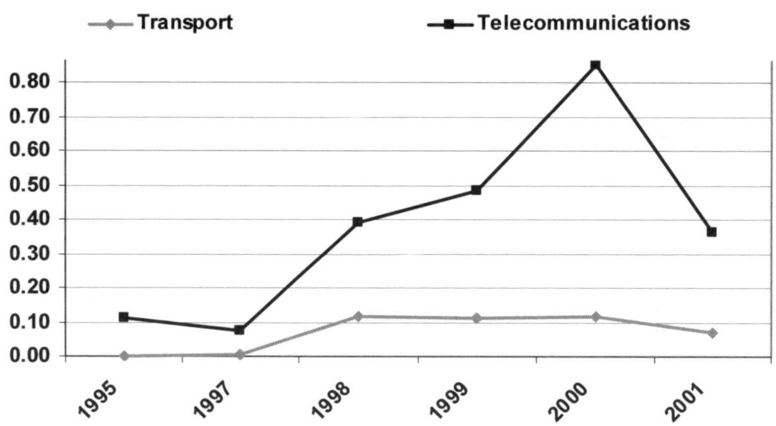

Source: Goskomstat (2004) and own calculations

Fig. 2.23. Shares of FDI in the total sectoral investments

[15] http://ppi.worldbank.org/resources/ppi_countryClassification.aspx

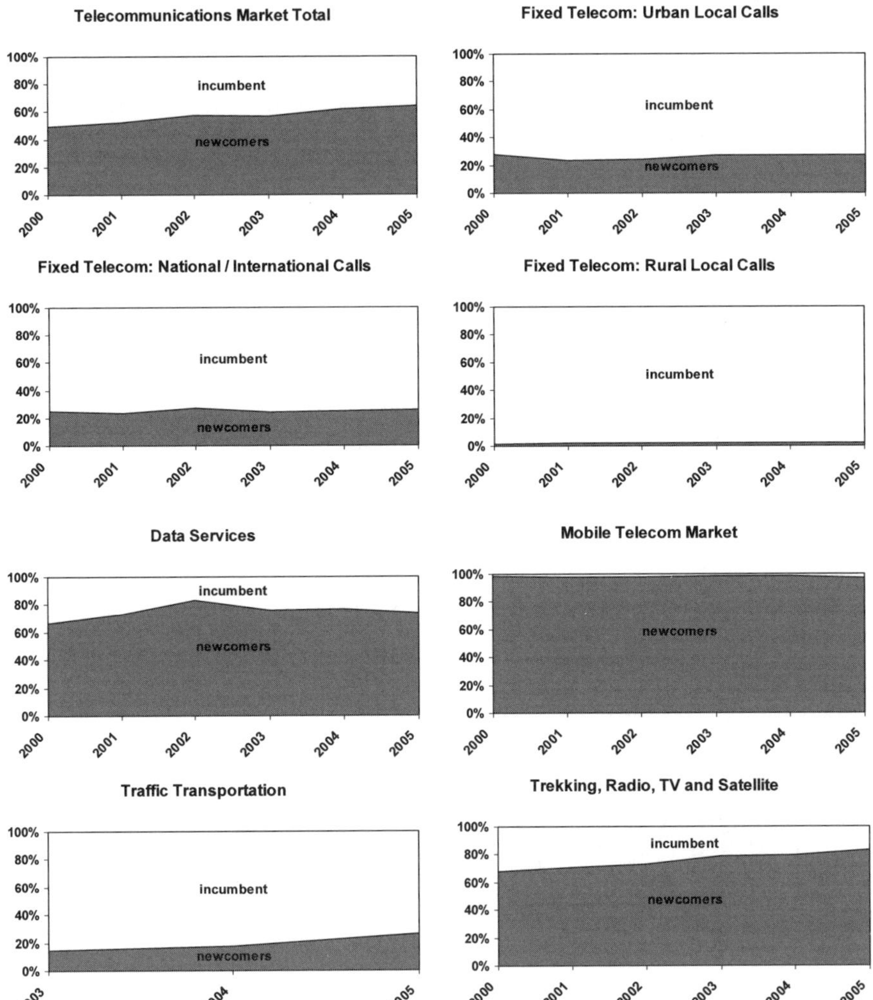

*Data (including telegraph services) are not identical between 2001/2002 and between 2002/2003.

Source: Minsvyaz (2006) and own calculations

Fig. 2.24. Trends in the Russian telecommunications revenues 2000–2005

However, among the Russian infrastructure sectors, the telecommunications sector is one of the most attractive. As illustrated in Fig. 2.23, the share of FDI in all investments in this sector is quite high.

Figure 2.24 illustrates the structure of the Russian telecommunications revenues in terms of their belonging to incumbent or newcomers. As one can see, in the Russian market more than 50% of revenues are earned by newcomers. The incumbent remains very strong in rural local calls and traffic transportation. It remains quite strong as well in long-distance calls and urban local calls (corporation clients are an exception, which are mostly served by the alternative telecommunications operators).

With respect to manufacturing of telecommunications equipment as an important element of the telecommunications industry, the figures indicate that the import of telecommunications equipment makes up to over 95% of all telecommunications equipment (ITU 2005). As one can see in Fig. 2.25, revealed comparative advantage in manufacturing of telecommunications equipment of Russia is very low and decreasing over time compared to other countries. For advanced transition economies like Poland, Czech Republic and Hungary, these indicators are higher and strongly increasing over the investigated period.

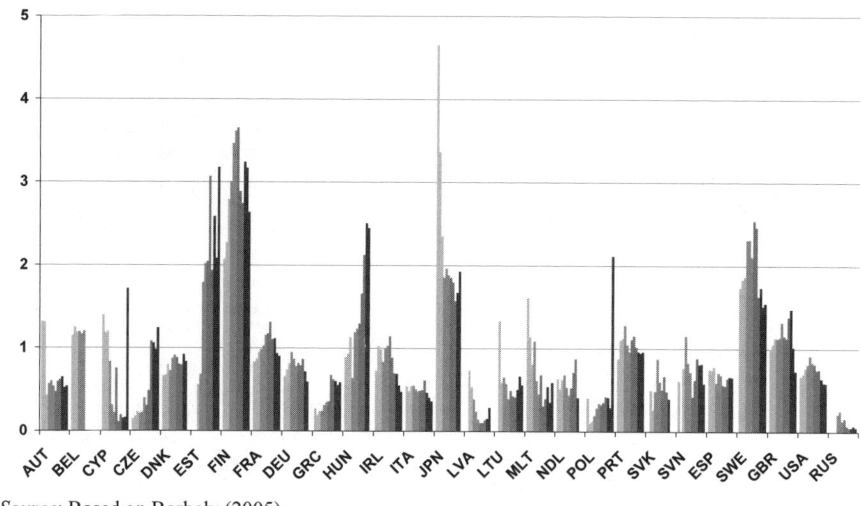

Source: Based on Borbely (2005)

Fig. 2.25. Modified revealed comparative advantage in telecommunications equipment manufacturing[16]

To access WTO accession, like other candidates, Russia has to adopt the WTO commitments in the telecommunications sector. According to negotiations over the last several years, two main points in terms of the Russian telecommunications sector were primarily mentioned:

1. Abolishment of the anti-competitive cross-subsidization between long-distance and local calls: This means primarily the de-monopolization of Rostelecom and market liberalization for long distance calls. However, the tariffs are still

[16] More on the estimation method see Borbely (2005).

not fully rebalanced in Russia. The long-distance and international calls markets were liberalized in 2006.

2. Removing the limits of foreign participation in the Russian telecommunications market (as well as other infrastructure sectors in general): in 2000, Russia set the limit of the maximum share of foreign participation in the Russian telecommunications sector to 49% (by leasing of Russian lines, 25%). In addition, the Russian party stated that the foreign management share in the telecommunications companies also had to be limited to a maximum of 49%. During negotiations, some of these requirements were shelved, e.g. a 25% limit on foreign participation in a telecommunication operator which leases its lines as well as limits on foreign participation in the long-distance call market segment.

Concerning other issues, which are included in multilateral trade agreements, Russia has started to introduce appropriate laws. The Federal Law on Communications involves topics such as interconnection rules, transparency and publicity of the licensing process, spectrum allocation procedure, and the introduction of universal service obligations. Nevertheless, a lot of additional documentation providing details on these issues is still missing.

2.4.2 Regulatory Institutions

Currently, the Russian institutions are undergoing an institutional reform leading to the development of a more efficient and transparent system. The first projects of this reform merged the old Ministry for Communications with the Ministry of Transport. However, at the end of June 2004, the Russian government returned to the idea of a separate Ministry in the field of telecommunications, post and information technologies.[17] The new Ministry for Information Technologies and Communications (Mininformsvyaz[18]) combines the function of policymaker and regulator. Russia does not have an independent regulator. Mininformsvyaz's competence covers the fields of TV and radio broadcasting. The new Ministry includes the following three departments:

- The Federal Telecommunications Supervision Services (FTSS), which handles control and supervision in the communications and information technologies sectors
- The Agency on Communications, which takes responsibility for the administration of government assets in the field of telecommunications, for the realization of public infrastructure programs as well as the universal services mechanism
- The Agency on Information Technologies deals with activities in the field of information technologies, similar to the Agency on Communications

---

[17] The Russian language often uses the words information technologies and communications separately and not information communications technologies (ICT) in its typical form.

[18] The old name Minsvyaz is often used.

The Russian State Radio Frequency Commission closed during the process of reformation, but was restarted again as an inter-ministerial collegial commission, and took the functions of allocation and assignment of radio spectrums. Price regulation in the telecommunications sector was taken over by the Federal Tariff Services. The latter was reformed from the Federal Energy Commission, which already regulated prices in the fields of energy and transport.

The Russian institutional framework demonstrates some imperfections and can be characterized by weak regulatory policy. Particularly in fast growing markets like mobile telecommunications, the regulatory mechanisms should work in an optimal way because each institutional, as well as operational weakness, can cause a slow-down of the diffusion process. This fact is particularly evident when one analyzes that the last Russian institutional reform brought about the following three main problems in the mobile telecommunication diffusion. Firstly, a lack of number capacity distributed by the Minsvyaz to the market operators slowed down the selling volume of all operating companies. According to Vedomosti, in July 2004, BaikalVestCom and SMARTS stopped accepting new users. VimpelCom, using the non-geographical codes 903 and 905 with a maximum capacity of 20 million numbers, decided to use numbers starting with 0.[19] Secondly, certification problems occurred and new kinds of mobile telecommunication equipment could not be certificated by the Minsvyaz. The losses were significant.[20] Thirdly, the awarding of licenses and license extensions were stopped. However, the new list of business activities in the field of telecommunications which requires licenses has been prepared but is still waiting for acceptance by the government.

The efficiency of the reformed New Ministry is partly still questionable. Independence and impartiality are issues to be worked on; the Russian institutional framework still requires improvement. The creation of an independent regulator with clearly defined duties and obligations anchored in telecommunications laws should be an advantage for the growth dynamics of the telecommunications sector.

2.4.3 Market Structure

In 2006, in the Russian telecommunication market, the four main holdings – Sistema Telecom, Alfa-Group, Telecominvest, and Svyazinvest – incorporated 90% of all telecommunications market revenues. Fig. 2.26 illustrates the market structure schematically. All holdings are active in many telecommunications subsectors: fixed telecommunications, mobile telecommunications and the Internet. In the following, each holding is presented, including some of its main subsidiaries and strategic investors.

[19] This is not common practice in the Russian telecommunications sector and was allowed for VimpelCom only in the spring 2004.

[20] In June 2004 alone, Motorola had estimated losses of Rub 7 mil. per month; experts referred to budget losses of $15 million per month.

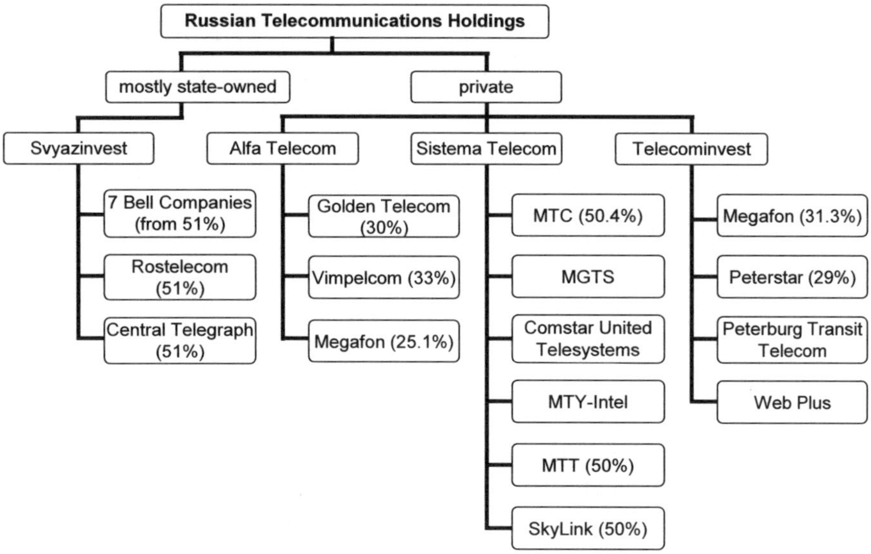

Source: Own description

Fig. 2.26. Main market players on the Russian telecommunications market

2.4.3.1 Svyazinvest Holding

The telecommunications holding company, Svyazinvest, was founded in 1994 to consolidate government-owned shares in the regional operators of Russia. In 2002, the fixed-line industry was reorganized, with 70 regional operators being consolidated into seven pan-regional companies. The Russian government owns 75% of Svyazinvest's shares. The other 25% are owned by the private company Mustcom Limited. Svyazinvest is a controlling shareholder of Rostelecom (50.67%), the nationwide backbone operator, and of the seven pan-regional companies. Svyazinvest and its subsidiaries make up the network of Incumbent Local Exchange Carriers. The Russian government intends to sell its shares in Svyazinvest; the procedure is ongoing but at the beginning of 2007 the incumbent company had still not been privatized.

2.4.3.2 Alfa Telecom

The Alfa Group is one of the most influential industry and finance groups in Russia. Its activities cover many sectors of the Russian economy. Alfa Telecom is a holding company dealing with telecommunications. In the telecommunications sector, Alfa Telecom owns 30% shares in the Golden Telecom group, which is a provider of a broad range of telecommunication services to businesses, other telecommunications service providers and consumers. This group provides telecommunications services through its operation of voice, Internet and data networks, international gateways, local access and various value-added services in the Commonwealth of Independent States (CIS), primarily in Russia, and through its fixed line and mobile operations in the Ukraine. A further 20% of Golden Telecom's shares are owned by the strategic investor of the Alfa Group: Telenor. In addition, the Alfa Group and Telenor are shareholders in the second biggest Russian mobile operator, VimpelCom, with 32.9 and 26.6% respectively. Moreover, Alfa Telecom own 25.1% in the third biggest Russian mobile operator, Megafon, through ZT-Mobile.

2.4.3.3 AFK Systema

AFK Systema also belongs to one of the most influential industry and finance groups in Russia. It operates in the Russian telecommunications market through its subsidiary, Sistema Telecom, which was set up in 1998.[21] Sistema Telecom is a shareholder in more than 50 telecommunications companies. Some of these companies are active in the Moscow fixed telecommunications market, e.g. MGTS, Comstar United Telesystems, and MTY-Intel. Sistema Telecom owns 50% of Multiregional TransitTelecom (MTT), which is the most important player in the field traffic services to the Russian mobile and fixed network operators. Moreover, this holding owns 50.4% of the biggest Russian mobile operator, MTS. The strategic investor of Sistema Telecom in MTS is Deutsche Telekom, with holdings of 10%. In the near future, Deutsche Telekom will sell its shares. Sky Link holding – founded in order to implement projects of creating federal mobile communications network operating in IMT-MC-450 (CDMA 2000) standard – also belongs to Sistema Telecom (50%). Sistema as a multi-profile telecommunications group is already developing to meet convergence challenges. It is planning not only to introduce unified branding across all its telecoms subsidiaries but also to develop unified retail outlets. These will offer products from all of Sistema's telecoms operations.

2.4.3.4 Telecominvest

The First Holding A.S. is the biggest shareholder of Telecominvest (85%). At the same time, 29.5% of shares in the First Holding A.S. are owned by Telia-Sonera and 70.5% by the Commerzbank. Telecominvest is mostly active in the North-West region. It is a shareholder with 31% in the third biggest Russian mobile operator Megafon and holds 29% in PeterStar, the leading alternative local exchange carrier in St. Petersburg. Petersburg TransitTelecom belongs to the Telecominvest group as well. Web Plus is the leading ISP in St. Petersburg and is owned 100% by Telecominvest.

2.4.4 Fixed Telecommunications

In 2005, the fixed penetration rate in Russia reached 30% (Minsvyaz 2006). This is close to the level of other CEE countries such as Poland (30.6%) and Latvia (31.7%) and relatively low compared to the level of industrial countries. The EU-15

[21] The other subsidiary of Sistema Telecom, Sistema Mass-Media, deals with business in the field of cable TV and is in the process of consolidation of many cable TV activities.

average penetration rates were about 56% in 2000, and 51% in 2005. Some of the industrial countries have achieved a penetration level of more than 70%, which – due to the high competition – has been significantly decreasing since 2001–2002, e.g. in Sweden, Denmark, and Switzerland (ITU 2006a). The Russian waiting list for basic services included approximately 5.8 million names in 2003 (WDI 2005).[22]

The main Russian population centers are quite well served, but large areas of this vast country have extremely poor or no access at all. In the Russian fixed telecommunications sector, one can see a clear increase in problems related to this digital divide between population in cities and population in rural areas. Figure 2.27 demonstrates the annually growing digital divide in fixed telecommunications.

The number of telephone lines per employee of telecommunications enterprises indicates the low efficiency of Russia's telecommunications firms. According to Russian incumbent's figures in 2003, one employee operated merely 63–130 telephone lines in the seven regional `mega companies` in 2000, while their counterparts in the USA had 172 and Poland 159 telephones lines per employee (WDI 2003).

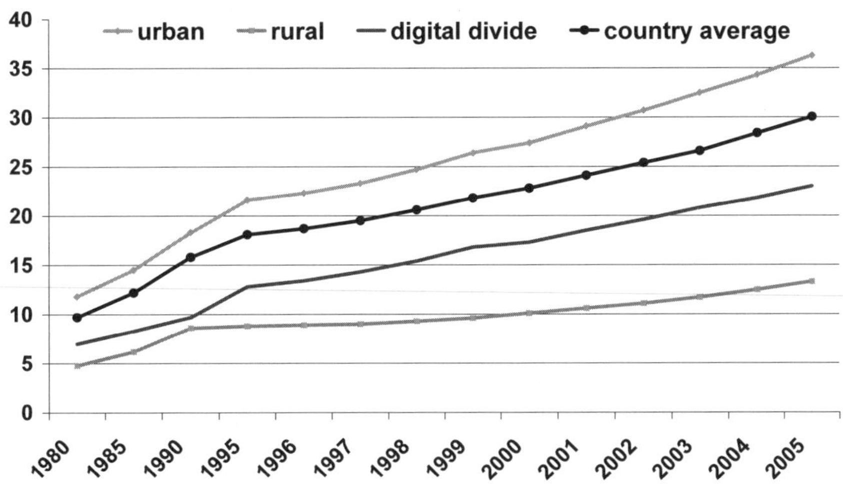

*digital divide between urban and rural regions (lines per 100 inhabitants) = density of fixed telecommunications users (100 person) in urban areas in the year i – density of fixed telecommunication users (100 person) in rural areas in the year i.

Source: Goskomstat (2004), Minsvyaz (2006) and own calculations

Fig. 2.27. Increasing digital divide in the Russian fixed telecommunications between urban und rural areas

[22] The latest available figure.

Prices in fixed telecommunications, when compared to other countries, reflect cross-subsidies. Rates for local calls and residential monthly telephone subscription are relatively cheap in comparison to other countries (see Fig. 2.28). In contrast, international calls are quite expensive. A 10-minute-call from the incumbent company in Russia to the USA costs about €6.7 (EU-25 average is €2.4); to Japan €8.2 (EU-25 average about €7).[23]

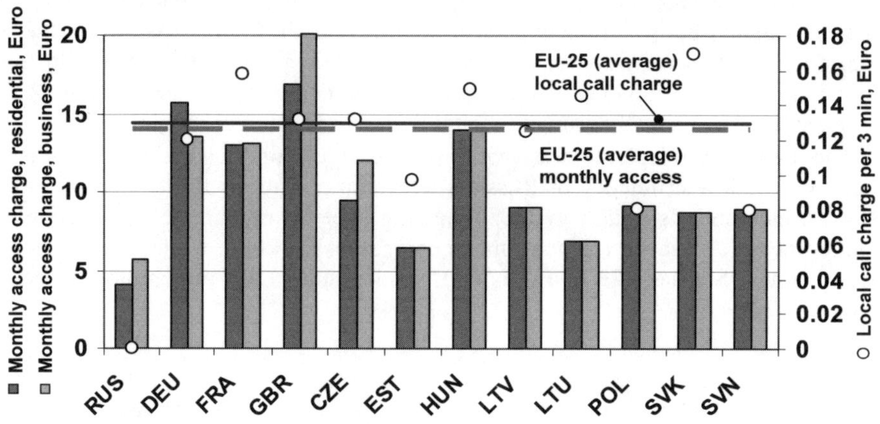

Source: www.svyazinvest.ru and EC (2005b)

Fig. 2.28. Monthly subscription fees and local call charges in transition countries 2004

The main players in the Russian fixed telecommunications market in terms of revenues are still the incumbent companies (MGTS, regional "mega-operators"). The newcomers like Golden Telecom and Peterstar mostly focus on the segment of corporate clients and the urban areas. Their share is about 25% of the urban and long-distance calls revenues. In terms of the number of access lines, the situation is similar. For example, in the Moscow market, one of the most competitive Russian markets, 80% of all access lines are owned by MGTS (incumbent company). However, in the residential and business segments the situations are different: in the residential segment MGTS has 97.5% of all residential users' phones; in the business segment its share is only 37%.[24]

2.4.5 Mobile Telecommunications

The role of mobile telecommunications in Russia is prominent. Mobile telecommunications arrived on the Russian market in the initial stages of transition, amidst poorly developed fixed telecommunications networks, low per capita income relative to the industrialized countries, and low demand for mobile telecommunications services. Due to this, as well as to relatively modest initial investments, the

[23] The data in Russia are for the Central region in 2004.

[24] www.sistel.ru

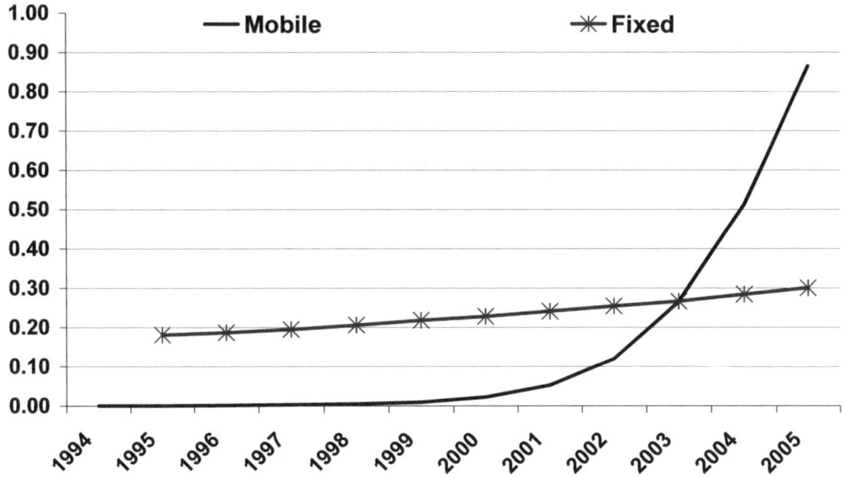

Source: ITU (2006a), Minsvyaz (2006)

Fig. 2.29. Fixed vs. mobile phone density in Russia

Russian government decided that the volume of the mobile telecommunications markets were very low, and did not regulate these services extensively. The lack of regulation in the mobile telecommunications market had a positive influence on its development. After 2003, mobile line density began to exceed the number of fixed lines and their revenues amounted to more than 50% of the entire telecommunications sector revenues. Mobile telecommunications are often, to some extent, a substitute for fixed telecommunications (WTO 2004). As illustrated in Fig. 2.29, after 2003, the mobile penetration rates in Russia are higher than fixed penetration rates.

Until 2005, mobile telephony in Russia grew rapidly, reaching saturation in 2007. In 2Q06, Russia had 140 million subscribers and a penetration rate of 96.6% per 100 inhabitants. However, according to Sotovik (2006a), penetration rates of active SIM-cards accounts for 2Q06 are only about 66%.

Diffusion of mobile telecommunications in Russia started from Moscow and St. Petersburg, as well as other urban areas, and then proceeded to spread across the rural areas, which offered a wide potential for market growth. One of the main factors behind the differences in mobile diffusion in the Russian regions was certainly GDP per capita in PPP (Markova and Ponder 2006, p. 174). However, the price level, resulting partly from the intensity of competition, has been and is quite important. Highly competitive Russian regional markets, with a leading operator's market share of less than 50%,[25] accounted for only 28% of all regional markets in 2004. In 26 and 16% of all regions, the market leader's share is more than 70% and 60–70% respectively. In spite of the Russian regional markets, three to four GSM operators exist and anti-competitive behavior from the respective dominant mobile operator is very likely in 72% of regions Sotovik (2004).

[25] e.g. Samarskay, Saratovskay, Nishegorodskay, Kaliningradskay distincts, Republic of Tatarstan.

In the early 90s, the enterprises which nowadays belong to the most significant players entered the Russian mobile telecommunications market. In the course of time, the Russian mobile telecommunications market has become dominated by three enterprises: Mobile TeleSystems (MTS), VimpelCom[26] and Megafon. They have successfully concentrated the market in their hands, attracting more then 80% of the market in the whole of Russia. The market share developments of the three main players in Moscow and in Russia as a whole are shown in Fig. 2.30.

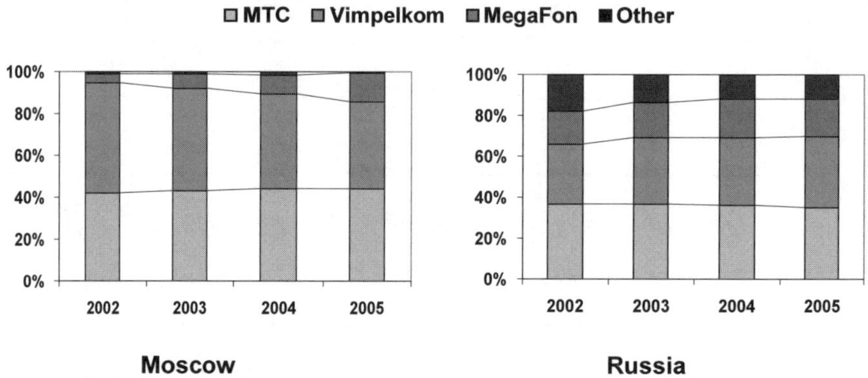

Source: Based on Sotovik (2006b)

Fig. 2.30. Market shares of the mobile operators in Russia and the Moscow region

The Russian market is characterized by a huge number of regional/local mobile operators such as Uralsvyazinform (subsidiary of Svyazinvest holding), SMARTS, Tele2 and SkyLink. Some of them are fighting to become the fourth-largest operator; however, success is still doubtful. Considering the aggressive expansion policy of the dominant operators especially at the beginning of the twenty first century, the regional operators were jeopardized by the anti-competitive behavior of the big players, who are interested in forcing them out of the market or acquisition. However, in 2007 after the "big three" decided to focus mostly on the revenues and not on subscriber acquisitions, the share of the regional operators grew to 20%

In the past years, one has observed a tendency towards consolidation in terms of capital structure in the Russian mobile telecommunication market, associated with numerous mergers and acquisitions. This trend is taking place on two levels: on the level of the holdings and on the level of the mobile operators. On the level of holdings, the process of market concentration was especially visible shortly after the crisis of 1998. Sistema Telecom, Alfa-Group and Telecominvest holdings respectively have a share in one of three main mobile operators of GSM standards: MTC, VimpelCom and Megafon with the exception of the Alfa-Group, who has shares in the VimpelCom as well as in Megafon.[27]

---

[26] The market label "Beeline"

[27] The legality of the purchase of 25.1% of Megafon's shares by the Alfa-Group is still questionable and brings about many court cases.

The leading mobile operators often used the following three ways to expand service provision in the regions: (1) acquiring of licenses, (2) acquiring a non-operating license as well (3) acquiring or merging with an existing operator and mergers and acquisitions. Since December 2003, VimpelCom and MTC have possessed the licenses for most of the Russian regions. Megafon already held a license portfolio enabling it to serve 100% of the Russian territory.

The Russian mobile telecommunication market is characterized by certain influences from integration through international stake holders, especially European companies. However, this dependence is sometimes limited. At the beginning of 2007, the biggest Russian company MTC was owned by AFK "Sistema" (52.8%), free float (46.7%) and others (2%). The structure of VimpelCom share holders was as follows: Telenor (Norway Telecom) (26.6%), Alfa Group (32.9%), free float (39.4%) and treasury stock and others (1.1%). Megafon, the youngest company, had many international stake holders: Sonera Holding (26%), Telecominvest (owned by international investors) (31.3%), ZT – Mobile (owned by Alfa Group) (25.1%), IPOC International Grant Fund (6.5%), Telia International AB (6.37%).

Svyazinvest, the biggest Russian telecommunication holding, has undergone numerous restructuring programs and its revenues in mobile telecommunications are continuously falling when compared to the others. The subsidiaries of Svyazinvest were less than 10% of the whole Russian mobile telecommunications market at the end of 2003. The holding is selling its unprofitable business and seeking to concentrate only on the three main regions: Povolsh'e, Ural, and Dalnyi Vostoc, where the mobile subsidiaries of Svayzinvest are quite strong. A special feature of the Russian telecommunications market is that the subsidiaries of the state company do not have a high market share in the mobile telecommunications market, which differs from Poland and many other countries.

Finally, the structure of the Russian mobile telecommunications market is characterized by one more feature. According to the decision of the Minsvyaz (2003a), the long-distance and international traffic of the GSM mobile network operators between the regions have to route only through the network of traffic transit companies; direct connections are not allowed. The main players on the traffic transfer market are Rostelecom (incumbent long-distance carrier) and MTT (private long-distance carrier). The latter gathers up long-distance traffic from mobile operators and passes it between the regions using channels rented from Rostelecom, for which it pays Rostelecom a flat rate. MTT controls 50% of Russia's mobile traffic and Rostelecom around 40% (Troika-Dialog 2004). However, the latest investigation by the Ministry showed that the three main mobile operators breached the rules and, in some cases, routed traffic directly.

At the beginning of 2000, in the Russian telecommunications sector, about 6,150 licenses[28] were issued, 526 (355 in 1995) in the mobile telecommunications sector. The scarce spectrum influences the diffusion of mobile telecommunications in Russia, e. g. due to the fact that the required 900 MHz band was mostly reserved by military or other government facilities, the Ministry of Communications initially

[28] http://light.minsvayz.ru/cgi-bin/show_site_document.cgi?parent=12&id=77&03.05.04

limited licensing of GSM-900 services to one per region. Referring to Minsvayz,[29] only 5% of radio spectrum in Russia is free for commercial use. The rest still remains under the control of military and other federal agencies (around 80%), or is shared by telecom operators and the military.[30] The Russian Telecommunications Ministry has started a couple of initiatives designed to release a portion of this spectrum[31]; it now depends on the efficiency of the Ministry as to how fast that might happen. Free spectrum, of course, plays a crucial role in the development of 3G mobile technology networks and fixed-wireless technology networks, as well as digital TV.

As a result of historical development, in 2005 in Russia, five standards of mobile technology networks were in operation: GSM, AMPS/D-AMPS, NMT–450, IS-95, as well as IMT-MC-450. At the beginning of 2005, the GSM standard had a market share of 98.2%, while AMPS/D-AMPS, NMT–450, IS 95 and IMT-MC-450 operators had respectively 0.8, 0.3, 0.5 and 0.2% of the market (IKS 2005). Currently the GSM standard is clearly dominant. The dynamics of the CDMA standard development is quite slow; in 2004 the CDMA subscriber share (IS-95 and IMT-MC-450) amounted to only 1%. The number of subscribers in NMT-450 and AMPS/D-AMPS standards has decreased over the last couple of years.

Within the clients structure of Russian mobile telecommunications, prepaid tariffs play a very important role. Especially after the Russian crises of 1998, when the financial situation was very unstable, pre-paid tariffs were the only possible way to provide services, taking into account the low liquidity in the country.[32] The share of prepaid subscribers varies across the companies but, for the whole of Russia in 2006, it was higher than 80%. For example, 96.6% of VimpelCom's subscribers had prepaid contracts in 2006, and the company ranks within the top-ten European mobile operators based on this indicator. In terms of active subscribers, 82.7% of the total VimpelCom subscribers are prepaid.[33] In recent years, the number of prepaid subscribers, especially in markets with low penetration rates, has grown and is helping to raise overall mobile penetration rates.

The three main Russian players are characterized by high subscriber growth rates until the end of 2005, this growth significantly decreased in 2006. The experts speak about market saturation in Russia. At this time, the "big three" decided to concentrate on the usage per subscription in order to shore up revenues. The indicator of monthly average revenues per user (ARPU) for the biggest Russian mobile operators decreased to $6.6–6.9 in 1Q06. However, in 2007 the ARPU leaped for

[29] Based on the Milovanzev's speech (2007).

[30] e.g. according to the Russian Newspaper Vedomosti, in 2004 SKY LINK shared the spectrum with the military-cosmos forces; because of this, the operator had to turn off the network for the connection to the international cosmos station for 20–30 min.

[31] The program of conversion is carried out by the state. The Mininformsvyaz's officials say that the operators do not need to participate in it; this is a challenge for the state.

[32] In October 1998, VimpelCom "launched a prepaid card program in an effort to reduce bad debt, eliminate monthly fees, and connection costs to its customers. Prepaid "Bee+" cards simplified the usage of cellular phones by eliminating deposits and monthly bills, and allowing customers to control their spending http://www.vimpelcom.ru/company/history1998.html.

[33] Company information.

MTS and VimpelCom to a high of $8.7–9.0 in 2Q07 "on the back of a number of one-off issues." The experts are sure that this increase is connected, not necessarily to price increases, but partly to the MOU increase as well as to the introduction of the CPP pricing regime, which gives an additional revenues source for the mobile operators.

For a long period, among the Russian mobile operators, MTS based on the ARPU as well as MOU was always above its competitors. Contrary to this, VimpelCom had lower costs in terms of subscriber acquisition and a lower rate of churn. As a result, MTC focused on the business customers and had better service quality and coverage. VimpelCom positioned itself on the market with attractive tariffs, especially with the introduction of pre-paid tariffs, and attracted a high portion of users, outstripping to some extent MTC. At the end of 2006, their market shares in the Russian market were quite close at about 33%.

In terms of CIS expansion, until 2006 MTS showed high expansion trends but in 2006 the situation changed. As a result, at the end of 2006 Vimplecom owned operators in six CIS countries. MTS, at the same time, had only four.

After the introduction of the CPI pricing regime, as well as the end of the price war to gain market share (saturation is mostly reached), the Russian mobile operators turned their attention to the content and advertising market. MTS had already tried to introduce I-Mode in 2005, but failed and stopped the project. VimpelCom was more successful and introduced data offering Chameleon, which pushed content to subscribers using only one handset. In total, mobile telecommunications earned $408 million on content, whereof music content had the highest share. In the first half of 2004, non-voice accounted for 11% of all mobile telecommunications revenues. These are, primarily, SMS/MMS (49%), content services (24%) and mobile Internet (6%). In the first half of 2006, non-voice revenues accounted for about 14%.

2.4.6 Broadband Infrastructure

Russia had only a small and scattered broadband installed base until very recently (Point Topic 2005). Up to 2004, most users were found in the business sector but considerable activity in the consumer/residential sector has started. In the middle of 2005, massive centralized investment programs were not an option in this country, but a plethora of smaller and localized companies were pushing broadband services through, whether DSL, cable modem or, increasingly, some form of "cable Ethernet" or "home networks". In 2006, the situation changed. The alternative operators' share of the broadband market fell in 2006 as a result of Svyazinvest's aggressive promotion of Internet services, in particular the introduction of new broadband service brands by some Svyazinvest units. As result, according to Point Topic (2007), the number of broadband lines achieved 3.1 million at the end of 2006; in 2005 they numbered 1.77 million, in 2004 only 890 thousand. As presented in Fig. 2.31, the informal 'Home Networks' which use Ethernet LANs to link up buildings, housing developments and sometimes whole neighborhoods to 'broadband' access as well as operators using Ethernet

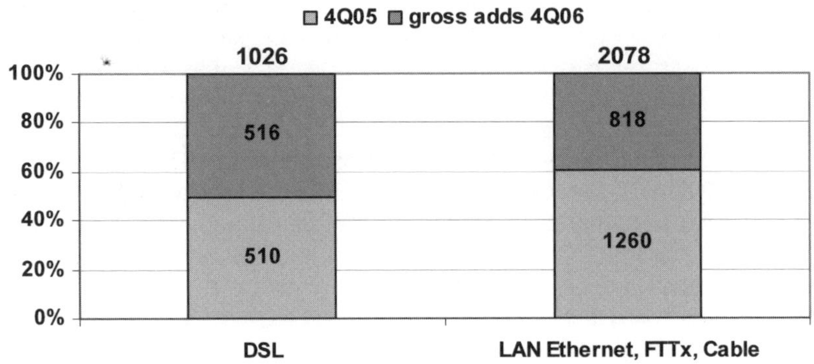

Source: Point Topic (2007)

Fig. 2.31. Russian broadband subscribers by the deployed technology 4Q05 vs. 4Q06

fiber-to-the-x connections (cable modem connections is only a very small part from 2.078 million connections) still has the leading position in terms of the number of lines. Comstar UTS opines that there are about 100 home networks in Moscow, most of which operate without operational or content licenses and charge about the same price as for an ADSL connection.

Furthermore, in 2007 the DSL, cable and mobile operators were already facing competition from providers offering services using Wi-Fi and WiMAX technologies. While WiMAX network operators currently focus mostly on lucrative corporate clients, Wi-Fi has already become available for individual users in Moscow and in some other major cities. According to Romir Monitoring, 16% of Muscovites regularly use Wi-Fi to connect to the Internet. J'son&Partners expected Russian operators' revenues from providing Wi-Fi wireless broadband services to double in the year 2007 to U.S. $100 million–$120 million (Parfenov 2006).

The most profitable and more developed segment of the Russian market is the Moscow region. According to data of Comstar-UTS (Systema Holding), the biggest player in the broadband market in Moscow, at the end of 2006, the following market shares could be observed in the residential and business broadband market in Moscow (see Fig. 2.32).

The Comstar UTS advantage in the Moscow market is due the fact that Sistema Holding has a majority ownership of the local incumbent MGTS, which served more than half of all business and residential subscribers in Moscow. This ensures access to last mile in Moscow for the Comstar-UTS. The main competitors of Comstar-UTS are operators of "home networks" providing services through Ethernet fiber-to-the-x (FTTx) connections. These are: Corbina, Centel, and Moscow Cablecom. Corbina, as the second-largest operator in the residential broadband market, was acquired by Golden Telecom in February 2007. Centel is a subsidiary of the Central Telegraph, owned by the Svyazinvest. Moscow Cablecom owns the leading Moscow cable TV operator and broadband provider Comcor-TV. It operates

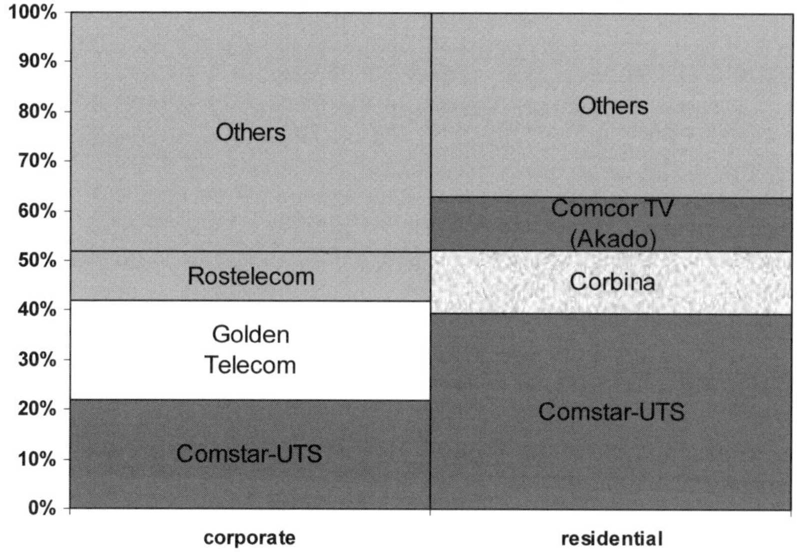

Note: 51% stake in Corbina was acquired by the Golden Telecom.

Source: www.sistel.ru

Fig. 2.32. Corporate and residential broadband markets in Moscow 4Q06

the FTTB network, covering 2.5 million apartments. This deal is important for Golden Telecom, because of Corbina's last mile access and a couple of licenses in the regions. Due to the fact that there is no local loop unbundling in Russia, Golden Telecom is constructing Wi-Fi hotspots in Moscow to bypass existing copper infrastructure.

Broadband operators are aiming to expand their customer bases beyond Moscow, into the Russian regions, through the rollout of new – very investment intensive – networks and acquisitions. Until 2007, they were mostly active in serving corporate networks in the larger Russian cities. With regards to acquisitions, the analysts say that "in Russia's regions there is virtually nothing to buy." In 2006, Comstar-UTS bought several companies, but they were all small. In the Russian regions, seven "mega-operators" have the best position to become leading broadband providers in their respective territories. Having full control over the last-mile infrastructure, they will be able to swiftly roll out DSL offers to most of their client base. All incumbent "mega-companies" have begun to roll out xDSL services and upgrade inter-regional backbone connections with fiber and/or radio. However, until 2006 the unique DSL development concept for Svyazinvest Holding was difficult to observe,[34] therefore e.g. 'mega-operators' buy DSL equipment separately that results in higher prices. In 2006, Svyazinvest's aggressive promotion of Internet services, in particular the introduction of new broadband service brands

[34] no DSL development plan is published (March 2006).

by some Svyazinvest units (e.g. J trade mark of Volgatelecom) as well as the promotion of new services and offer of unlimited tariff plans (e.g. Dalsvyaz, as a bundle with IPTV), brought about positive developments for Svyazinvest and its share increased. Svyazinvest's share in the Russian broadband access market accounted for 30% in 2007; the plans were to boost the share to 50% in the next 5–6 years.

The competitive situation in the DSL access market for the whole of Russia is difficult to observe. For example, in the Volga region, VolgaTelecom and 70 ISPs provide Internet access. The share of VolgaTelecom is 65% in the dial-up market and 45% in the dedicated access market. The situation in the regions of the Volga area is, however, different. The market share of VolgaTelecom in the dial-up connection segment varies between 24% (Samara region) and 96% (Republic of Mordovia); in the dedicated connection segment it varies between 19% (Yuljanovsk region) and 100% (Kirov region) (Electronic Russia 2004b, p. 28).

Last year, the Russian holding AFK Sistema's subsidiary Comstar UTS bought a blocking stake in national telecommunications holding Svyazinvest and was one of the candidates to gain the control share during Svyazinvest's privatization. This movement was interpreted as Comstar UTS seeking access to Svyazinvest regional networks. The privatization of Svyazinvest will not happen in 2008. Disagreements over a development strategy for the telecommunications giant between Svyazinvest and Sistema management are already spilling into the public arena. However, the experts predict that there are several market segments in which Comstar UTS could successfully cooperate with Svyazinvest units, e.g. business or ADSL segments.

However, though many cable TV companies exist in Russia, their cables often do not enable bi-directional carriage of signals to provide Internet access and need additional investment to achieve it. The share of cable providers in the Russian broadband market is not high. In the Moscow market, there are a couple of cable TV operators. Comcor TV (AKADO brand), the biggest one, uses the Comcor Moscow fiber optic network to provide all services over last mile. Comcor TV has the third-largest share in the Moscow broadband market. In the Russian regions, the consolidation process in the cable market has been observed since 2004. The main players are National Cable Networks (1.5 million subscribers, 30% are broadband and pay TV subscribers) operating in St. Petersburg, Moscow as well as Yekaterinburg, Novosibirsk, Kurgan and United Cable Networks (1.2 million subscribers) owned by Sistema. Most of the cable operators, which work on uni-directional carriage of signals, are announcing plans to upgrade their networks in the future to be able to provide a wide range of broadband services.[35]

2.4.7 Internet Dynamics and Information Society

Internet user penetration in Russia has very high growth rates but is still lagging behind other advanced transition countries and the EU-15 (see Fig. 2.33). In 2006, Internet user penetration in Russia reached 17.5%.

[35] In 2007, the Russian cable companies provided cable TV and broadband Internet. Telephony was seldom included in the bundling offers.

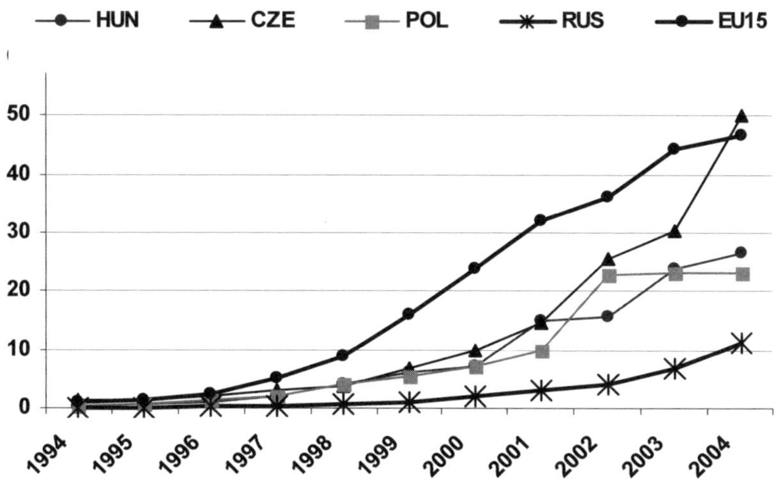

Source: ITU (2005), Minsvyaz (2005)

Fig. 2.33. Internet user penetration per 100 inhabitants

As mentioned above, the broadband market in Russia is still in an early stage of development. The broadband penetration rates are quite low: 2.2% per 100 inhabitants. However, a comparison of the number of personal computers per 100 persons in Russia with Poland, the Czech Republic and Hungary shows that the number of computers in Russia is quite close to the number in the Czech Republic and Poland (see Fig. 2.34). However, as one can see in Fig. 2.33, in both new EU member countries, the number of Internet users is significantly higher. The reasons for this could be manifold, e.g. prices, skills, public Internet access or Internet contest.

With respect to the computerization of the Russian population, in February 2007, the Mininformsvyaz started the Pilot project "PC in each house" cooperating with the Russian Post, Intel and Microsoft. This project is aimed at the Russian population in the remote regions to decrease the digital divide between rural and urban areas. Four different computer models, which will be put together by Russian manufacturers, will be offered with about 10% discount in comparison to the market price. It will be possible to buy and pay for a computer at all post offices, which also deals with the computer delivering services. The Ministry is very optimistic about this project, which was planned for 3 years.

With respect to the prioritization strategy, the issues of relatively high computerization and relatively low Internet participation seem quite controversial to the actions of the Mininformsvyaz's in terms of the program "Computer in each house". To keep a balance between supply and demand, in this case, one would expect more efforts on the development of a broadband infrastructure, price decreasing through promotion of competitions, encouragement of people to work with the Internet, as well as the creation of useful content rather than prioritizing the computer promotions.

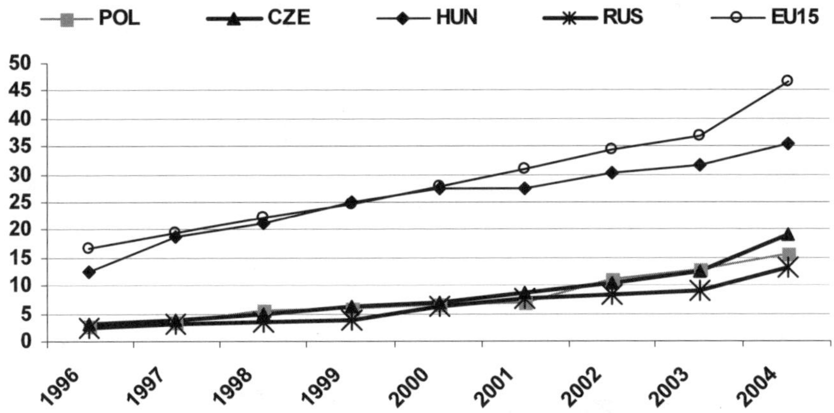

Source: ITU (2005), Minsvyaz (2005)

Fig. 2.34. Personal computers per 100 inhabitants

Internet usage in Russia, especially by governmental organizations, is quite low. The survey on local governments (Electronic Russia 2004a, p. 29) serves as an example. In the Astrachan region, only 39% of local leaders have worked with the Internet. On a local level, 92% do not have Internet access at all.

Broadband Internet connections offer the wide advantages of the Internet and the building of an advanced information society. According to J'son&Partners', as of late 2006, around 2.6 million households in Russia used broadband connections and 2.73 million used dial-up connections. The trend of users switching to broadband from dial-up is continuing, as the share of dial-up connections is still high, except for Moscow and St. Petersburg. Moreover, the broadband providers in Russian regions have recently started offering unlimited tariff plans, which is another driver for broadband development in Russia.

An interesting fact is that, in 2006, even low-speed dial-up access was still growing rapidly in Russian regions. VolgaTelecom (regional subsidiary of Svyazinvest) serves as an example and shows an increase of Internet users in both the dial-up and dedicated segments (see Fig. 2.35). However, the rates of growth in the dedicated sector are significantly higher than in the dial-up segment.

The Russian government has started a series of large Public Infrastructure Programs (PIP) in each infrastructure sector, including the telecommunications sector. The main financing in these programs come from the Russian government. The volumes of these programs are impressive but the question is whether these programs will actually be carried out or whether this is only a written plan.[36] Electronic

[36] These programs are typical for Eastern European countries and are analyzed by Von Hirschausen (1999) with respect to the Baltic countries, where similar programs were started but carried out with only a low degree of success (e.g. in 1995 only 29% of PIP in Lithuania was realized). A better result can be seen in Estonia, with a fulfillment ratio of the 1995–1997 PIP of 95.5%. This, however, seems to be strongly similar to the Soviet-type plan fulfillment ratio. In the opinion of von Hirschausen, efficient infrastructure investment policies are more easily "planned" than actually carried out and his lesson is not to waste time or resources drawing up the "plans" as long as they can be executed only marginally.

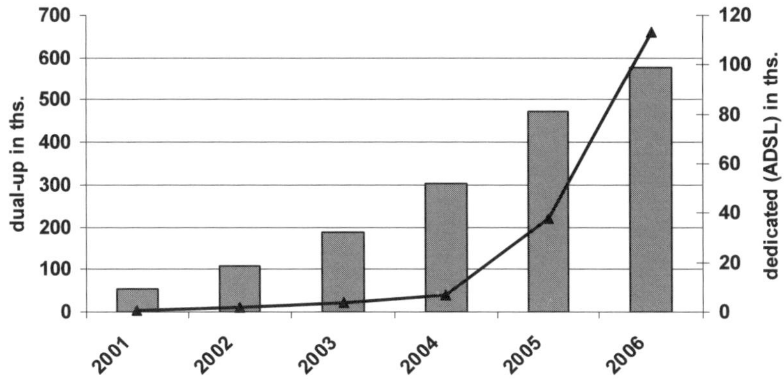

Source: Electronic Russia (2004b, p. 28) and press releases

Fig. 2.35. Internet connections of Volga Telecom (in thousands): dial-up vs. dedicated

Russia 2002–2010 is a Public Infrastructure Program of the Russian government in the field of ICTs with a financing volume of about US$ 2.4 billion from 2002 to 2010. This was 0.7% of GDP in 2002. Only 20% of this amount is planned to be from non-government budget sources. The program is aimed at the following main goals: improvement of the legal basis in the field of ICT, e-government, e-learning/ e-skills, development of telecommunications infrastructure and opening of public Internet access points, e-commerce and actions to increase public support of this PIP. Some results are already visible; as mentioned above, the Internet users penetration is increasing, number of personal computers is growing, in several regions e-government programs, e-learning and e-commerce programs have started. However, especially in the early years, a rather low ratio of fulfillment of this program is observable, e.g. in 2003 on the federal budget level, this program was financed only to about 20% (Minsvyaz 2003b, 2004). In 2006, it is claimed that this program was fully financed. However, in the first 9 months the financing volume accounts for about 10–20%.

By the Russian President as well as by the Russian regions, different smaller programs, such as Internet to all schools or "Student notebook", were or are realized which is certainly reasonable and positive for the formation of an information society in Russia.

3 Theory of Privatization and Liberalization in the Telecommunications Sector

3.1 Basic Theory of the Telecommunications Sector

The telecommunications sector, as many other network infrastructure sectors, is characterized by two sub-parts: telecommunications network infrastructure and telecommunications network services, which complement each other. In the following part of this study, the special characteristics of the network infrastructure sector, especially the telecommunications sector, are considered from a theoretical perspective.

3.1.1 Telecommunications as a Network Sector and Network Effects

The most fundamental economic characteristics of the telecommunications sector are network effects (e.g. Liebowitz and Margolis 2002, p. 77; Shy 1999, p. 4). The value of telecommunications networks increases as the number of subscribers grows. A positive external effect is created each time a new subscriber is connected to a network, because the telephones of existing subscribers increase in value as the potential number of subscribers grows (Saunders et al. 1994, p. 271). Liebowitz and Margolis (2002, p. 77) insist that network effects should not be interpreted as network externalities unless the participants in the market fail to internalize these effects. Network effects raise two concerns in terms of the outcome in the conditions of decentralized decision making of laissez-faire markets (Liebowitz and Margolis 2002, p. 77). The first focuses on the sizes of networks. Potential market failures can arise if network participants do not capture the benefits that their participation confers on others. The second arises because scale economies may result in the survival of only one network among the conceivable alternatives, which in turn may prevent decentralized individual choices from being properly counted in the market.

Network effects will be internalized in many empirically important circumstances. Owners of the networks have an incentive to internalize these effects. Such internalization can address both the size of network and the choice among competing networks.

In addition to network effects in the telecommunications sector, there are also call externalities. Call externalities arise because those receiving calls do not, as a rule, pay for them, even though for most calls the recipient enjoys a benefit from receiving the phone calls (Cullen international/WIK 2001, p. 25). Vogelsang and Mitchel (1991, p. 61) argue that call externalities are relatively more important in developed economies because they involve interactions among all consumers, while network externalities only involve interaction with marginal consumers. Many economists seem to be prepared to accept that internalizing call externalities are not so large to warrant regulatory intervention.

3.1.2 Natural Monopoly and Telecommunications

For a long time it was argued that the telecommunications sector is a natural monopoly, and this sector was served by one public enterprise. A natural monopoly is characterized by the fact that one company can serve a certain market cheaper than many. In economics language, this means that the firms' cost functions are subadditive over the total relevant output range. A cost function $C(y)$ is strictly and globally subadditive with regard to the quantity of goods $N = \{1,....,n\}$, if for each set of output vectors $\{y^1,...., y^m\}$, $y^i \in R^n$:

$$C(y^1 + ... + y^m) < C(y^1) + ... + C(y^m), \tag{3.1}$$

and at least two $y^i \neq 0$ (Baumol 1977, p. 810).

In the single product case, a cost function $C(y)$ is strictly and globally subadditive, if

$$C(y) < \sum_{i=1}^{m} C(y_i), \text{ with } y = \sum_{i=1}^{m} y_i, \ y_i \in R^n \tag{3.2}$$

(Baumol et al. 1982, p. 17). In the past, existence of economies of scale was interpreted as a reason for a natural monopoly. Based on the research of Baumol, Willing, Panzar and others, this opinion partly changed. As a result, in the single product case, economies of scale and existence of natural monopoly have a direct connection; in the multi-product case, this connection is more complex. In the following we consider characteristics of a natural monopoly in detail:

1. *Economies of scale*. For long time it was typical to say that economies of scale and natural monopoly are two identical concepts. Baumol (1977) was the first, who specified the concept of natural monopoly and analyzed their connection to economies of scale. Strict economies of scale in the production of outputs in N are present if for any input-output vector $(x_1,..., x_r; y_1,..., y_n)$, and for any $w > 1$ there is a viable input-output vector $(wx_1,..., wx_r; v_1y_1,..., v_ny_n)$, where all $v_i \geq w + \delta$ and $\delta > 0$ for all i (Baumol 1977, p. 810). To sum up, economies of scale exist if a proportional increase of all input factors brings about an over proportional increase of all output components. In the single-product case, economies of scale ensure decreasing average costs and are sufficient for the existence of a natural monopoly. However, they are not necessary. In the multi-product case, economies of scale are neither necessary nor sufficient for subadditivity (Baumol et al. 1982, p. 172).
2. *Economies of scope.* They result from the simultaneous production of several goods within a single firm and constitute a special case of cost subadditivity, where only such output vectors are chosen that are orthogonal to each other; i.e. that have no shared positive components. In the multi-product case, economies of scope are necessary for the existence of natural

monopoly. The general definition of economies of scope was introduced by Panzar and Willing (1981, pp. 268–269). Let $N = \{1,\ldots, n\}$ denote the set of products $y = (y_1,\ldots, y_n)$. If $T = \{T_1,\ldots, T_k\}$ denotes a non-trivial partition of N (i.e. $\cup_i T_i = N$, $T_i \cap T_j = \emptyset$ for $i \neq j$, $T_i \neq \emptyset$ and $k > 1$), then there are economies of scope in supplying output vector y with respect to partition T, if $\sum_{i=1}^{k} C(y_{T_i}) > C(y)$, with $y_{T_i} \in R^n$, $y_i > 0$ for $i \in T_i$ and $y_i = 0$ for $i \notin T_i$. To sum up, if there are economies of scope it is cheaper for one single company to produce all products together compared to different companies producing these products. According to Baumol et al. (1982, p. 173), economies of scale and scope do not imply subaddititivity.

3. *Cost complementarity*. The cost complementarity is the next cost concept which is sufficient for the existence of a natural monopoly. A cost function fulfils the conditions of cost complementarity if $C(x+z) - C(x) \geq C(x+y+z) - C(x+y)$ for all $x, y, z \geq 0$, and $x, y, z \in R^n$ (Sharkey 1982, p. 69). If C is cost complementary then C is subadditive.
4. *Decreasing average incremental cost and economies of scope.* It should be differentiated between a natural monopoly for all output vectors and a natural monopoly for one certain output. The incremental costs of a product $i \in N$ in producing an output vector y are $IC_i(y) = C(y) - C(y_{N-i})$, with $y_{N-i} \in R^n$, $y_i = 0$ and $y_{j \neq i} > 0$ (in y_{N-i}), and $AIC_i(y) = \frac{IC_i(y)}{y_i}$ the average incremental costs of the ith product. According to Baumol et al. (1982, p. 176), if for each good in output vector y the average incremental cost decreases and if C has economies of scope in the production of y then C is subadditive in y.

3.1.3 Price Setting in Natural Monopolies

In Fig. 3.1, the pricing options for a natural monopolist are presented. In the absence of intervention, an unregulated monopolist would charge a high price p_M. In these circumstances, a monopolist will maximize its profits by the relatively higher price, which lies above average cost and hence delivers a monopoly profit. As a result, service prices paid by consumers will be high, and those consumers will suffer to the benefit of shareholders in the monopoly, who will enjoy excess profits. In the ideal case, the prices of goods and services, sold in the economy, should be set at their marginal costs. The ideal price would be p_{MC}, where the demand curve DD cuts the marginal cost curve MC, because output has been expanded up to the point where the buyers' willingness to pay for an additional unit of services provided exactly equals the marginal cost to the economy of producing that final unit of output. At a price higher than this, the buyers' willingness to pay would exceed the marginal cost of providing an extra unit. At a price lower than this, the marginal cost to the economy of providing the last unit of output is greater than the buyers' willingness to pay for it. Therefore, the best price for the service is a price equal to marginal cost (the first-best solution). By this price, allocative efficiency in service provision is achieved. However, a price equal to p_{MC} would fail to cover the firm's average cost AC; hence the firm could not survive in the long run. p_{AC} is the lowest price being consistent with the firm breaking even (the second best). By this price, productive efficiency is achieved.

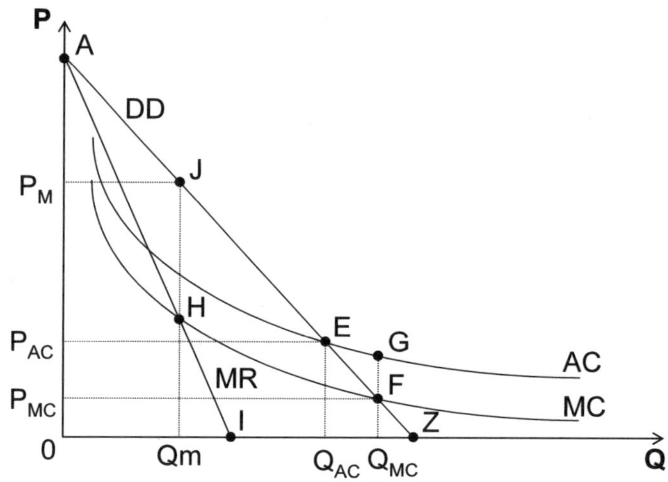

Source: Baldwin and Cave (1999, p. 206)

Fig. 3.1. Pricing options for a natural monopolist

In the case of a multi-product firm, however, it is not possible to identify individual average costs for separate services because these services will typically have common inputs such as capital equipment and, as a result, it will not be possible to attribute all costs unambiguously to individual services. The marginal costs of each service will be possible to establish, by identifying the increases in overall costs associated with increasing the output of any services when the output of other services is held constant.

As presented in Fig. 3.2, in the case of a multi-product firm, the ideal prices are where the demand curves DD^a and DD^b cut the marginal cost curves MC^a and MC^b. A firm charging such prices would, however, make losses as both products are produced in conditions of economies of scale. There is a need for a mark-up

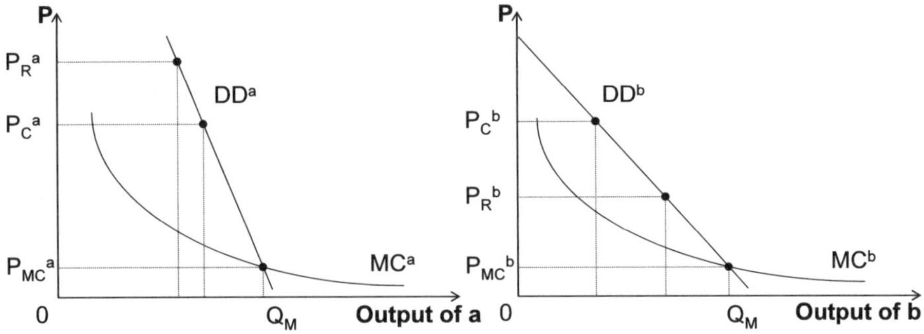

Source: Baldwin and Cave (1999, p. 208)

Fig. 3.2. Efficient pricing for a multi-product natural monopoly

above marginal costs. One option is that this mark-up would be an equal mark-up to cover common and fixed costs, i.e. P_C^a and P_C^b. The resulting prices would have distorting effects on the demand for both services. A better option is so-called Ramsey pricing (or Ramsey-Boiteux pricing),[1] P_R^a and P_R^b.

The main principle of the Ramsey pricing is the following: when prices are being set for a regulated monopoly, which produces a variety of services and which is required to break even, they should embody the minimum mark-ups above marginal costs that are necessary to allow the firm to break even. Services with relative elastic demand should generally have a lower than average proportionate mark-up, while the services with relative inelastic demand should have a higher than average mark-up over their marginal costs. Due to this principle, common costs will be recovered in a way that reduces the harmful effects of distortion in output caused by the mark-up over marginal costs to a minimum.

3.1.4 Competition and its Effects: Static and Dynamic Efficiency

Competition involves rivalry among firms for the customer's business across all the dimensions of the service – price, quality, and innovation. Competition is not something which is either fully present or fully absent – it is a matter of degree. The degree of rivalry encountered also depends upon firm behavior, which ranges from out-and-out competition in all dimensions of the service, through more limited forms of competition in which, for example, firms compete in terms of quality but not in terms of price, to openly or tacitly collusive or parallel behavior in all the dimensions of service provision (Baldwin and Cave 1999, p. 210).

A monopoly causes a static and a dynamic inefficiency. The static inefficiency means that for given technologies, monopoly pricing results in a welfare loss. This kind of inefficiency includes allocative and productive inefficiency. There is an

[1] Marcel Boiteux (1956) spoke about the mark-up rules for public monopolies. These are very closely related to that of Frank Ramsey (1927) on optimal taxation.

inverse relationship between market power (the ability of firms to set prices above marginal costs), of which monopoly power is the most extreme form, and (static) welfare. Market power brings about a welfare loss due to prices being too high. This welfare loss is labeled "allocative inefficiency", and is highest when market power coincides with monopoly power. By looking only at allocative inefficiency, one might actually underestimate the welfare losses from market power. High market power might also result in productive inefficiency. This inefficiency is connected to the fact that a monopolist charges not only a too high price, but it might also be insufficiently innovative, since – sheltered from competition – it is not pushed to adopt the most efficient technologies and to invest much in R&D. The statement that high market power decreases productive efficiency is based on two arguments: (1) competition pushes managers to make efforts and be more productive; (2) competition selects the more efficient firms, which results in lower market prices. However, it is not necessarily true that the larger the number of firms in an industry, the higher the welfare due to the inefficient duplication of fixed costs.

Dynamic efficiency[2] refers to the extent to which a firm introduces new products or processes of production – in other words, whether competition pushes them to move the efficient frontier of production further forward. In general, a monopolist might indeed have lower incentives to innovate, thus adding dynamic inefficiency to the list of welfare losses created by a monopoly. However, between market power and innovation, the following relationship exists: firms are unlikely to make any investment unless they can expect it to pay off, i.e. the expectation of market power has an important role as it gives firms incentives for R&D.

3.2 Theory of Monopolistic Bottlenecks and the Disaggregated Approach

Based on the above considerations, there are good reasons for permitting and, in some circumstances, even encouraging as much competition as is possible in the utilities sectors. The scope for competition, however, depends upon a variety of factors. The following concept for the localizing of market power of monopolistic bottlenecks in the context of the disaggregated approach in the network industries is elaborated by Knieps (1997, p. 327). Its theoretical basis was set up in the framework of the theory of contestable markets. The concept of contestable markets deals with influence of potential competition on the disciplining of natural monopoly behavior. A contestable market is one into which entry is absolutely free, and exit is absolutely costless (Baumol 1982, S.3). The crucial feature of a contestable market is its vulnerability to hit-and-run entry.

For specification of influence of potential competition in a contestable market, one considers the concept of the sustainability of a natural monopoly. A natural monopoly is sustainable under the following assumptions:

---

[2] As opposite to dynamic inefficiency.

1. Free market access: There is a large number of potential competitors that have unlimited access without loss of time to the same, most cost-efficient technology as the active provider.
2. Absence of irreversible cost: The investment necessary for market entry can be fully recovered in case of market exit. Market exit is possible without incurring cost or time loss. Active and potential competitors have the same decision-relevant cost function.
3. Bertrand–Nash-behavior: Potential competitors calculate their market chances by taking the incumbent's current price as given and undercutting it (assuming there is perfect information, i.e. there are no search costs).

Let's denote m and e as a single monopoly supplier and newcomer. The price vector p^m is sustainable if $p_S^e\ y_S^e - C(y_S^e) < 0$ for all $S \subset N$, $p_S^e \leq p_S^m$, $y_S^e \leq D^s(p_S^e, p_{(s)}^m)$, $y_S^e \neq D(p^m)$, $N - S \equiv (S)$ and $\Pi(p^m) = p^m D(p^m) - C(D(p^m)) \geq 0$. The natural monopoly is sustainable if there is at least one sustainable price vector (Panzar and Willing 1977, p. 5).

The next question is to what extent potential competition can be a substitute for the absence of competition between active suppliers in the market, i.e. to what extent is a natural monopoly contestable? Necessary conditions for sustainability of a natural monopoly include the following three points:

1. Natural monopolists have to produce efficiently: $\pi(p^m) = p^m\ y^m - \overline{C}(y^m) \geq 0$, Market entrant: $y^e = y^m$, $p^e < p^m$, $C(.)$, then it follows $\pi(p^e) = p^e y^m - C(y^m) = 0$.
2. Natural monopolists win no profit: if $\pi(p^m) > 0$, market entrant: $y^e = y^m$, $p^e < p^m$, consequently: $\pi(p^m) = p^m\ y^m - C(y^m) > 0$ and $p^e < p^m$, so that $\pi(p^e) = p^e\ y^m - C(y^m) \geq 0$.
3. There is no internal subsidization: if for all $S \subset N$: $\sum_{i \in S} p_i^m\ y_i^m \leq C(y_S^m)$, where $y_i^m = D^i(p^m)$.[3]

[3] This definition of internal subsidization formulated in Panzar, Willing (1977) based on Faulhaber (1975). According to Faulhaber, the price structure is subsidy-free if the provision of any commodity (or group of commodities) by a multi-commodity enterprise subject to a profit constraint leads to prices for the other commodities being no higher than they would pay by themselves. Knieps (1987) simplified this sustainability condition and arrived at the following result. Assume a cost function $K(N)$ and for the coalitions $S,T \subset N$ the following to apply: $K(S)+K(T) \geq K(S+T)$. (1) a revenues vector meets the criteria for cost covering if $\sum_{i=1}^{N} E_i = K(N)$, with $E_i \geq 0$. (2) a revenue vector passes the stand-alone cost test if $\sum_{i \in S} E_i \leq K(N)$, $\forall S \subset N$; (3) a revenue vector passes the incremental cost test if $\sum_{i \in S} E_i \leq \overline{K}(N)$,

If these three points are not fulfilled, there are incentives to abolish a natural monopoly. If the above mentioned assumptions and conditions are, however, fulfilled, there is no market power even though, based on the economies of bundling, only one active supplier presents in a market. By the absence of irreversible costs and Bertrand-Nash-behavior potential, competition is sufficient for the disciplining of an established operator.

The central conclusion of the contestable markets theory contests that not the existence of a natural monopoly itself but at the same time presentation of irreversible cost as a market entry barrier gives a reason for market power. Irreversible costs are not decision relevant for established suppliers; however, these play an important role for the newcomers. By achieving a sufficiently high share of irreversible cost in total costs, market entry can be excluded at all (Knieps and Vogelsang 1982, p. 240).[4]

Several authors also consider consumer switching costs and network effects to be market entry barriers. Motta (2004, p. 79) concludes that, although an unqualified proposition is not possible, especially in the light of the various strategic effects that they bring into play, switching costs are generally detrimental to welfare, because they make entry more difficult and market less competitive among other reasons. Klemperer (1995, p. 536), in his study analyzing switching cost in detail, arrived at the conclusion that "public policy should discourage activities that increase consumer switching costs (such as airlines' frequent-flyer programmes), and encourage activities that reduce them (such as standardization that enhances compatibility and reduces learning costs of switching, and quality regulation and information sources that reduce consumer uncertainty about untested brands)." Knieps (2001a, p. 93) postulates, however, that switching costs are not the reason for the monopolistic bottleneck and do not justify any special regulations – the technical regulation should solve problems concerning this issue.

The same situation concerns network effects. Motta (2004, p. 82) holds that, in some cases, if completely new networks are introduced, expectations about what other people will do are relevant. The expectations play a crucial role in network industries. This is why a potential entrant might find it very difficult to challenge an incumbent in these industries. Incumbents can also adopt a number of strategies which might delay or completely deter new entrants. First of all, incumbents will want to make sure that the new product cannot be compatible with theirs. Secondly, they might also engage in anti-competitive practices, e.g. announcing an upgrade in the near future to achieve product quality of a newcomer when it is not true. Knieps (2001a, p. 93) argues, however, that network externalities are not the

$\forall S \subset N,$ where $\overline{K}(S) = K(N) - K(N-S)$ is the incremental cost of S. The conclusion is that a price vector is free of internal subsidization, if (1) plus (2) or (1) plus (3) are fulfilled.

[4] A natural monopoly is sustainable (given an efficiently producing monopolistic firm), if $k > \frac{1}{2} C_o(D(p_o))$ where $k = K_o - K_1$ is the irreversible cost, and $p_o = \min_q \frac{C_o(q)}{q} = \min_q AC_o(q) = AC_0(q)$ as well as $q_0 < D(p_0)$.

reason for sector-specific regulation and technical regulatory instruments can be found to solve associated problems.

As a result, according to Knieps (2001a, p. 32), regulatory instruments, aiming at the disciplining of monopoly power, should be applied only to the parts of a natural monopoly which are characterized by irreversible cost. The latter is a barrier to entry in line with Stigler's concept (Stigler 1968, p. 67).[5] A barrier to entry may be defined as a cost of producing (at the same time or rate of output) which must be borne by firms already in the industry. This concept of market entry barriers helps to discover stable market power in the parts of network sectors which are characterized by high fixed costs and irreversible costs (see Table 3.1). These are monopolistic bottlenecks, such as airports, railways, electricity networks and local telecommunication networks.

To sum up, the disaggregated approach for the localization of market power in network industries is crystallized in the following main points: (1) process of market liberalization and abolishment of market entry barriers creates high competition potentials in all network sectors; (2) the disaggregated approach for the localization of market power is tailored by the concept of monopolistic bottleneck; (3) in most network sectors, monopolistic bottlenecks exist which require regulation for the disciplining of remaining monopoly power; (4) sector-specific regulation can be phased out if competition is created through technological progress; regulatory review is needed; (5) generally, competition potential on the de-regulated markets can provide efficient solutions as far as there is a symmetric access to the monopolistic bottleneck.

Table 3.1. Localizing monopolistic bottlenecks

	With irreversible costs	Without irreversible costs
Natural monopoly	Monopolistic bottlenecks	Potential competition
No natural monopoly	Competition between active suppliers	Competition between active suppliers

Source: Knieps (2004, chart 13)

The situation focusing on the telecommunications sector is presented in Table 3.2. The market for public telephone services is contestable, because suppliers of value added services are also prepared to offer telephone services if the legal

[5] Stigler's concept of entry barriers plays an important role in the regulation theory. In industrial economics, Bain's concept found its central position. Both concepts aim at advantages of the established firms compared to newcomer firms and resulting market power. However, advantages by Stigler are coming through cost asymmetries; by Bain, they also resulted from historical/accidental differences. According to Bain, condition of entry is "the extent to which, in the long run, established firms can elevate their selling prices above the minimal average costs of production and distribution (those costs associated with operation at optimal scales) without inducing potential entrants to enter the industry."

entry barrier disappears. The large market share of the incumbent company plays a minor role due to the fact that inefficient suppliers would lose their customers.[6] But contestable sub-areas can also be identified in the area of telecommunications infrastructure. An essential condition for the functioning of potential competition in order to discipline firms already providing network services is that the incumbent company does not have cost advantages over potential entrants.

If, however, the economies of bundling in combination with sunk costs are relevant, market power is to be expected and neither active nor potential competition can fulfill the function of disciplining the active supplier. According to Knieps (2004, chart 13b), sunk costs are only relevant in the cable-based telecommunications infrastructure. In a long-distance telecommunications network, economies of bundling do not exist; competition between active and potential firms will prevent the existence of market power. To multi-route in long distance networks, every network carrier can easily be substituted by an alternative (or potential) one. By contrast, the local cable based networks are considered as non-contestable networks. Based on the economies of scale in providing local network access, only one active provider of a local cable based network will exist. In addition, irreversible costs create market power for the incumbent firm. The essential point is that the local networks are an important input to complete long distance telecommunications, so they are also referred to as monopolistic bottleneck. For the effectiveness of actual and potential competition in long-distance telecommunications networks, it is important that all (active and potential) suppliers have equal (symmetric) access to the complementary monopolistic bottleneck. Due to this fact, it is necessary that actual market power in networks is regulated in an effective way, as long as the conditions of a monopolistic bottleneck are valid. In all other subparts of telecommunications networks, competition will lead to efficient market results.

Table 3.2. Local telecommunications networks as monopolistic bottleneck facilities

	Economies of bundling	Irreversible costs
Terminal equipment	No	No
Telecommunications services (including voice telephone services)	Yes	No
Satellite/mobile networks	Yes	No
Long-distance cable-based networks	No	Yes
Local cable-based networks	Yes	Yes

Source: Knieps (2004, chart 13b)

As a result, the aim of future regulatory policy should not be the global regulation of markets. Instead, only a disaggregated regulation of non-contestable networks is

[6] A precondition for this is implementation of number portability (Knieps 1997, p. 327).

justified. The aim then is to localize the market power in monopolistic bottleneck areas and discipline it by regulatory intervention. Asymmetry of market power due to monopolistic bottleneck facilities, however, does not by itself require asymmetric regulation. Instead, the symmetry principle requires that all firms have access to local telecommunications networks on terms identical to those of the incumbent (non-discriminatory access). The symmetry principle demands that only bottleneck facilities are regulated, irrespective of whether the owner is the incumbent or a newcomer (Knieps 2001b, p. 280). The detailed consideration of regulatory policy is presented in part 4 of this investigation.

3.3 Privatization in the Telecommunications Sector

The political and economic policy of privatization, defined as the deliberate sale by a government of state-owned enterprises (SOEs) or assets to private economic agents (Megginson and Netter 2001, p. 321). A broader definition of enterprise-level privatization includes any takeover of property rights (control over use, benefits from property, transfer or sell, exclusion rights) on companies or parts of companies by a private subject. Property rights can be time-limited and without limits and can be transferred fully or partly.

3.3.1 Privatization Objectives and Possible Trade-Offs

In general, many different privatization objectives can be encompassed in the three following categories:[7] (1) increase of economic efficiency at the level of individual firms, markets as well as the whole economy (efficiency objectives). In transition and developing countries, the attraction of foreign direct investments (FDI) through privatization can be a special objective. Due to the fact that the major objective of the FDI promotion is an increase in efficiency, for example, through the transfer of technology and managerial know-how, in this study it is analyzed under the efficiency objectives; (2) raise of revenues for government activities (the fiscal objectives). In developing and transition countries, the objectives of the state can also be related to monetary policy; (3) seeking of political advantage by means of income redistribution (the distributional objectives). These three categories of the privatization objectives, with possible trade-offs between each other, which are described below, are summarized in Fig. 3.3.

It is prudent to assume that governments are driven primarily by efficiency considerations in their initial decision to divest public assets. Schipke (2001, p. 128) argues that other objectives have often been the driving force behind divestment.

[7] For example, Jasinski and Yarrow (1996, p. 9), Schipke (2001, p. 9ff), Welfens (2000, p. 23), Guislain (1997, p. 18).

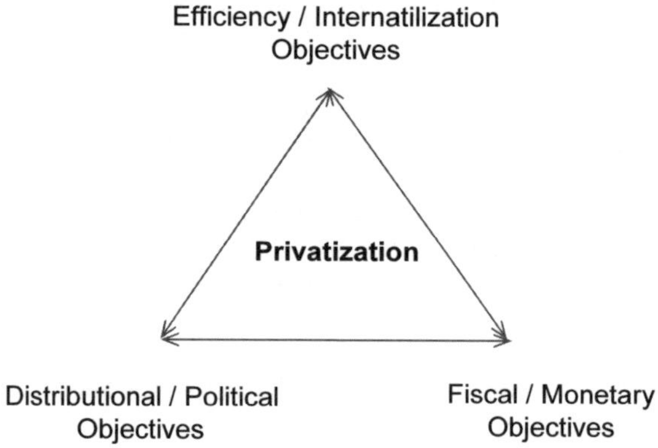

Source: Modified based on Welfens (2000, p. 23), Schipke (2001), Jasinski and Yarrow (1996, p. 9)

Fig. 3.3. Privatization objectives

3.3.1.1 Efficiency/Internationalization Objectives

With respect to private ownership, it is assumed that owners are profit maximizers and more interested than their public counterparts in the financial performance of the firm. Financial performance is, for example, measured by profits or share price. Given the fact that public enterprises are controlled by the government and foreign ownership has traditionally been limited, privatization might especially profit from the attraction of FDIs. These could be capital accumulation as well as a transfer of technology and managerial know-how. With respect to public ownership, an economist would naturally assume that the objective will be to maximize social welfare, which is defined as economic efficiency, usually measured by the sum of consumers' and producers' surpluses. The latter leads to the term public interest theory of state-owned enterprises, which suggest that in markets, where there are market failures, public enterprises can do better by correcting the misalignment of public and private objectives. This theory does not, however, take account of two important results concerning the fact that the relative efficiency performance of public and private enterprises will tend to depend upon: (1) whether or not the relevant market is subject to inefficiencies on account of monopolization or other types of market failure; and (2) where there is market failure, the effectiveness of alternative regulatory instruments. To sum up, factors such as competitive conditions and regulatory environments are important determinants of the likely performance of different types of ownership (Jasinski and Yarrow 1996, p. 9).

The studies on privatization cited almost unanimously reports of increases in performance associated with privatization. The studies of post-performance examine the effects on groups such as workers but rarely the welfare effects on consumers. Only a few studies control the possible use of market power by privatized firms. That is, performance improvement could be due to greater exploitation of monopoly power, which has harmful effects on allocative efficiency (Megginson and Netter 2001, p. 347).

3.3.1.2 Fiscal/Monetary Objectives

An important motive for privatization is the government's need to raise revenues or reduce expenditure, in other words, selling SOEs gives governments opportunities to capitalize future streams of earnings and thereby raises immediate revenues. In this respect, privatization is to be compared with selling government bonds as a means of raising funds. A preference for equity over bond sales might arise when a government is constrained in its ability to sell bonds, e.g. negative consequences of the perceived risk of default on bonds, which is an increasing function of an economy's debt-to income ratio, are greater than those associated with equity risk (Jasinski and Yarrow 1996, p. 26).

Governments can use privatization in such cases as balance-of-payments crises and monetary policy. The privatization revenues may be used as an additional instrument for dealing with temporary surges in capital inflows (Schipke 2001, p. 128).

3.3.1.3 Distributional/Political Objectives

In practice, the transfer of ownership is likely to give rise to non-trivial shifts in income distribution. Government policies can be heavily influenced by demands from income redistribution from various interest groups. This means that privatization presents opportunities to politicians for income and wealth transfers to favored groups and it would be naive to simply ignore this aspect of the policy process.

Three factors give rise to redistributional effects (Yarrow 1986, p. 355). The first is the change in both the level and structure of output prices that may occur following privatization, e.g. significant adjustments in the relative prices of business/residential or long-/short-distance calls as cross-subsidization is reduced. The second is the price at which shares in an enterprise that is being sold are offered to the market. Discounts on the market-clearing price represent a transfer of wealth to the new owners from the wider public and, more particularly, from taxpayers. Thirdly, privatization may also redistribute income towards those associated with the provision of services that can be regarded as inputs into the process of selling assets: for example, financial institutions responsible for underwriting and placing or advertising agencies running the campaign.

There can clearly be significant conflicts between these three privatization objectives, and hence the resolution of these conflicts or trade-offs can be an important determinant for the shape of individual privatization programs. When selling a state-owned monopoly, promotion of efficiency may require the introduction of competition and/or regulatory measures to contain the firm's monopoly power. But the revenues from asset sales are likely to be higher if such steps are not taken. The search for maximum revenue may also come into conflict with distributional/political goals that might be better served by selling the enterprises equity at a low price (Jasinski and Yarrow 1996, p. 19).

3.3.2 Forms of Private Participation

Private activity in telecommunications is defined by a strong focus on private ownership and management. This trend is reflected in the fact that the dominant form of private participation in telecommunications in terms of investment and projects are greenfield projects and divestitures.[8]

Divestitures in the sector – a private entity purchases an equity stake (100% or a part) in a state-owned enterprise through an asset sale, public offering, or mass privatization program – took different forms across regions. In East and South Asia, divestitures were commonly carried out through public offerings of minority stakes on local or regional stock exchanges, with the government keeping control of the companies. In other developing regions, divestitures were usually structured as the sale of controlling stakes to strategic operators.

Greenfield projects, with "build, own, and operate" as a main form, were used mainly to introduce mobile services and to create competition in the telecommunications sector. Thus, the rapid growth of their share in annual investments reflects the rapid development of mobile telecommunications and introduction of competition in basic services.

From the period 1990 to 2003, of the US $362 billion committed to telecommunications projects with private participation, about US $159 billion has gone to 477 greenfield projects and US $197 billion to 113 divestitures. The resources captured by divestitures have been directed to network expansion and modernization (55%) and divestiture revenues (45%). By 2003, most developing economies with private participation in the sector had exposed mobile phone services to competition, though they were taking a more cautious approach to basic services. A regional breakdown of projects by 2003 showed that Latin America and the Caribbean led the way of private participation in telecommunication (47%); the share of Europe and Central Asia accounted for 22%. Among segments, stand-alone mobile operators and fully integrated providers dominated investment. The stand-alone mobile operators are the leaders that reflect the worldwide boom in mobile telephony. Almost all stand-alone mobile service companies were created through greenfield projects.

3.3.3 Telecommunications Privatization Experiences Around the World

National telecommunications companies, or "telecoms", have been in state hands since the dawn of the electronics era in most rich countries (with exception of the

[8] According to the classification of the World Bank, all private participation activities in infrastructure projects can be classified into four categories: (1) management and lease contracts, private participation forms where a private entity takes over the management of a state-owned enterprise for a fixed period while ownership and investment decisions remain with the state; (2) concessions (or management and operation contracts with major private capital expenditure), the forms where a private entity takes over the management of a state-owned enterprise for a given period during which it also assumes significant investment risk; (3) greenfield projects; (4) divestitures.

United States) as well as in virtually all the developing nations. Therefore, many authors e.g. Wallsten (1999, 2000), Noll (1999) see telecoms' privatization as a truly epochal shift in the balance of state power within every economy where denationalization is attempted. In addition, like in the other infrastructure sectors, citizens have a direct economic stake in the cost and quality of telecommunications services being provided, so their privatization is always controversial. The financial impact of telecom sales is also huge due to the fact that telecommunications share issue privatizations are almost always one of the largest share offerings in national history. Furthermore, telecommunications shares become the "bellweather" stocks on national exchanges, often accounting for 30% or more of total capitalization and an even greater share of total trading volume (Boutchkova and Meggison 2000). Besides these facts, the sizable share of population involved in the telecommunications share issue privatizations, e.g. in France 16% of the population purchased shares in the initial public offering of France Telecom and became shareholders for the first time. Finally, an efficient communications sector is vital for a modern economy. However, it requires high sector investments, so only a few governments can either achieve or effectively manage it. All these reasons make privatization of telecoms high-stakes gambles, and selling governments typically approach divestment with great anxiety (Bortolotti et al. 2002, p. 244).

Due to the economic importance of national telecommunications industries and a rich variety of regulatory and financial issues following their privatizations, many researchers have examined effects of telecommunications privatizations empirically. Their studies, e.g. Wallsten (1999, 2000), Ros (2003), Ros and Banerjee (2000), McNary (2000), Bortolotti et al. (2002), generally indicate that in developing and developed economies, deregulation and liberalization of telecommunications services are associated with significant growth in teledensity and operating efficiency, also with a significant improvement in quality and a fall in prices of telecommunications services. The impact of privatization is less obvious, but most studies agree that privatization ensures its positive impact on rates of phone penetration and efficiency only when linked with deregulation, liberalization and efficient regulation (as a rule with an independent regulator).

In the transition economies, due to the lack of adequate or reliable data, there is still limited empirical evidence concerning this issue. Vagliasindi (2004) bases her investigation on enterprise surveys. This does not allow her to estimate a panel regression, but it does allow the implementation of both qualitative and quantitative measures in terms of infrastructure service access and reliability. She can also capture the variation of these measures across several enterprise types (including ownership, size, and location). Her results are as follows: at the enterprise level, the reduction of utility areas is significantly associated with lower costs in terms of interruption of telecom service provision. At the country level, increased investment, tariff increases and the establishment of an independent regulator are all significantly associated with the reduction of telecom outages.

3.3.4 Obstacles for Privatization in Transition Countries

Privatization is only part of the massive changes in the economy as transition countries move from communism to more market oriented methods of allocating resources and organizing production, so this process is particularly challenging.

In market economies with predominantly private ownership of productive assets, privatization can be analyzed against a background of relatively constant economic institutions. Transformational privatization is characterized by the fact that the institutional background is not relatively fixed, but rather is changing as a result of processes that are closely linked with privatization, e.g. creation of a domestic stock market and democratization of the state.

Many of the insights gained from the study of privatization programs in market economies are relevant to transformational privatization, but they often have to be developed and extended to take account of the more general economic, social and political changes that occur together with privatization (Jasinski and Yarrow 1996, p. 31).

The Soviet-type economies were based on concepts of socialists in general and Marxists in particular, who began systematically to question the legitimacy and effectiveness of private ownership of the means of production, and who argued for an economic system in which this form of ownership would be abolished. Before the collapse of Soviet-type economies in the late 1980s, there had been many attempts to reform, e.g. give some degree of autonomy to individual enterprises or provide appropriate incentives for managers and workers.

From a theoretical point of view, central planners were just like ministers supervising state-owned enterprises in market economies, in that they did not tend to benefit greatly from improved performance of the firms under their control. In practice, however, given the lack of private capital markets and general suppression of product market competition, agency problems under central planning had to be solved with a much reduced set of instruments and with very little access to reliable information.

In Soviet-type economies, competition understood as rivalry in and for market places was not only present but impossible. This also was considered by planners to be highly wasteful and therefore undesirable. The state-owned enterprises compete with each other in order to gain administratively allocated resources; most often to force central planners to give them as much as possible in return for as little as possible. This competition for investment funds as well as for raw materials and other inputs had little to do with the competition in and for markets that can be observed in market economies.

The situation did not change much with attempts to give autonomy to enterprises and to introduce better incentives. As long as most assets belonged to the state and money played only a passive role, and as long as the higher-level political agency problem remain untackled, there was a very strict limit to the performance improvements that could be made.

Jasinski and Yarrow (1996, p. 31) argue that the ubiquitous character of public ownership and the absence of competition imply that it is regulation (in a very general sense) that plays the decisive role in "solving" resource allocation problems in Soviet-type economies. It is possible to argue that central planning was nothing but an expanded version of the kind of regulation imposed on public utilities in market economies. On the other hand, it should be recognized that such extension of regulation is likely to have a material impact on its effectiveness. In particular, the scope of regulation can be expected to have substantial effects on information conditions, and hence on incentives, throughout the whole economy. However, it can be argued that central planning and the regulation of natural monopolies in market economies are similar. Most market economies have the advantage that most input prices will be set in reasonably competitive markets, and hence that information for monitoring costs will be superior to that typically available under central planning.

Among the advantages that have been claimed for transformational privatization are: (1) an increase in the productive efficiency of the existing assets, which, since inefficiency was an endemic characteristic of the socialist economies, offers the prospect of larger gains than in market economies; (2) help to eliminate soft budget constraints (i.e. the willingness of the state to provide further finance to state-owned enterprises if targets are not met), which again are much more pervasive in Soviet-type economies than in market economies; (3) establishment of a sounder basis for general micro-economic policies which, in the absence of privatization, may continue to be set and implemented via bureaucratic bargaining; (4) extension of economic freedom and a limit to the power and authority of the state; and (5) help to create political stability by giving more people a well defined stake in the new system.

Much transformational privatization is accompanied by deregulation, i.e. the regulatory aspect of state-ownership disappears in the moment of privatization and the activities of the given enterprises become subject only to general legal regulation. However, by considering the utility sector, as in market economies, the relationships between privatization and regulation become much more complex. As was expected, privatization of public utilities including telecommunications was given a relatively low initial priority in transition economies. Jasinski and Yarrow (1996, p. 31) point out two main arguments against delaying utilities privatization. Firstly, it is a pressing requirement to raise finance for investment in utility infrastructures. It does not necessarily mean that existing state-owned enterprises should be privatized but, at the least, it will require reforms to open up the relevant sectors to private capital, including foreign investment. Secondly, utility privatizations can be a political advantage to governments in gaining popular support for the transformation process.

3.3.5 Transformation and Timing, Sequencing and Staging in the Sector Reforms

A very important aspect of privatization of SOE and market liberalization in transition economies is timing, i.e. which arguments exist in favor of delayed privatization and liberalization. The interrelated questions are; what order should be followed in privatizing (sequencing), whether to sell an SOE all at once or in stages (staging), and whether to restructure an SOE prior to sale.

In the ideal type reference model of a market-oriented infrastructure policy, there is no reason to delay the restructuring process (Von Hirschhausen 2002, p. 82). Concerning transition economies, two opposite options exist on this issue. The first, the prevailing view in the early 1990s, is to carry out privatization particularly rapidly before the firms are restructured. This is called the big bang strategy (e.g. Lipton and Sachs, 1990). The arguments in favor of this strategy were the following: (1) the same factors and incentives that led the state to be inefficient – and often corrupt – managers of state-owned firms would prevent them from properly restructuring (Roland 1994); (2) a danger of a coalition against competition-oriented reforms was particularly high in the traditional infrastructure sectors, and the danger of a roll-back of reform efforts was in general high in the early phase of reform; (3) a successful implementation of reforms in one sector could have positive external effects for the reform process as a whole.

Arguments in favor of delayed deregulation and privatization usually rely on assumptions of incomplete information and institutional instability. It is argued that, given high uncertainty in the early transformation stage, delaying the reform process may be welfare-enhancing: the option value of delaying reforms is higher than the expected loss of welfare from not having reformed immediately. By the privatization of an infrastructure enterprise in the early transformation period, there is a risk of selling to a "wrong" investor. This risk is lower with decreasing information asymmetry. On the other hand, extending state ownership increases the risk of productive inefficiency, the welfare losses of which have to be weighed against the welfare gains of delaying privatization.

One main argument for delaying liberalization, market opening for potentially competitive segments and regulation of the remaining natural monopoly, is the high uncertainty of what the optimal sequencing might be for a transition economy. Hirschhausen (2002, p. 83) argued that, given the large political, macro- and micro-uncertainty that is a reasonable argument for the impossibility of direct transfer of established Western European regulatory models, "waiting" can be a dominant strategy in the transition countries.

Objective need for large investments in an institutionally unstable environment – i.e. a high regulatory risk – is a transformation-specific argument for delayed liberalization. Armstrong and Vickers (1996) have developed a model that accepts urgent investment requirements as a (politically) given external constraint, and then asks what this implies for the speed of liberalization. They consider the optimal timing of liberalization as a function of the two risks that an investor faces in transformation conditions: (1) expropriation risk is the danger of losing the quasi-rent once the investment is sunk; (2) liberalization risk is the possibility of the opening of the formerly monopolistic market without prior notice, and thus the expected monopolistic profits do not materialize. From the model of Armstrong and Vickers (1996) it follows that, if the expropriation risk is high in relation to the liberalization risk, then early liberalization has a positive effect on infrastructure capacity and thus on investment, because revenues with liberalization exceed regulated monopoly revenue adjusted for regulatory risk. A low expropriation risk would suggest that a later date of liberalization is conducive to increasing investments. As result, delaying liberalization in transition economies can be justified if short-term investment requirements are high, and the institutional environment is unstable (high regulatory risk).

According to the summarizing study of Meggison and Netter (2001, p. 341), several authors have theoretically modeled the sequencing and staging of SOE sales. Their models illustrate the importance of sequencing and staging by the privatizing government to build reputation capital with investors, encourage domestic support for the program, and identify bidders that will maximize efficiency.

A related practical question about privatization is whether governments should restructure SOEs prior to selling or leave this to the new owners. Early advice from the World Bank was that governments should restructure SOEs prior to divestment, since governments are able to cushion the financial blow to displaced workers better than private owners by using unemployment payments or pensions (Nellis and Kireri 1989). However, over time this opinion altered. Nellis et al. (1992) opine that small and medium-sized SOEs should be sold as is at the best price possible, as quickly as possible. In addition, they argue that in all cases new investments "should be left to private owners once a decision has been made to privatize the enterprise". Lopez-de-Silanes (1997) examines whether prior government restructuring of SOEs improves the net price received for the company, and finds evidence that it does not. However, his investigation is based on a small sample of banks, which limits its usefulness. Dewenter and Malatesta (2001) find some evidence that the improvements brought about by privatization occur before the SOE is privatized.

According to Wallsten (2002), who empirically proves the sequencing issues in telecommunications based on data for 197 countries from 1985 to 1999, regulatory authority prior to privatization will facilitate improvements in the sector following privatization; failure to put in place the regulatory framework prior to privatization will reduce the value of the firm to investors.

3.4 Liberalization of the Telecommunications Sector

Substantial evidence reveals that privatization can lead to performance improvements. However, privatization has yielded significant benefits; the sale of a public enterprise has little immediate impact on market structure (Yarrow 1986, p. 333). Allowing entry and competition into the sector appears to bring far greater benefits. A monopoly provider, whether state-owned or private, faces fewer incentives to improve service and lower prices than do firms operating in a competitive environment. As Ambrose et al. (1990) postulated, "simply moving a monopoly from the public to the private sphere will not result in competitive behaviour". Empirical research finds that competition drives the biggest improvements in the sector. In the next section, we turn our attention to and investigate in detail the liberalization process in the telecommunications sector.

3.4.1 Restructuring as an Element of Liberalization

The disaggregated approach for the localization of market power in the network industries shows that in virtually every infrastructure sector, there are some services that can be provided competitively, while there remain some services that are likely to be monopolistic bottlenecks in the production chain. In practice, there are three main institutional options of infrastructure restructuring to consider (World Bank 2002, p. 155):

Option A, in which the owner of the monopoly bottleneck enterprise continues to operate in the "competitive" sector in competition with other providers in that sector (that is, an integrated firm subject to competition in the non-bottleneck market).

Option B, in which the owner of the monopoly bottleneck enterprise operates as a monopolist in the (otherwise) competitive sector as well (that is, an integrated monopolist).

Option C, in which the owner of the monopoly bottleneck enterprise is not permitted to operate in the competitive sector but, rather, provides connecting service to the competitive firms operating there (that is, vertical separation with competition).

Option C brings the great advantage that it overcomes problems associated with vertical integration, when a monopolist in one area of activity has an opportunity to extend its market power from that area into related competitive markets. The disadvantage of such break-ups, however, is that they prevent the realization of those economies of scope that might be available to a firm undertaking several connected activities. For example, a single telecommunications operator running both a local and a long-distance network may have lower costs than two separate firms operating the networks independently. The World Bank writes in its report on infrastructure in the developing world (2002, p. 157) that telecommunications appear to be a sector where competition can often coexist with vertical integration (option A).

3.4.2 Liberalization of Market Entry

The first step in introducing competition in utilities is achieved by liberalizing entry into what had formally been a statutory monopoly. Usually, entrants into utilities markets have to acquire a license from the relevant government department. The argument for the licensing necessity is related to the fact that certain conditions relating to consumer protection have to be imposed and integrity of the network has to be maintained. In the competitive situation of mobile telecommunications, frequencies are scarce resources, which suggest licensing.

If competition is introduced in a utilities sector, the situation is highly unusual, since the incumbent has the 100% market share. Where the incumbent is vertically integrated (involved in up-stream and down-stream markets) additional problems arise. Newcomer firms have to use networks of the incumbent company, in particular to terminate calls made by its subscribers to the incumbent's network. As a result, there are two linked problems, the first arising from the existence of a highly dominant firm in the market, the second – that is often the case – from vertical integration of the dominant firm. In order to deal with the problem of dominance, some additional regulations, compared to ordinary competition law, are appropriate in the early stages of the development of competition. These regulations can be justified as interim measures necessary for the competition development in the markets which had been an "unnatural monopoly" over a long time (Baldwin and Cave 1999, p. 218). However, this approach overlooks potential medium-term problems in establishing nationwide competition for Internet services (provided mobile telephony is a full substitute for fixed lines).

3.4.3 Price Liberalization and Cross-Subsidizing Mechanisms

The other factor, influencing the scope of competition, is the fact that many utilities have pricing structures that embody considerable amounts of cross-subsidies. In the past, telecommunications services, in particular the telephony service, were generally considered public services, to be provided to all members of society at a reasonable cost. When competition is introduced into a market involving cross-subsidies, there is a risk that this competition will be distorted. With liberalization debates, fulfillment of universal service obligations is the main argument against liberalization of the telecommunications market because, under market conditions, service would either fall short of full coverage or lead to unfair trading conditions. The proponents of liberalization argued, to the contrary, that competition would help extend service coverage and that market shortfalls could be prevented through regulatory measures (Cullen international/WIK 2001, p. 13).

Traditionally, before the deregulation of telecommunications, the universal service objectives, realized mainly through cross-subsidizing mechanisms, relied on the practices of market power to support above-cost pricing in some services or to some customers, in order to generate profits to allow the below-cost pricing of others.[9] The cross-subsidization policies were adopted by both state-owned and privately-owned operators during most of the twentieth century.

Generally two types of internal cross-subsidies were implemented by the incumbent. Inter-service cross-subsidization features low cost pricing of access and usage charges for local calls and high cost pricing of long-distance and international calling; the subsidy flows from long-distance and international calling to access and local calls. Intra-service cross-subsidization is the subsidization by the geographic tariff averaging between access price in rural and high-cost areas and urban and low-cost areas, or between business and residential access services. Figure 3.4 presents these situations graphically.

[9] The theoretical aspects of internal subsidization are presented in the Sect. 3.2.

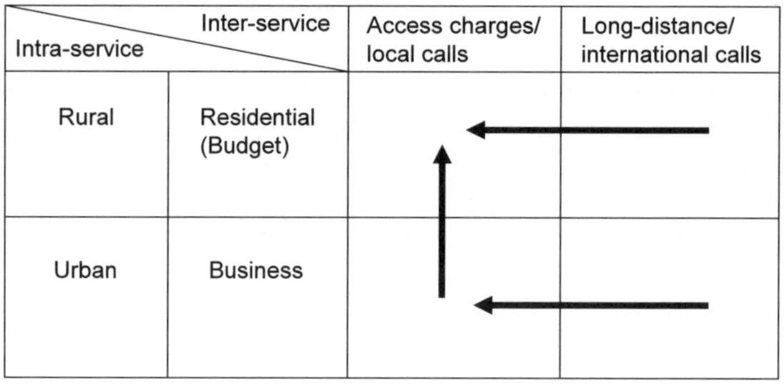

Source: Borrows et al. (1994, p. 45), own modification

Fig. 3.4. Types of cross-subsidization

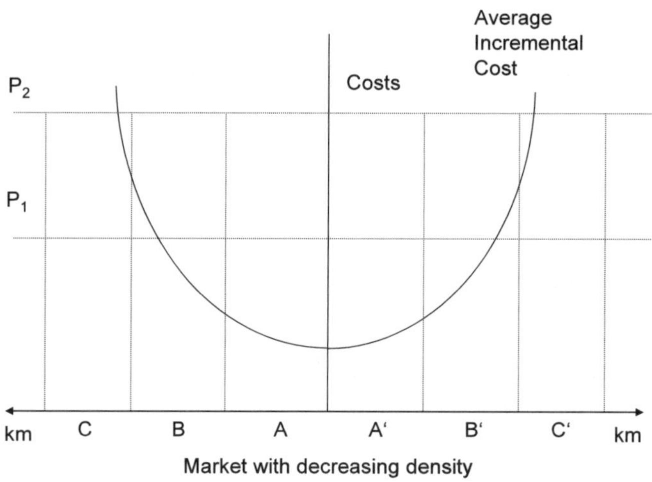

Source: Knieps and Blankart (1994, p. 241)

Fig. 3.5. Instability of cross-subsidization in the process of market liberalization

Although cross-subsidization policy was commonly used in most countries, it is being phased out in many countries. The main reason is the un-sustainability of this mechanism. Competitive un-sustainability creates problems by opening up the market for competition. New entrants target profitable market segments or services which provide subsidies and, because of this, the possibility of cross-subsidization is reduced or eliminated. Knieps and Blankart (1994, p. 241) introduced this situation (Fig. 3.5) with the unit price requested by the universal services and economies of density which characterizes the telecommunications sector. The cost of proving telecommunications services is lower the closer the users are together.

The low density in remote areas means that the average marginal cost of service provision is higher than in urban areas. The unit price P_1 is not stable. In the profitable area there will be many "cream skimming" telecommunications companies. P_2 could be the profitable price and stable price for the remote areas which could bring telecommunications services to the rest of country's territory.

A unit price like P_1 encompasses inter cross-subsidizing between different user groups. However, these user groups can be served independently and, in most cases, pay lower prices. In addition, they receive the subsidy, it does not depend on whether they can afford this service or not. The same situation can result from cross-subsidization between different products.

The fact that subsidies lower demand for the higher cost services which provide the subsidies is an acknowledged weaknesses of cross-subsidization mechanisms. They can be used by the anti-competitive subsidization; subsidies are aimed only at existing users. Rebalancing of tariffs so that they better reflect the underlying cost structure is considered as a pre-requisite for full competition. It is clear that the process of tariff rebalancing could be painful in the short term and the need to raise tariffs for local telephony could have a negative impact on the universal service objectives (Cullen International/WIK 2001).

4 Theory of Network Regulation and Regulatory Policy Options in the Telecommunications Sector

Regulation is very often associated with the post-privatization control of utilities. However, regulation has been practiced in many countries for many decades, e.g. in Britain since the Tudor and Stuart period at least.

Based on Baldwin and Cave (1999, p. 223), three phases involved in the transition process from monopoly to fully competitive markets can be primarily differentiated (see Fig. 4.1). In phase one, pre-competitive markets, competition is emerging, and regulation can be used to prevent any firm monopolizing a distribution network, giving an advantage to an affiliated supplier over any others or disclosing the access for market newcomers. Price regulation of suppliers (end-customer prices) as well as of monopoly distribution elements (access prices) are used to protect end-consumers as well as newcomers; and sector-specific measures, covering such matters as service standards, are again necessary to protect consumers. In phase two, emerging competitive markets, price regulation can be withdrawn from fully competitive parts of the market (but retained for monopoly network provision) and firms allowed to compete. As competition increases, there may be a regulatory retreat from detailed prescriptive controls over such matters as service standards and growing reliance on market pressure to protect consumers. In phase three, fully competitive markets, economic regulation becomes largely unnecessary and general competition laws can be used to secure the operation of the market. The need to regulate becomes confined to the use of special rules to ensure such matters as the compatibility of networks and the ability of consumers to purchase from a range of suppliers. Limited social objectives (such as universal service) can be achieved through special arrangements which are designed to avoid distorting competition.

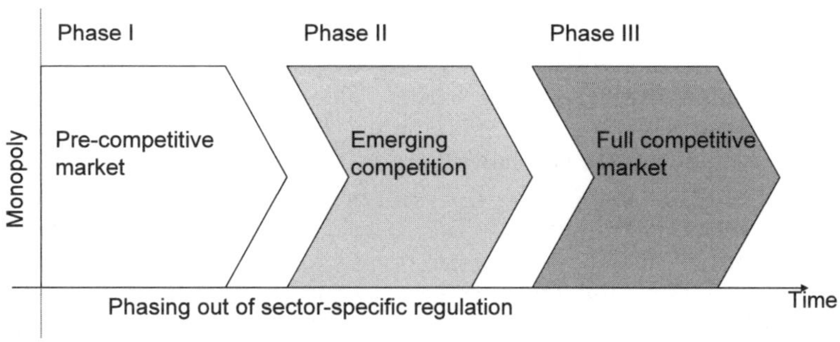

Source: Baldwin and Cave (1999, p. 223)

Fig. 4.1. Three phases of sector-specific regulation

The economics of regulation, pioneered by Baron and Myerson (1982) and Laffont and Tirole (1993), analyzes the optimal design of regulation to encourage efficiency. One of the main insights coming from this literature is that high powered incentive schemes (price-cap) should be preferred to low powered schemes (rate of return regulation) to encourage short run efficiency. However, there is no clear consensus on the impact of different regulatory schemes on long-run investment, which depends significantly on the way different regulatory schemes are implemented (Vagliasindi 2004, p. 303).

4.1 Ramsey–Boiteux Pricing: The Second-Best Price Solution

On the assumption that the regulator has full information about cost and demand, the optimal price structure for a multi-product firm, given that the overall price structure must enable it to break even, is the Ramsey-Boiteux pricing. As a result, the basic principle of second-best price solution (or Ramsey-Boiteux pricing) is as follows:[1]

$$\frac{p_i - MC_i}{p_i} = -\frac{\lambda}{1+\lambda} * \frac{1}{\varepsilon_i}, \tag{4.1}$$

where p_i is price of the product i, MC_i is the marginal cost of the product i, ε_i is the own elasticity of demand of product i.

In practice, the regulators have less information about the firm's demand and cost function than is presumed by the Ramsey-Boiteux approach. The question arising in many studies is should utility prices still abide by the business principles enunciated by Ramsey and Boiteux? According to Laffont and Tirole (2000, p. 65), deviations from the Ramsey-Boiteux precepts would be warranted only if they facilitated the regulator's extraction of the firm's rent. Departures from Ramsey-Boiteux pricing raise the prices of some services and lower those of other services. Laffont and Tirole (1990) provide sufficient conditions under which such a rebalancing of rates away from the Ramsey-Boiteux structure does not help to alleviate the informational asymmetry and reduce the firm's rent, and is therefore undesirable. Prices are confined to their allocative role, and rent extraction is performed through the earnings-sharing scheme. This dichotomy seems a reasonable benchmark, unless there is a good presumption that raising the price of a service and lowering that of another helps to reduce the firm's rent.

The applicability of the Ramsey-Boiteux pricing is wide. However, sometimes some reinterpretations are required. The Ramsey-Boiteux model is apparently a static, "one-period" model. The intertemporal situation is considered to be that the same service offered at different dates should be thought of and treated as different services. Thus, formally, the Ramsey-Boiteux model with n services and T regulatory periods can be reinterpreted as a static one with nT services. The Ramsey-Boiteux model, assuming linear prices can be adjusted to nonlinear pricing. For example, a two-part tariff with fixed and variable charges should be analyzed

[1] For mathematical details see e.g. Laffont and Tirole (2000, p. 64), Knieps (2001a, p. 84–85).

as the provision by the firm of two services "connection" and "consumption". In the case of externalities, the Ramsey-Boiteux pricing should be corrected to adjust to the externalities. A positive (negative) externality amounts to a reduction (increase) in the cost of producing the service. Therefore, ignoring interdependences among services, the firm should lower its prices in the case of positive externalities and raise them in the case of negative externalities (Laffont and Tirole 2000, p. 72).

Laffont and Tirole (2000, p. 73) review four factors which limit the use of Ramsey pricing. (1) Ramsey-Boiteux markups are levied primarily on services with inelastic demands. These may sometimes be primarily purchased by poor consumers who have no other alternative than using the service; (2) one of the main concerns about Ramsey pricing is that the likelihood of regulatory capture is high. In particular, if interest groups A and B, consuming the same service, pay different prices, each will lobby the regulator to pay the lower price. In certain circumstances, the main determinant of price discrimination between the two interest groups may be the relative political strength of the interest groups; (3) non-discrimination rules may sometimes protect the firm against its own "bad behavior". Lafont and Tirole (2000, p. 75) argue that price discrimination should, in general, be favored, but they also see some benefits from non-discrimination and do not think that utilities should be given blanket permission for price discrimination; (4) treating the regulated firm in the Ramsey-Boiteux pricing as a single entity means that the various fixed costs incurred in different activities are lumped together, and the overall costs must be recovered through markups on all services. "Single-cost-recovery-problem" implies that a service may be financed largely by consumers who do not purchase the service. There are three main critiques of the concept of a single budget constraint: Firstly, many regulatory choices involve lumpy decisions. Generally, compartmentalization avoids situations in which undesirable activities are undertaken or perpetuated. A proper application of Ramsey-Boiteux prices requires consideration of the learning and experimentation process. Then prices differ from the Ramsey-Boiteux prices that would be obtained were the provisions of the service a foregone conclusion. Some compartmentalization may be considered, although it may have serious drawbacks. Secondly, the one-budget principle is that it dilutes the impact of a deficit or inefficiency on a product line over many different categories of users. Thirdly, even if the provision of the service is taken for granted, the regulator may favor low prices (below Ramsey level) to provide greater benefits to the users, to the detriment of users of other services.

4.2 Regulation of End User Pricing: Historical Developments

In this practice, where the full information about demand and supply is not always available, there is a number of ways in which price control can be achieved. The simplest means constraining market power through profit regulation. Under such a regime, the regulator sets prices for the utility in a way that means they cover the utility's costs of production and include a rate of return on capital. This is sufficient to maintain investors' willingness to replace or expand the company's assets. This is the reason why cost-plus regulation is also known as "rate-of-return" regulation.

4.2.1 Rate-of-Return Regulation

Many economists, especially in the USA, have dealt with the investigation of the impact of rate-of-return regulation, and it is well known that this method is subject to one obvious flaw and one that is more subtle. The obvious flaw is that the company, having ensured the recovery of increasing costs with a subsequent increase in price, has no incentives to operate efficiently. Due to the fact that the price reviews take place with sufficient frequency, the firm pays no penalty for inefficiency. The less obvious flaw is that the arrangement may give an incentive for the firm to over-invest in capital equipment (Baldwin and Cave 1999, p. 225).

Averch and Johnson (1962) modeled the rate-of-return regulation approach and found significant distortions of incentives already for the one-product-case. The main idea is as follows:[2]

$$p_c < p_s < p_m, \tag{4.2}$$

where p_c prices under perfect competition, p_s maximum permitted price, p_m monopoly price.

$$r < s < m, \tag{4.3}$$

where r rate of return in perfect competition, s rate of return allowed by the regulator, m rate of return of an unregulated monopolist. The production function has two production factors, labor and capital, which can substitute each other. The maximization problem of regulated firms is

$$\max \pi(L,K) = R(L,K) - wL - rK \tag{4.4}$$

under the rate-of-return constraint as an auxiliary condition

$$\frac{R(L,K) - wL}{K} \leq s, \quad r < s < m. \tag{4.5}$$

In the single-product case:

[2] For more mathematical details see e.g. Borrmann and Finsinger (1999, p. 345f)

$$p(q) * q(L,K) - wL = sK \rightarrow p = \frac{wL}{q} + \frac{sK}{q}, r < s < m \text{ and} \quad (4.6)$$
$$q = f(K,L).$$

The objective function of a regulated firm is:

$$\max \pi(L,K) = R(L, K) - wL - rK \quad (4.7)$$

From the rate-of-return constraint $R(L, K) - wL \leq sK$ follows the profit constraint:

$$R(L,K) - wL - rK \leq (s-r)K, \text{ i.e. } \pi(L,K) \leq (s-r)K. \quad (4.8)$$

The maximization problem then is $\max(s-r)K$, given the side condition:

$$\frac{R(L,K) - wL}{K} = s, \; s > r. \quad (4.9)$$

The result is that the factor balance condition is not fulfilled

$$\frac{\frac{\partial q}{\partial L}}{\frac{\partial q}{\partial K}} \neq \frac{w}{r}. \quad (4.10)$$

This result is called the Averch–Johnson effect (Averch and Johnson 1962). A profit-maximizing firm, regulated on fair rate of return "operates inefficiently in the sense that (social) cost is not minimized at the output it selects," and, that "the firm adjusts to the (regulatory) constraint by substituting capital for the cooperating factor (labor)." The latter is particularly important for the interpretation to avoid misunderstanding, interpreting the Averch–Johnson effect as a tendency of regulated firms toward all forms of overcapitalization (Zajac 1970, p. 117). Zajac (1970) presented a simple geometric analysis of the Averch–Johnson model (see Fig. 4.2). He visualized in a K, L, π coordinate system the function $\pi = \pi(K, L)$ as a surface, the "profit hill", spanning the K, L plane. Regulation may limit the firm so that it cannot operate at the very top of the profit hill. The constraint $\pi \leq (s-r)K$ requires that the firm operates below or on the plane $\pi = (s-r)K$ in the K, L, π coordinate system. Maximum profit occurs at the point of maximum K along the intersection of the constraint plane and profit hill.

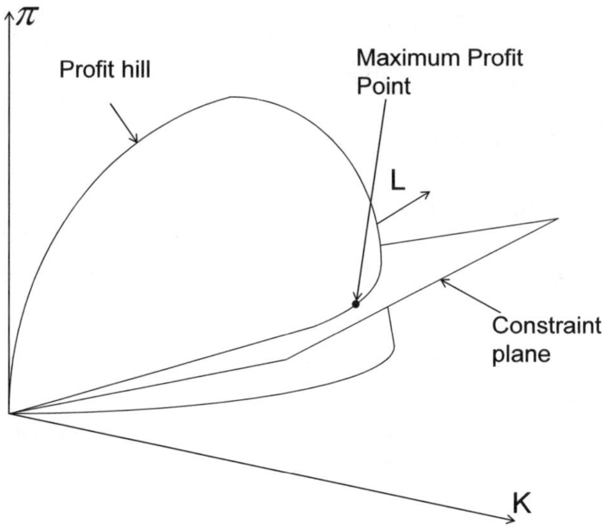

Source: Zajac (1970, p. 119)

Fig. 4.2. Profit hill and constraint plane

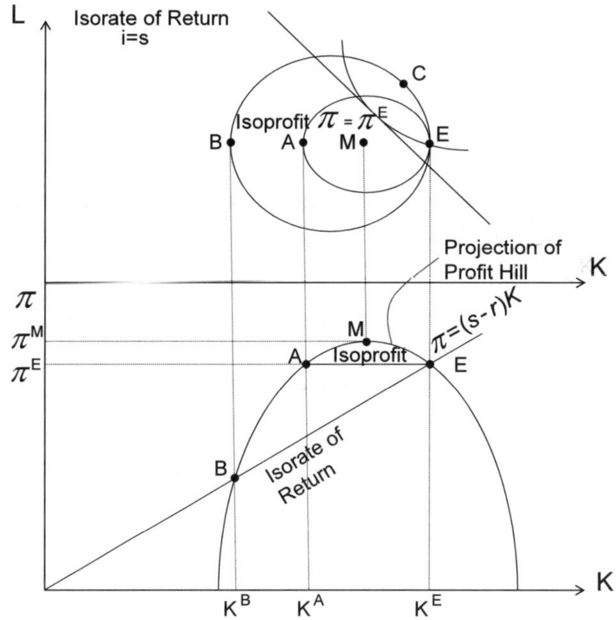

Source: Baley (1973, p. 71)

Fig. 4.3. Averch–Johnson effect

It is convenient to look at a two-dimensional representation of Fig. 4.2. Figure 4.3 has two components: the bottom depicts a projection of the profit hill into the $K\pi$ -plane while the top shows the projection into the KL-plane. AE is an isoprofit line in the bottom part of Fig. 4.2. The lowest and highest K points on the isoprofit contour $\pi = \pi^E$ correspond precisely to the K^A and K^E value of the lower figure. Since all points on the line segment *BE* have lower profit than all points on the isoprofit segment AE, it is apparent that the isorate-of-return contour $i = s$ in the $K\pi$ -plane lies everywhere outside the isoprofit contour $\pi = \pi^E$, except at the point E where the two curves touch.

4.2.2 Mark-Up (or Cost-Plus) Regulation

Mark-up regulation is another form of market power regulation (Finsinger and Kraft 1984; Braeutigam 1981). This method was very often implemented in Europe, e.g. in Germany. The basic principle consists of limiting revenues by the mark-up on the real cost of production $\overline{C}$. The mark-up rule is the following:

$$p\,(x)\,x = \sum_{i \in N} p^i\,(x)\,x_i \leq \overline{C}(x) = (1+m)\,\overline{C}\,(x), \tag{4.11}$$

where $p^i(x)$ is the inverse demand function for i[th] product, $i = 1,\ldots, n$; $p(x) = (p^1(x),\ldots, p^n(x))$ is the price vector; $x = (x_1,\ldots, x_n)$ is the output vector; $\beta = 1 + m > 1$, where $m > 0$ is the allowed mark-up. As a result, a firm does not need to produce to minimal costs $C(x)$ and aims at $\overline{C}(x) \geq C(x)$.

The single product case is considered. $p(x)$ inverse demand function; x is output; $C(x)$ production costs. The mark-up rule states that $p(x)x = (1+m)\overline{C}(x)$, $m > 0$. Which can be re-written into $\pi(x) = p(x)x - \overline{C}(x) = \frac{m}{1+m}p(x)x$.

In order to describe the possible incentive distortions, it is differentiated between $C(x) = c * x$, that is the minimal cost, and $\overline{C}(x) = \overline{c} * x$, that is the actual cost. The decision problem of the firm is:

$$\max(p(x) * x - \overline{c} * x), \text{ so that } p(x) = (1+m)\overline{c} \text{ and } \overline{c} \geq c. \tag{4.12}$$

The corresponding Lagrange function is:

$$L(x,\lambda) = \frac{m}{1+m}p(x) * x + \lambda\left(\frac{p(x)}{1+m} - c\right) \tag{4.13}$$

Derived for x this yields

$$\frac{\partial L}{\partial x} = \frac{m}{1+m} p' * x + \frac{m}{1+m} p(x) + \lambda \frac{p'}{1+m} = 0. \tag{4.14}$$

Denoting marginal revenue by MR, the first order condition requires $m * \text{MR} = -\lambda * \frac{\partial \text{p}}{\partial \text{x}}$ and the complementary slackness condition $\lambda(\overline{c} - c) = 0$.

Generally, as illustrated in Fig. 4.4, mark-up pricing on the one hand achieves an output increase beyond the level x_u chosen by an unregulated firm. On the other hand, the mark-up pricing output remains below the welfare-maximizing output x_u where price is equal to marginal cost. Two cases can be distinguished (1) $\lambda > 0$ production is efficient. Due to the complementary slackness conditions $\overline{c} = c$, i.e. the firm produces at minimum cost c. (2) $\lambda = 0$ resources are wasted and production is inefficient. This case is illustrated in the next figure. The condition $\lambda = 0$ implies that $MR = 0$. Hence the firm produces the revenue maximizing output x_2. The maximum revenue can only be attained by a waste of resources (Finsinger and Kraft 1984, p. 502).

By describing the rate of return and mark-up in a revealing way, one can observe that these regulation methods are low-powered incentive mechanisms due to the fact that the firm benefits little from any efficiency gains. The reason for this is

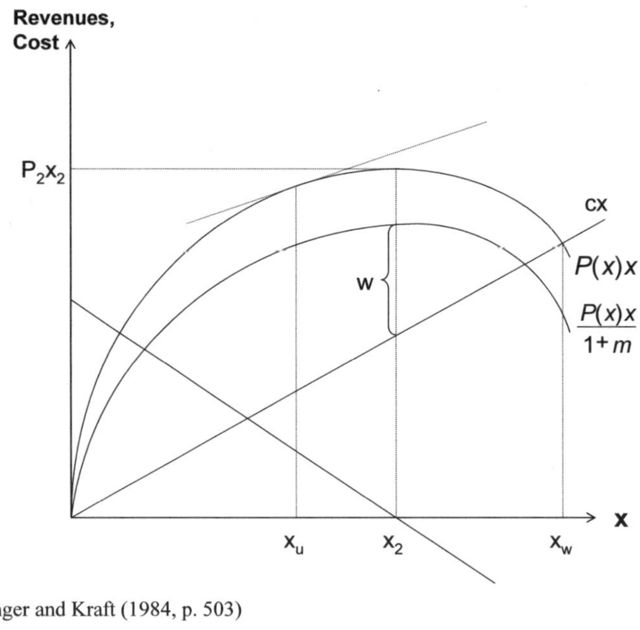

Source: Finsinger and Kraft (1984, p. 503)

Fig. 4.4. Revenue maximization and waste

that if cost savings are realized, they will almost immediately be taken from the firm and given to consumers in the form of lower prices. In a "high-powered" incentive mechanism, the clear distinction must be that the firm retains, at least temporarily, a substantial proportion of the benefits of any greater efficiency.

4.2.3 Price-Cap Regulation

Operating by setting a trajectory of prices for the firm's products indefinitely into the future, e.g. requiring them to fall by two per cent per year in real terms, would be a very high-powered incentive mechanism. In this case, a firm not challenged by competition would be able to "keep" the benefits of any achieved cost savings in perpetuity. Setting prices in advance for an indefinite period is either likely to drive the firm into bankruptcy, if they are set too low, or to allow profits to grow to a politically unacceptable level, if they are set too high. An intermediate variant exists, under which prices are set in advance for a period of 4–5 years, allowing the firm to benefit from any cost savings made during that period, but recalculated at regular intervals in order to bring them back into line with underlying costs (Baldwin and Cave 1999, p. 226).

This regime is known as price-capping or $RPI - X$ regulation. Littlechild (1983) was the first who proposed this method in the Report of British Department of Industry. He referred not only to the well known disadvantages of rate-of-return regulation, such as the Averch–Johnson effect, but also to the impossibility of applying this method on the single steps of the production chain following the disaggregated approach. Price-capping was applied in the United Kingdom to British Telecom in 1984.

The main idea of $RPI - X$ is relatively simple. It usually permits a utility to increase its overall level of prices by the previous year's rate of inflation in the economy, as measured by the retail price index (RPI), which is then varied by a percentage (the X) that reflects the real cost reduction that the regulator is expecting.

To model the $RPI - X$ rule, the following approach is used by Knieps (2001a, p. 107).

$$\sum_{i=1}^{n}\left(\frac{w_{i,t-1} * (p_{i,t} - p_{i,t-1})}{p_{i,t-1}}\right) \leq RPI - X, \tag{4.15}$$

where $p_{i,t}$ is the price of the ith product in period t and

$$w_{i,t-1} = \frac{p_{i,t-1} * q_{i,t-1}}{\sum_{j=1}^{n} p_{j,t-1} * q_{j,t-1}} \tag{4.16}$$

is the share of revenues of the ith product in total revenues of the previous period; $q_{i,t-1}$ is the quantity of the ith product, which is sold in period t–1. From this follows that

$$\sum_{i=1}^{n} p_{i,t} q_{i,t-1} \leq \sum p_{i,t-1} * q_{i,t-1} * (1 + RPI - X). \tag{4.17}$$

According to this formula, the prices in the present time period will be set up in a way that the amount of the present tariffs, weighed with quantities of the previous time period, should not be higher than the amount of the previous tariffs, weighted with quantities of the previous time period and corrected by the factor $1 + RPI - X$. In other words, it should be possible to buy a certain quantity of services from the previous period at the present prices to the same amount, corrected by the retail price index and productivity.

Through price-caps, the choice of Ramsey-Boiteux prices can be decentralized to the firm. Supposing that the utility maximizes its profit subject to the price-cap constraint $\max_q \{R(q) - C(q)\}$ subject to $\sum_{k=1}^{n} w_k p_k \leq \overline{p}$. Letting v denote the shadow price of the price-cap constraint, the first-order condition with respect to q_k is $p_k - c_k + \sum_{j=1}^{n} \frac{\partial p_j}{\partial q_k} q_j - v \sum_{j=1}^{n} \frac{\partial p_j}{\partial q_k} w_j = 0$ and so if the weights w turn out to be the quantities q, and letting $\lambda \equiv (1/v) - 1$, one obtains the Ramsey-Boiteux conditions.

A price-cap is typically set every 4–5 years. When calibrating the cap (choosing the value of X in the formula) the regulator will typically try to achieve a balance between costs and revenues over the four- or five-year period as a whole. Compared to low-powered incentive schemes, the regulator makes a projection of costs into the future, and sets overall prices so that they will cover those expected costs. If the regulated firm is able to increase its efficiency and reduce costs further than the regulator anticipates, its profits will go down. The incentives for greater efficiency introduced by the price-capping regulation are higher. In the empirical investigation of productivity in the various states of the USA, one found productivity increases by the implementation of high-incentives schemes (Sappington and Weisman 1996, p. 310). Moreover, the price-capping mechanism demonstrates administrative convenience. A price-cap of four or five years involves intensive periods of work in the period before it comes into effect. However, once established, regulation is confined to the relatively simple arithmetic task of checking that price changes prepared by the regulated firm do, in fact, satisfy the constraint. Per annum this process requires just few days of work.

However, possible distortion of incentives might be in the service quality (Laffont and Tirole 2000, p. 5). Because the firm bears a higher fraction of its expenditures, it is more prone to skimp on services, and so the regulatory reform should be accompanied by increased attention to quality issues. In the UK, the regulator was forced to design new quality measures in response to a degradation of BT service quality a few years after the introduction of a price-cap; in the USA, customers of US. West complained of increased delays after it laid off many workers in response to a switch to incentive regulation.

Some modifications of the price-capping mechanism exist. Profit sharing means that price-capped utilities, which earn a rate of return on capital above some specified level, have to return a proportion of their excess profits to customers through lower prices within the period of the price-cap. It could also be accompanied by a symmetric arrangement under which, if the firm's profits fall below a certain level, the firm is entitled to raise its prices to recover a proportion of the deficit. As an alternative, prices can be linked to dividends paid to shareholders. This mechanism is called "sliding scale", when dividends exceed the stipulated levels but prices have not been reduced. The main advantage of linking prices to dividends is that companies are less able to manipulate figures on dividends than on profits (Baldwin and Cave 1999, p. 235).

Error correction mechanisms mean that price-caps are set at levels based on a number of assumptions about economic growth rates, investment spending of the regulated firm and so on. Under an error correction mechanism, a price-cap can be fine-tuned within the period if the assumptions mentioned above turn out to be mistaken. For example, if a regulated firm was able to undertake its investment at a much lower price than anticipated by the regulator, prices would be adjusted downwards automatically.

Both profit-sharing and error correction mechanisms reduce incentives for cost reductions, and may lead to price-capping closer to rate of return regulation. Nevertheless, they do bring advantages, notably bolstering the political acceptability of the regulatory system and increasing the level of fairness between consumers and investors.

4.3 Regulation of Access and Interconnection Pricing

As a consequence of the recent developments towards deregulation and subsequent vertical disintegration of networks, problems of network access – e.g. local loop unbundling, shared line or bitstream access – as well as network interconnection – e.g. "local" level, "single transit" or "double transit" interconnection – are gaining increasing importance (Knieps 2001b, p. 275). Moreover, an obvious regulatory trend is the shift from the end-user price regulation discussed above to access or wholesale price regulation.

An intelligent access and interconnection policy is the key to harmonious development of competition in the telecommunications sector (Laffont and Tirole 2000, p. 98). Due to this fact, access and interconnection charges must reflect multiple objectives, such as induction of an efficient use of networks, encouragement of their owners to invest while minimizing cost, generation of an efficient amount of entry into infrastructure and services; all this should be at reasonable regulatory costs.

The setting of access and interconnection charges is a highly difficult exercise (Laffont and Tirole 2000, p. 7):

1. The stakes are high, and negotiations are highly contentious. Often half of the entrants' costs are access charges and thus are controlled by their competitors. Conversely, access charges are a substantial source of income for the incumbent (for the regional Bell operating companies in the USA it is about 30%). Intense lobbying by interest groups and political intervention do not simplify the regulator's task.
2. The setting of access charges regulates the rate of return on the incumbent's investment in infrastructure. In general, there is a trade-off between promoting competition to increase social welfare once the infrastructure is in place and encouraging the incumbent to invest and maintain the infrastructure. The aim of regulators should be to encourage entry without expropriating incumbents.
3. The information requirements of regulators in order to compute the access charges and to monitor the compliance must be reasonable. This helps to reduce the regulatory costs and limits the influence of politics in the determination of access charges.

Traditionally, the interconnection services are classified based on the criteria of reciprocity or reversibility (Economides and White 1994, p. 625). If, in order to provide a complete service to end-users, firms or networks must purchase essential inputs from other firms and vice versa, there is a reciprocal network access (two-way access). If reciprocity lacks, it is known as one-way access. The typical situation is that the incumbent firm has a monopoly over important inputs needed by its rivals, but it itself needs nothing from other firms (Armstrong 2002, p. 298). For example, a long-distance entrant or information service provider needs access to the incumbent's local network. Figure 4.5 presents these situations. Operator 2 buys both originating and termination access from operator 1 in order to be able to offer the long-distance service. In a "two-way" interconnection situation, customers calling each other belong to two different local networks. Each carrier must then buy termination access from the other network.

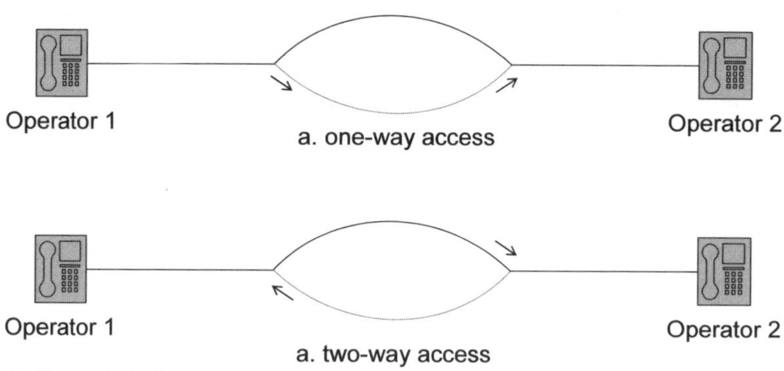

Source: Laffont and Tirole (2000, p. 6)

Fig. 4.5. Types of interconnections

In one-way and two-way access there are "competitive bottlenecks". These occur in the following situations: call termination on mobile networks or access pricing for competing Internet networks. The basic underlying features of these kinds of markets include: (1) there are several networks competing vigorously for the same pool of subscribers, and (2) even though networks compete vigorously for subscribers, they have a monopoly position in providing communications services to their subscribers. It is argued that in such markets it is undesirable to leave network access arrangements entirely to the discretion of individual networks and, in many cases, the regulator intervenes and sets access charges at the appropriate level (Armstrong 2002, p. 337).

Moreover, a common fallacy is that small players do not have market power and should therefore face no constraint on their termination charges. A network operator may have a small share in terms of subscribers, but is still a monopolist on the calls received by its subscribers. Under the assumption that retail prices do not discriminate according to where the calls terminate, the network has more market power the smaller its market share. A big operator must account for the impact of its wholesale price on its call inflow through the sensitivity of its rivals' final price to its wholesale price; a small network faces a very inelastic demand for termination and thus can impose higher mark-ups above the marginal cost of terminating calls (Laffont and Tirole 2000, p. 186).

4.3.1 Theoretical Approaches on Access and Interconnection Pricing: From Pricing at Marginal Cost to Global Price-Caps

Although interconnection among contestable networks may play an increasing role in the future, especially in telecommunications, there is still the problem that non-contestable network infrastructures may be involved. The market power involved in non-contestable network fundamentally disturbs the bargaining process. One extreme alternative could be vertical foreclosure of competitors on a complementary service market. Another way of abusing market power within the bargaining process on interconnection conditions could be by providing insufficient network access quality or excessive (monopolistic) interconnection charges (Knieps 1997, p. 330).

An option to overcome the discrimination incentives would be vertical separation. The regulator prohibits the incumbent to enter the competitive segments of the market (option A in Sect. 3.4.1). In this way, the discrimination problems may be solved. The incumbent in the conditions of price-cap regulation could increase its efficient profits. The vertical separation ensures a level-playing field for all firms in the competitive segment. As a result, principally, all aims, price regulation and non-discrimination incentives are achieved. However, in practice, this method is very seldom used because it often limits private ownership. Due to this fact, governments often restructure the firm and only privatize it afterwards. Moreover, economies of scope and transaction costs are often the arguments against vertical separation. Based on the above mentioned arguments, the regulator, as a rule, regulates the access charges and deals with discrimination incentives (Brunekreeft 2003, p. 35).

An adequate instrument for government interventions when market power is involved in the interconnection/access process seems to be the Essential Facilities Doctrine, which was applied in US antitrust law. Its focus is on access on equal terms for all competitors to the "monopolistic bottleneck". Liability under the Essential Facilities Doctrine is based on the following characteristics: (1) control of an "Essential Facility" by a monopolist (endowing monopoly power); (2) a competitor's inability practically or reasonably to duplicate the facility; (3) the denial of the facility's use to a competitor; and (4) the feasibility of providing the facility (Knieps 1997, p. 284).

The next question is how efficient access charges should be determined. From a theoretical point of view and following the first-best solution, a necessary condition for optimality would be that entrants internalize the bottleneck's marginal cost so the access charge would be cost-based and the retail goods would obey marginal cost pricing. The incumbent, however, would demonstrate deficit, equal to the non-traffic sensitive cost of the local loop, which should be covered from the other sources, e.g. government subsidies. In the absence of these sources, the incumbent must balance its budget by offering at least some, retail or wholesale, services at prices above marginal cost. To avoid distortions, the Ramsey–Boiteux prices, as a second-best solution, could be applied. Reflection of marginal costs and demand elasticities minimizes the distortions brought about by the recovery of fixed costs. Reinterpreting demand as a residual demand given competitive offers, Ramsey–Boiteux prices must also reflect competitive pressure on the firm's various segments. It is inefficient to tack a substantial mark-up over marginal cost on the price of a wholesale or retail service if this induces customers to purchase from a less efficient competitor or a product less adapted to their needs. Moreover, Ramsey–Boiteux prices take the complementarity or substitutability between services into account. For example, the price of a service should be higher when a price increase boosts demand for another service; controversially, the prices of complementary services should be set below the "myopic" levels that result from looking at the demand of individual products in isolation. To conclude, wholesale and retail prices must contribute to the recovery of the network's fixed costs together. A cost-based pricing of access generally tilts the level playing field toward inefficient entry in the contested segments and forces the incumbent to shift the burden of recovery to consumption in monopolized retail segments (Laffont and Tirole 2000, p. 104f).

The very popular rule of the efficient pricing of access is known as the efficient component pricing rule (ECPR), which was proposed by Robert Willing (1979) and called the parity pricing principle or the Baumwol–Willing rule. It is a partial (incomplete) regulatory rule that links retail and wholesale prices. Suppose that entrants supply a service in competition with the incumbent, for which, however, they need access to the incumbent's facility. According to the ECPR rule, the efficient interconnection/access charges for a single-supplier covers the incremental costs of this component plus the opportunity costs, which include any foregone revenues from a concomitant reduction in the single-supplier's sale of the complementary component.[3] Based on this rule, the new entrant on the competitive segment should only enter if he is more efficient (Knieps 1997, p. 282). The advantage of the ECP rule is that the incumbent does not have discrimination incentives. However, the disadvantage of this rule is a monopoly result and allocative inefficiency (Brunekreeft 2003, p. 32). When there is asymmetry along at least one of the four dimensions (access cost, market power, retail demand, or retain cost), ECPR is, in general, not satisfied by optimal prices (Laffont and Tirole 2000, p. 104f). A correction should be made in order to take the access price below or above the ECPR level. However, the practical use of the ECPR approach was refused by several regulatory agencies, e.g. in the United States and the United Kingdom.

In theory, the Ramsey pricing structure can be obtained by imposing a global price-cap on the incumbent. The intermediate good (access) is treated as a final good and is included in the computation of the price-cap. Weights used in the computation of the price-cap are exogenously determined and are proportional to the forecasted quantities of the associated goods. The global price-cap forces the firm to internalize the increase in consumer net surplus in proportion to the weights in the cap.

Under a global price-cap, the operator manages its product lines "symmetrically", as it has no built-in incentive to favor one over another. A global price-cap provides the operator with a choice of which product lines, retail or wholesale, are profitable. Exclusion of rivals raises the cost of the operator or limits its demand and tends to reduce the operator's profit. In a nutshell, the exclusionary practice is then tantamount to the operator raising its own cost of providing the retail service through the competitive rivals. Global price-caps thus provide an opportunity for regulation to be more light-handed; they reduce perverse incentives and therefore diminish the need for regulatory oversight of the operator's decisions. However, the global price-caps still involve problems concerning setting of weights in the cap and their revision process.

Moreover, global price-caps raise the possibility of predatory behavior. However, in general, this fear may be exaggerated because a global price-cap tends to eliminate, rather than create, incentives for exclusion, which is a more common practice. Price squeezing is easy to carry out under a global price-cap. The operator can raise the access charge and decrease its final price, keeping the price-cap constraint satisfied. It has a negative influence on its rivals in the retail market. This strategy might be used for predatory purposes. As a result, the operator might reduce its profit until the next price review, but eliminate rivals who otherwise would be used by the regulator as benchmarks in the future. Laffont and Tirole (2000, p. 178) postulated that ECPR is a reasonable rule against predation. Using ECPR as a predation test unduly constraints the incumbent.

[3] Opportunity costs here mean monopoly profits.

4.3.2 Practical Approaches of Access and Interconnection Pricing: Backward-Looking vs. Forward-Looking Cost-Based Pricing

The traditional approach for computing access and interconnection charges is based on the methodology of cost-of-service regulation to the operator's wholesale offerings. There are a variety of possible cost allocations. The most common are (1) additive or usage-proportional mark-ups, which are tantamount to a fixed (price-independent) excise tax, whose magnitude is computed so as to cover the unallocated cost; (2) uniform or price-proportional mark-ups are proportional to the marginal cost of service and akin to a proportional (VAT-type) tax. The advantage of fully distributed cost pricing is that it commits the regulator to allow the operator to recoup its investments and to break even. By the large investment an operator needs not be concerned that this investment will later be expropriated by the regulator setting low access charges.

Despite the above mentioned advantages, fully distributed cost pricing is often criticized by economists. The main reasons are the following: (1) fully distributed cost pricing is a cumbersome process; (2) this method is cost-based and therefore does not encourage cost minimization; (3) it may subsidize inelastic-demand segments to the detriment of elastic-demand ones. Under competitive conditions, fully distributed cost pricing tends to create an inefficient amount of entry. To lessen the cost of the first and third drawbacks (delays in price revisions, inefficient entry in the competitive and bottleneck segment), the prices set by fully distributed cost methods have sometimes been interpreted as ceilings or caps, especially in the conditions of competitive entry. This flexibility might bring actual prices closer to Ramsey level, however, its applicability is still limited (Laffont and Tirole 2000, p. 144).

The dominating and younger approach is the forward-looking cost-based pricing and, in particular, forward-looking long-run incremental cost (LRIC). The main idea of this approach is to set access prices on the basis of an efficient cost benchmark rather than on the operator's embedded costs; that should provide much better incentives for static cost efficiency. However, Laffont and Tirole (2000, p. 149) argued that its impact on incentives for dynamic efficiency (investment, innovations) is quite mixed. In practice, the computation of the LRIC of an element of the network is based on the cost of the current most efficient technology derived from an engineering model, using a forecast of the likely usage of the element, and a rule for treating depreciation.

However, a broad regulatory consensus in favor of LRIC has been achieved but is supported by little economic argument (Laffont and Tirole 2000, p. 148):

1. LRIC regulation gives regulators a key role in managing entry. On the one hand, the determination of long-run incremental costs is highly discretionary. On the other hand, LRIC precludes operators from making money in the access activity and gives them strong incentives to favor their competitive affiliates by biasing access against their competitors. These wrong incentives call for heavy-handed supervision of the incumbent. In addition to a high cost in terms of regulatory staff, this creates scope for interest-group politics.

2. In the case that LRIC could be determined objectively and rivals' exclusion could be prevented costlessly, the associated access prices would still not be efficient prices and would result in economic distortions.

Laffont and Tirole (2000, p. 162) hold that, when facing a stringent ceiling on access charges and a looser constraint on final services, perhaps no constraint at all (as in the case of the deregulated competitive segment), an operator has a strong incentive to deprive its rivals in the final segments from access to the bottleneck through non-price methods. The operator has an incentive to deny access to its competitors or to raise their costs, in order to loosen the competitive pressure on the final segment. This incentive is stronger the lower the cap on the access charge. They conclude that the operator would have much less incentive to exclude rivals if its final price itself were constrained, as he would not be able to exploit his monopoly power in the competitive segment once the rivals were excluded. As a result, deregulation of competitive segments is costly, since it substantially increases the monitoring requirements.

4.4 Regulation of Universal Services

Universal service policies in general focus on promoting or maintaining "universal" availability of connections by individual households to public telecommunications networks. The term "Universal Service Obligation" encompasses the objective of connecting all or most households to public telecommunications networks. A policy of universal services (US) is practiced in many industrialized countries. In developing countries, universal access (UA) is a more feasible policy objective. Universal access can generally be described as a situation where everyone has access to a publicly available telephone (it can be pay telephones, community telephone centers, teleboutiques, and community Internet access terminals). The policies of US and UA can be quite different but their concepts are closely related and they are sometimes used interchangeably (Hank 2000, pp. 6–9).

In many countries, access to telecommunications services is the basic right of all citizens (the right to communicate) and extending US or at least UA to unserved members of the public finds strong political support. There are the following motivations for the universal services policies:

1. Allocative motivation is based on the existence of beneficial externalities: network externalities and call externalities. The network externalities could be very important, especially in a competitive environment, to achieve the critical mass of subscribers (Knieps and Blankart 1994, p. 239). The universal service policy should help to overcome this problem. In addition, network externalities arise because, when considering whether or not to join the network, people tend not to consider the benefit their subscription would provide to those who already have telephones (Cullen international/WIK 2001, p. 25). The universal service policy aims to achieve social equilibrium by expanding the network as far as the marginal benefit of network participation is equal to marginal cost (Liebowitz and Margolis 2002, p. 82). Laffort and

Tirole (2000, p. 230) argued that, in industrialized countries, the network externalities have been no longer "at the forefront of the universal service debate (except perhaps for new services such as the Internet), partly because networks are largely developed in these countries and partly because it is recognized that network externalities are to a large extent internalised by operators." However, some researchers, e.g. Riordan (2002, p. 445), hold that the magnitude of network externality remains an empirical issue on which evidence is scant. Concerning call externalities, Vogelsang and Mitchel (1991, p. 61) argue that they are relatively more important in developed economies because they involve interaction among all consumers, while network externalities only involve interaction with marginal consumers. However, most analysts seem prepared to accept that internalizing call externalities are not so large as to warrant regulatory intervention.

2. Distributional motivations focus on the redistribution toward low-income consumers or toward high cost areas (1) to encourage a more balanced distribution of population, eliminating disparities between rural and urban areas as well as decreasing congestion costs arising from the urbanization (Knieps and Blankart 1994, p. 239), (2) to decrease the digital divide problems, a democratic society has a interest in keeping its citizens informed about development throughout the world, the state is interested in preventing social fragmentation in which households live with few connections to the rest of polity and in permitting full participation in twenty first Century society, (3) to provide the basic safety nets, which include a limited number of goods and services which the majority of citizens in many countries consider of sufficient importance (Cullen international/WIK 2001, p. 27).
3. Promotion of economic development can be a motivation, especially in low and middle income countries. As mentioned in Sect. 2.1, the relationship between telecommunications and economic development is complex; nevertheless telecommunications are increasingly recognized as a key component in the infrastructure of economic development (Saunders et al. 1994, p. 3). In general, the amount of revenue available to fund telecommunications networks and services depends on per capita income levels within countries. It is, however, obvious that per capita income does not absolutely determine teledensity levels, e.g. the distribution of income within a country can determine phone penetration levels.

Universal services are a knotty and explosive problem. Behind the official universal services discourse lays interest-group politics (Laffont and Tirole 2000, p. 224). On the consumer side, the interest groups receiving those subsidies (e.g. residential customers and rural inhabitants) lobby heavily, of course, for their preservation. On the other side, powerful interest groups such as large business users push for deregulation in order to remove the subsidies and enjoy lower prices. On the producer side, incumbent operators have often used universal services as an argument against liberalization (Laffont and Tirole 2000, p. 218).

When defining universality, one must clarify which telecommunications services are subsumed under this term. Important factors here are country economic and sector conditions such as the level of national income and its distribution, the distribution of a country's population, national geography, topology and security matters. Universal service requirements which have been set out in order to address the telecommunications environment in affluent Western societies may not be the correct recipe for middle and lower income countries. They could lead to the setting of virtually unobtainable targets that it would not be in the country's interest to meet (Cullen International/WIK 2001, p. 1). Typically, basic access is defined to include voice-grade access to the PSTN. The definitions of universality are not static and require reconsideration based on market conditions and public demand. Compared to industrial countries in developing economies, the regulatory bodies should focus on public access services, and the expansion of new access services, rather than supporting existing services (Hank 2000, pp. 6–9).

4.4.1 Measures to Promote Universal Services

There are a couple of measures to promote universal service policy. With the liberalization of telecommunications markets, cross-subsidization as a mechanism to promote universal service policy showed its inefficiency around the world. Market-based reforms such as privatization, competition and cost-based pricing are an alternative to achieve higher phone penetration. In many developing and transition economies, outdated sector policies are the cause of universality problems. The reforms in these countries aim at the un-served population, those who are willing and able to pay for personal or community telecommunications access. The experiences in many countries provide evidence that, since starting the market-based reforms, the supply of telecommunications services is increasing.

As considered in Sect. 3.3.3, only privatization accompanied by efficient regulation (as a rule, with an independent regulator) ensures a positive impact on rates of phone penetration, and competition in most cases has a positive influence. Cost-based pricing includes primarily the tariff rebalancing reform. Empirical evidence for the OECD and developing countries indicates that rate rebalancing policies lead to increasing levels of teledensity and lower overall prices for telecommunications services. Ros and Banerjee (2000) provide empirical evidence on this issue in Latin American countries; Vagliasindi (2004) investigates and finds a positive influence of tariff rebalancing in transition economies.

Other possible mechanisms to provide universality are mandatory service obligations, which some governments and regulators have imposed on newly licensed or newly privatized operators. Mandatory service obligations are imposed by license conditions or other regulatory measures. These may include obligations to provide service throughout certain areas (e.g. for wireless operators) or to install a specific number of lines within a certain period. Mandatory service obligations are used in most privatizations and new license grants. The main advantage of this mechanism is that the funding is generally provided by the private sector. The disadvantage is that an operator is tied to specific roll-out obligations. If these are partly uneconomic, this operator will have to finance such obligations through monopoly profits, cross-subsidies or other mechanisms that result in inefficient output and market distortions. (Hank 2000, pp. 6–19).

If the process of tariff rebalancing is not completed, or is completed but net USO cost is not avoidable, the possible deficit could be financed by one or other of the following two mechanisms: Access Deficit Charges (ADCs) and Universal Service Fund (USF). Noam (1997, p. 116) asserts that any new type of revenue raising measures to finance universal services should meet the following neutrality requirements as closely as possible: (1) competitive neutrality (not skewing the relative market strength of any carrier or of consumers' choice); (2) structural neutrallity (not favoring or disfavoring integrated or unbundled provision of a service); (3) technological neutrality (not favoring any type of transmission technology over others); (4) applications and content neutrality (not favoring any particular use of telecommunications or type of message); (5) geographical neutrality (not burdening any parts of the country disproportionately); (6) traditional neutrality (no shocks or windfalls to any participants due to transition to a new system); (7) jurisdictional neutrality (the new system should be integratable into the federal-state's regulatory system). In addition, he points out that the following "friendliness" criteria have to be complied: political friendliness, collection friendliness, administrative and user friendliness, integrability, productivity friendliness.

ADC is paid by all providers of subsidizing services to subsidize the access deficit of incumbents; they are a variation on traditional mechanisms of cross-subsidy. The "subsidy-tax" is expanded beyond the incumbent and spread across all competitors for example in the long distance market. ADCs cross-subsidies have been criticized as being inefficient and anti-competitive. Some regulators have rejected or reviewed their ADC regimes.

ADCs are often collected in a similar manner to interconnection charges based on per minutes, trunk or some other basis. They may also be collected by means of a levy on telecommunications services revenues. Nevertheless, they should be collected in a transparent, non-discriminatory and competitively neutral manner. This means they should be separated from interconnection charges.

The reasons for abolishing and replacing the ADC regimes in many countries were as follows: (1) ADCs inflate the prices of the subsidizing services and reduce demand for them. (2) ADCs encourage service providers to bypass the PSTN resulting in inefficient duplication of network facilities and depriving the incumbents of interconnection revenues they would otherwise have earned. (3) The development of new technologies undermines the viability of ADC regimes. (4) ADCs as traditional cross-subsidies are internal to the incumbent and this brings the same problems.

The second and most popular mechanism of USO cost financing is the universality fund, which can realize most neutrality requirements and friendliness criteria. The universality fund is an independently administered fund that collects revenues from various sources and provides targeted subsidies to implement universality programs, which could ideally be new network rollouts as well as the maintenance of existing services (Hank 2000, pp. 6–21). A good universality fund is administrated in a transparent way independently from the telecommunication operator and does not favor incumbent operators or new entrants. The funding of the universality fund has to target specific beneficiaries, whereby the subsidies should be relatively small and subsidize the uneconomic part of costs.

The "collection mechanisms" of such a fund include the following possible sources:

1. Direct funding from general government revenues
2. Contributions from telecommunications operators (e.g. in proportion to their revenues from specified services)
3. Proceeds from telecommunications privatizations, spectrum allocations and/or license/concession payments
4. A subscriber levy (e.g. on a per access line basis) collected by telecommunications operators; and
5. Funding from international development agencies.

Regulators have established different criteria for the best method to collect revenues (Hank 2000, pp. 6–24). All collection mechanisms induce distortions on the competitive entry process, on the equilibrium market structure and, therefore, on the *economic efficiency issues*. The goal thereby should be to collect revenues by minimizing economic efficiency losses. The best way could be based on the Ramsey pricing rule; to charge the services with relative inelastic demand more than the services with relatively elastic demand. In practice, regulators take into account administrative and equity considerations and prefer the widely-based uniform universality charges, which will reduce the inefficiency associated with operators trying to avoid or by-pass highly-taxed services in favor of low or untaxed services. The other important efficiency issue is whether to collect universal service fund revenues from the government budget based on the observation that the government as a tax collector has the best economic vision and mandates to tax all sectors of the economy and can therefore opt for the best taxation level and method.

The collection mechanism should aim at *administrative efficiency*. The revenues can be collected by the government, who already has the infrastructure to collect taxes. However, experience suggests that the administrative costs of setting up a universality fund are relatively low. A comparatively simple interpretation of the collection mechanism and its broad definition is the way to clear misinterpretation and controversy.

Collection mechanisms should be designed based on the *sustainability* principle and assure a relatively stable revenue base. Developments in digital and IP technology bring into question whether minutes will continue to be the basic unit of measurement for telecommunications; maybe this unit can be replaced by a bit- or IP-packet. Therefore, for the sustainability of universality fund revenues, experts recommend selecting a stable revenue base (e.g. operator's revenues) as a constant measure rather than a technology or service specific measure.

The collection mechanism should be fair and take into account *equity* considerations. The option to collect revenues as a levy on access was rejected by many regulators due to equity considerations because such levies would increase local access rates for all, including low-income subscribers. Many observers argue that universality is the subject of government's social policy and should be funded through the government budgets rather than exclusively from telecommunications. According to the Atkinson–Stiglitz theorem, the best way to redistribute income may be the direct way, through the taxation of income, and (indirect) manipulation of the relative prices of goods and services may be an inefficient policy. If not all assumptions of this theorem are fulfilled, e.g. existence of imperfect observability of income or of constraints on tax schemes, then the arguments in favor of indirect taxation may be appropriate.

For the viability of the universality program, the developed financial models calculate, in general, the difference between the cost of providing services in specific regions and the projected telecommunications revenues available in those regions. Cost projections can be based on specific network construction studies, or on local or international benchmark costs for building new lines. The revenues can be based on the assumption that around the world people spend, on average, about 2.2% of their income on telecommunications. This is true for a whole country, region or for an average household (Wellenius 2000). If the costs of providing telecommunications access is greater than 2.2% of local income, external subsidies may be required to promote universal access or/and universal services. Mechanisms of funding, such as a universal access fund, can be designed based on this rule.

For the determination of subsidy, there are two complementary methods. The first is to estimate the subsidy cost using the financial model. The second approach is to let the market determine the final amount of required subsidy through a competitive bidding process. The latter approach is always preferable, but the first can assist the fund budgeting and determination of maximum subsidy that will be available for the projects. The cases of Chile and Peru are good examples of a successful bidding process. As a result of competitive bidding in these countries, many licenses were granted with zero-subsidy or significantly lower subsidies. The Peruvian case indicates another advantage of the competitive bidding process. There are often synergies in providing services to different localities or across various regions. By tendering more than one designated service area, fund administrators can capture economies of scale by allowing applicants to bid to serve different combinations of areas at different levels of subsidy. Another advantage of a competitive bidding process is that it can transfer the value of the intangible benefits of universal service or universal access operator to the universality fund. These intangible benefits mean that financial or other benefits accruing to univcrsal services or universal access providers exist, which are not taken into account in the cost or revenue models.

4.4.2 Theoretical Aspects of Universality Policy in Transition Countries

In general, in transition countries the following range of policy types were implemented relating to universal services: (1) untargeted universal service subsidies; (2) targeted universal service subsidies; (3) tax shifting schemes (Cullen International/WIK 2001, p. 30). The latter is not investigated in the study due to the fact that it includes measures which are not related to the provision of telecommunications services per se but which use the telecommunications industry as an alternative source of tax revenues. Internet access for schools or medical organizations serves as an example of this.

Untargeted policies provide assistance in a way that is not effectively designed to improve residential subscription rates, and/or are not targeted effectively on those who need it. They have a tendency to shift costs away from residential subscribers as a whole, or shift costs away from a group, who are not identified by whether they presently subscribe or not, or whether they are low or high income earners. In general, untargeted schemes include the following policies: (1) universal access subsidies; (2) free or below costs local calling; (3) tariff averaging.

Externality benefits explain why, in most countries in the world, the subsidization of access deficits is practiced. But here the problem is that this policy does not target in any refined way. If the average price of access (line rental and connection) is high enough to cover the forward-looking LRIC of providing an access service as a whole, access service provision cannot be said to be cross-subsidized. However, if cross-subsidies from within the service still exist then there is a degree of tariff averaging.

The empirical evidence indicates that the price elasticity of demand for access to the telephone network is very low (e.g. about $\varepsilon_A = -0.02$ for residential subscribers),[4] the price elasticity of demand for local calls is a little bit higher, conversely the price elasticity of toll and international services are quite high ($\varepsilon_A = -0.35$ to -0.75). Figure 4.6 indicates this situation. P_b is the price level of access charges (this includes the local calling services to simplify the situation) when prices are roughly balanced; P_r is the regulated price level of access charges. $0Q_r$–$0Q_b$ is the decrease in demand for the access, $P_b d''d'P_r$ is the loss of revenues due to the fact

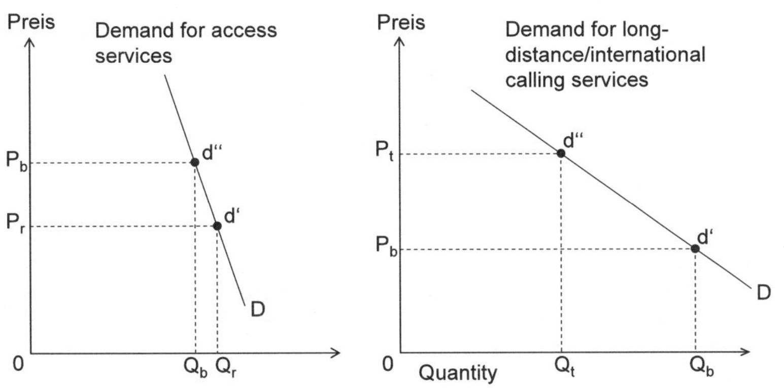

Source: Cullen International/WIK (2001) and own modification

Fig. 4.6. Elasticity of demand for access and long-distance/international calling services and price rebalancing

[4] These figures are derived from empirical evidence in the industrialized countries, such as the USA and Canada, see e.g. Taylor (1994). In transition countries, with lower penetration rates, the elasticity figures for access demand would be expected to be sufficiently higher. According to expectations in the report of Cullen International/WIK (2001, p. 37), ε_A for transition countries is -0.1 or even higher. With penetration rates between 40–70%, due to network externalities, the value of the telephone network is lower. In addition, the income of the population in transition countries is lower and the relative share of telecommunications expenditure in income is higher.

that the access price is lower than required to cover long run incremental costs. The loss of revenues needs to be recovered from another source, e.g. toll and international calls. Hereby $0Q_b$–$0Q_t$ is a significant reduction in the number of long-distance/international calling services.

The abovementioned market situation arises because of a telecommunications demand feature: access to telecommunications networks and telephone calling services (usage) are complementary; a decrease in the price of usage will result in an increase in demand for access services. This means that demand for access is influenced at least as much by the level of usage as by the access charge (Taylor 1994, p. 31; Hank 2000, pp. 6–17).

As a result of subsidizing access, there may be a small increase in the demand for household subscriptions. If supply was not constrained by the un-remunerative pricing of access, an increase in the subscriptions themselves may be possible. This consequence has resulted from the need to cross-subsidize access from the long distance and international services that are very much higher than cost, causing a very large negative effect on the quantity. In the liberalized markets, a high degree of tariff averaging will eventually result in a competition problem and become a difficult and inefficient policy to sustain in the long term.

Very cheap or free local calls are the other common practice. A large part of the cost of such calls involves switching costs; if the operator is pricing the local calls at a level which is insufficient to cover these costs, prices of other services will have to be higher in order to pay the necessary cross-subsidies for local switching. The result may be a situation where there are insufficient funds to invest in new switches or, ultimately, to maintain existing ones. The quality of services will be poor and technologies will be outdated.

Tariff averaging occurs when a service is priced at the same level for all subscribers, where the cost of providing that service varies significantly between them. According to the report of Cullen International, existing access cost models indicated that LRAIC of access in high-cost rural areas could be three and possibly five times higher than the equivalent costs in a very low-cost urban area, depending on the level of averaging retained within the de-averaged groups.

In middle and low income countries, an obligation to serve all at averaged prices implies much higher levels of cross-subsidization because the average access price is lower than in the higher income countries, while costs according to the Annex of Cullen International/WIK Report (2001, p. 5) can be assumed to be roughly the same.

Tariff averaging substantially contributes to network development with urban bias. This fact is illustrated in Fig. 4.7 P_{AD} is the average price of access, which is below the LRAIC. The marginal readiness to supply curve traces out the area specific LRAIC for each local office area. Firstly, if the network has been built up, the lowest cost applicants receive subscription. The shaded area represents the access deficit. Due to the connection of subscribers from very rural areas (highest cost end) the access deficit for the 20,000 new connections is much higher. Because of this, the subscribers from the low-cost end will be connected first, for the financing of access deficit cross-subsidies will be required, which is quite

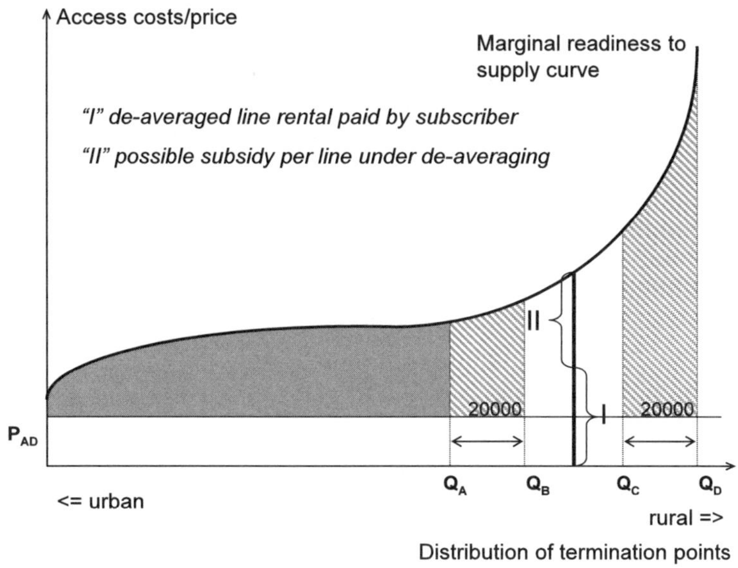

Source: Cullen International/WIK (2001)

Fig. 4.7. De-averaging in the situation of access deficit

limited. This situation, faced by many low and middle income countries, would partly be overcome with tariff de-averaging. In particular, tariff de-averaging could bring higher penetration rates to the rural areas because there will be a large number of rural households with strong enough demand for a connection to the network, instead of being placed on the waiting list.

Tariff averaging is considered to be an untargeted assistance scheme because, in most of the accession countries, tariff averaging is unlikely to have been pursued so as to advantage rural householders. For many households, tariff averaging with a large access deficit has meant that a telephone subscription is not available to them. In the rural communities with high phone penetration, tariff averaging-might be classified as a targeted scheme, as it will certainly subsidize rural telephone access. The USA serves as an example of this, with higher rural penetration rates than urban rates.

(2) Targeted schemes. Probably the greatest problems with untargeted "universal" access subsidies are their opportunity costs and the implication for industry revenues as well as profits (and even GDP) of subsidizing price inelastic services with excessive revenues earned from price elastic services. The targeted subsidies, following on rebalancing, can potentially keep all those subscribers on the network who subscribed under "universal" access subsidies; they are a much more cost effective universal service policy. Moreover, targeted subsidies give the operators the chance to charge remunerative prices. In most accession countries, non-remunerative prices have stifled network rollout and universal access, and resulted in a very large un-satisfied demand for residential subscriptions, particularly in non-urban areas.

If the targeted policy is intended to internalize positive network externalities, the lowest economically justifiable price could be below the long-run incremental cost of access charges. The efficient discount below this price would be the amount required to internalize the beneficial externality for those households who have not jet joined the network. An important role in their internalization is played by self-selective service packages. They result in an increase of output and in a welfare-enhancing effect. Fig. 4.8 illustrates this situation. The two-part tariff system serves as an example.

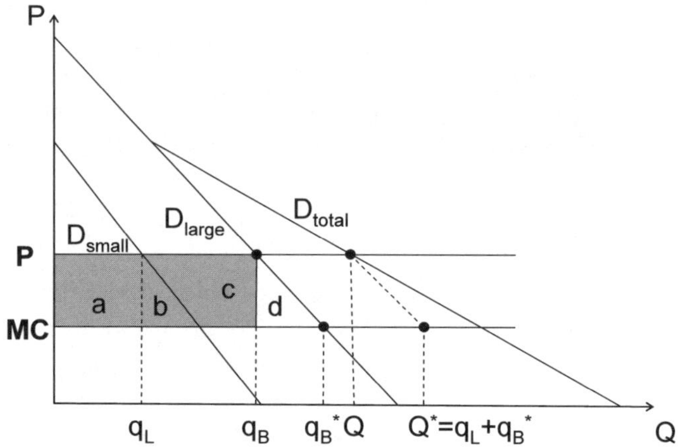

Source: Berndt and Kunz (2003, p. 196)

Fig. 4.8. Efficient targeting policy

D_{small} and D_{large} are two different kinds of demand; D_{total} is the aggregate demand of private householders. At price P, which means the same mark-up for both subscribers' groups, the resulting quantity would be Q. If a two-part tariff will be offered on the market, a subscriber could decide to either pay the same price P or to pay a certain fixed amount plus usage charges which are close to MC. If the amount of fixed charge accounts for $a + b + c$, low usage subscribers will choose the first option, i.e. will continue to pay price P, because in this case their benefits are higher. For high usage subscribers, it is profitable to pay a fixed charge $a + b + c$ because its profits account for $a + b + c + d$. As a result, low usage subscribers will use the same amount q_L, high usage subscribers will increase their usage from q_B to q_B^*; the total output will increase from Q to Q^*. The welfare-enhancing effect can be observed.

In practice, in many transition countries, the target groups include pensioners, invalids, the unemployed or those with low income as well as public sector workers (policemen, judges and teachers) and war veterans. In discussion, these groups are often called "privileged groups" and targeting of these groups might better be explained within a political, rather than an economic, framework.

Targeted assistance programs need to be focused towards non-subscribers, who nevertheless place a relatively high value on having a telephone. This means targeting those who have the strongest demand among those whose demand is nevertheless too weak to pay full fees. The strength of such programs is that neither the authorities nor the incumbent operator will have information about subscribers willing to pay; self select service packages offer the option of exogenous choice.[5]

Offering alternatives to standard services can do much to help low-income customers to become or to remain connected. If a customer has a choice between different options differentiated by service quality and price, he will pick the most suitable for him. Many options can be built by repackaging components of the standard service. Effective programs include: low up-front charges; low fixed recurrent charges, ways for the customers to control expenses as well as the ability to make small, frequent, regular payments (Wallenius 2000). Taking the USA as an example, Cain and MacDonald (1991) provide empirical evidence that, by the existence of self selective package schemes, increases in flat rates for monthly services, the most commonly chosen local rate option, had no effect on access demand.

As an answer to this situation of large access deficits, transition countries have started tariff rebalancing reforms and implementing access deficit financing schemes. Tariff rebalancing needs to be thought of as a program with several accompanying policies; one of these is especially important. This is the implementation of targeted universal service programs which, in many cases, will have the considerable benefit of reducing rather than expanding existing cross-subsidization. The usual case in most transition countries is that rebalancing faces very weak demand. There will be areas, and large numbers of subscribers, where it will not be possible to raise line rental and connection prices sufficiently to cover the full cost of providing an access service, without forcing large numbers of households off the network. There is, however, a loss-minimizing strategy if a network has already been built in the un-remunerative areas. This is a pricing strategy to cover at least variable costs. Prices should move in the direction indicated by their relative demand elasticities. In order to lose as little money as possible on its original investment, price should equal the point where TVC and TR are farthest apart.

In the Cullen International/WIK Report (2001), the following aspects for new pricing strategies in accession countries are presented. They are also recommendable for other transition economies. (1) rebalancing of access charges and (2) de-averaging in accordance with rural and urban supply costs to reflect the large difference in the cost of providing rural as opposed to urban connections. Special self select packages should be available to minimize the level of disconnections caused by tariff rebalancing.

If de-averaging occurs into two categories (rural and urban), the situation with respect to demand, supply and pricing appears to be as follows (Fig. 4.9). For rural (D_RD_R) and urban (D_UD_U) demand, there are the obvious pricing points around which self select packages may be constructed. $LRAIC_{AR}$ ($LRAIC_{AU}$) represents the long-run average incremental cost per subscriber of providing residential access

[5] See more on second price degree discrimination in Knieps (2001a, p. 212)

to profitable rural (urban) areas; $LRIC_{AR}$ ($LRIC_{AU}$) represents the long-run incremental cost of providing an access service to scattered residential subscribers in otherwise profitable rural (urban) areas. VC_R (VC_U) represents the variable cost of providing an access service to scattered individual subscribers in a rural (urban) area. The balanced "standard" prices are indicated by P^*_R and P^*_U. A package that successfully selects those subscribers with weak demand is sustainable over the long term, as subscribers at P^*_R (P^*_U) are paying in common the cost associated with the area as a whole. In the long term, existing subscribers below P_{LRICr} (P_{LRICu}) on the demand curve cannot be served except at a loss.

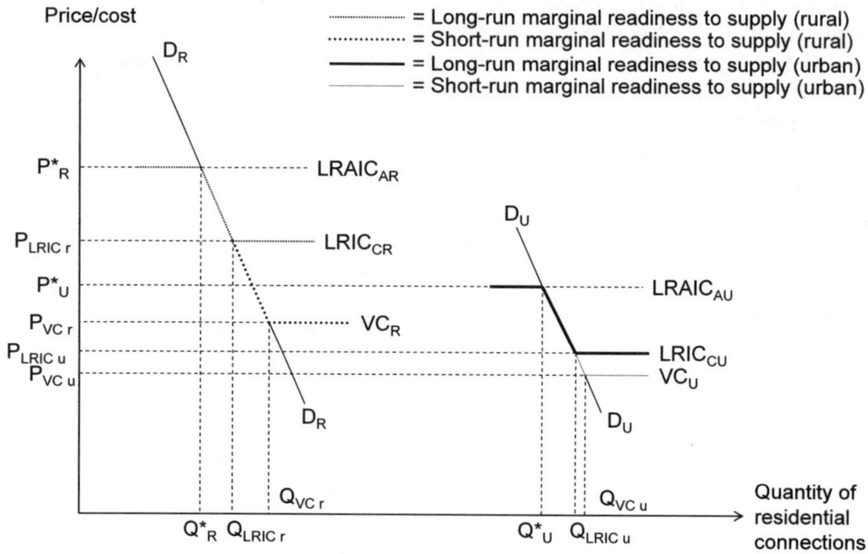

Source: Cullen International/WIK (2001)

Fig. 4.9. Common and joint costs and pricing service packages with partially de-average tariffs

As a result, in the transition countries, universal service problems are partly caused by pricing rigidities. Rigidities such as tariff averaging and "universally" subsidized residential access are often the result of regulatory and political intervention. Tariff rebalancing and de-averaging in accordance with rural and urban supply costs can improve the situation. Special self select packages should be available to minimize the level of disconnections caused by tariff rebalancing.

4.5 Regulation of Service Quality

While it is a familiar proposition of economic theory that an unregulated monopolist can usually distort both prices and product quality from efficient levels, the methods of regulation are often initially focused on pricing decisions (Rovizzi and Thompson 1995, p. 336). In general, regulators find it easier to regulate price than quality, because price has the great advantage of being (in certain markets at least) both one-dimensional and objectively measurable. Quality is harder to pin down due to many dimensions, some of which typically rest upon subjective evaluations by the purchaser or consumer. In many cases, the true quality of a product only comes to light some time after it has been consumed; in some cases, it never comes to light. In many markets, customers appear to attach more importance to quality than to price; commercial users need continuous and reliable telecommunications services in order to transact their business, and residential customers need such services in order to meet domestic emergencies (Baldwin and Cave 1999, p. 251).

Consider first the case of an unregulated monopolist supplying a product of uniform quality to its captive market. In pricing output of a given quality, its route to profit maximization is clear: raise prices to the point where any further increase will reduce demand so much as to lower profits. If quality is a choice variable, the incentives of an unregulated monopolist will be either undersupply or oversupply quality to outcome depending on demand conditions (Spence 1975). The departures from the optimum arise due to the fact that the monopolist chooses the quality level with an eye to the preference of the marginal consumer who, at the price charged, is just on the margin of buying or not buying the product. The welfare of others is ignored.

In the case of rate-of-return regulation, consumers are likely to benefit chiefly because the price of output of a given quality is controlled. Moreover, encouraging capital intensity, the rate-of-return regulation may raise the quality of output; the result may be excessive quality.

With the price-cap regulation, the situation becomes less ambiguous, as the regulated firm with a given price-cap will be able to make extra profits by degrading the quality of service. Quality degradation is a means of evading the price-cap. A natural complementarity exists between powerful incentive schemes and a close monitoring of quality standards. If the regulator is unable to specify the standards or to monitor compliance with these standards, then there may be no other choice than the adoption of low-powered incentives (Laffont and Tirole 2000, p. 55).

If the service quality can be differentiated ex ante or ex post across customers, one can offer customers a choice of tiered levels of service, and to require compensation to be paid for failure to deliver these as due to individual customers. The arising question is how the gradations of service or conditions of eligibility for compensation should be set and how prices for each should be determined. In the case of compensation, damages should ideally equal losses borne by the representative consumer divided by the probability that compensation will be sought. This gives the firms an appropriate deterrent against breaching standards, which takes account of the problem that not everyone will complain. Thus, if only one half of the customer base complains, the payment will have to be twice the actual damage imposed in order to give the operator a strong incentive to maintain service standards.

If the quality attribute is public, one superficially attractive means of combining price and quality regulation is to incorporate quality measurements directly into the price-cap. This is possible by adding an extra term $\alpha \Delta Q$ to the $RPI - X$ formula, where ΔQ is the improvement in quality. As a result, by the increase of quality, a regulated firm can increase the price faster than if quality level remains constant.

As quality increases, it becomes more and more expensive to raise it further because the marginal costs of quality improvement (MC) rise as quality rises (see Fig. 4.10). In contrast, as quality rises, the extra benefit consumers gain from a further increase (MB) declines. These two factors determine an optimal level of quality (Q*), where marginal benefits and marginal costs are equal. To reach this optimum, the firm chooses the coefficient α in the price-cap formula $RPI - X + \alpha \Delta Q$. But it is obvious that the marginal costs or marginal benefits could be misestimated. This leads to an incorrect choice of the quality coefficient in the price-cap and, as a result, to oversupply or undersupply of quality.

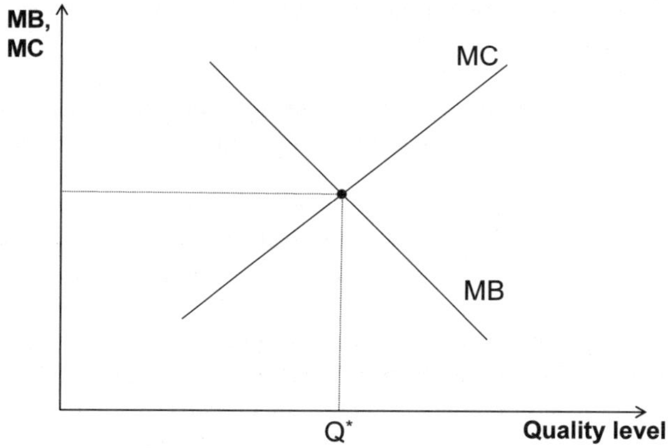

Source: Baldwin and Cave (1999, p. 253)

Fig. 4.10. Optimal level of quality

Moreover, the obvious problem arises from the multidimensional nature of quality and the troubles with its objective measuring. In the telecommunications industry, there are many quality attributes which should be reflected in a coefficient of the price-cap formula. By omitting some attributes, serious deterioration might be the result. Quality levels would also have to be measurable by objective, or at least agreed, methods, but the difficulties in making measurements would almost certainly mean that many quality attributes would not be covered in the formula. This is the main reason why quality of service has not been incorporated in the price-cap of any regulated industry.

Instead of the approach above, the regulators have used measures such as publishing comparative quality data, where a number of supplies are in operation; criticizing regulated firms publicly when service standards have fallen; using their standard-making powers. Thus the "command and control" method of setting standards has generally been adopted in preference to the price-guided method. The regulator determines Q* and then enforces it as a minimum standard.

How the optimal standard should be determined in practice remains ambiguous (Cave et al. 1993). The obvious way is to ask the customers directly. This approach has been used relatively rarely, because there are a number of well-known difficulties in eliciting reliable information about households' willingness to pay for public services. A well-established but worrying finding is that consumers typically exhibit a willingness to pay for an increment in the level or quality of a public good only a fraction of the sum they would require in compensation for the loss of the same quantity or quality. The sources of bias arise for a number of reasons, including the following: market inexperience, difficulties in understanding probabilities, strategic or policy bias, spill-over effects. Ideally, an experiment would be contrived in which stated willingness to pay was tested against actual behavior or revealed preference.

Even if accurate willingness to pay responses are available, a decision still has to be made about ways of averaging them in order to set the overall standard, which will be too high for some and too low for others. Given the difficulties noted above, it is natural to look for alternative techniques with which to elicit households' valuations. One possibility is a technique called stated preference or conjoint analysis. There respondents are asked to choose between alternative packages of attributes. Then the chosen set of alternatives is ranked, individuals show their preferences for particular attributes, either in terms of a willingness to pay or in terms of willingness to trade (Baldwin and Cave 1999, p. 251).

4.6 Positive Theory of Regulation: Regulatory Capture

After an explanation of "regulatory model" themes or normative theory of regulation, the attention is directed to "political economy" themes or positive theory of regulation, which focuses on the self-interested interactions in the political marketplace of regulators and various constituencies.[6] Two main theories have been proposed as an explanation of the pattern of government interventions or regulation in industries. According to the "public interest" theory, the government's role is correcting market imperfections such as monopoly pricing and environmental externalities. The regulatory agencies, facing some informational constraints, are viewed as benevolent maximizers of social welfare. In the second theory, the "capture" or "interest group" theory, the role of interest groups in the formation of

[6] Normative and positive theories of regulation have developed substantial insight into the problems of regulation, but each has borrowed surprisingly little from the other. Only some papers try to bridge this gap, e.g. Laffont and Tirole (1993) develop a model of interest group politics within the overall framework of agency theory; essentially, it is an agency model with enforceable side payments. Faulhaber (1996) asks the question whether the inefficiencies of regulation outweigh the inefficiencies of market failure and develops a model to compare aggregate surplus from unregulated monopoly with aggregate surplus from price setting in a median voter model in a framework of (perfectly) regulated monopoly.

public policy is emphasized (Posner 1971, p. 22).[7] Originally, the main idea was that big business controls institutions. This paradigm was considerably extended by Stigler (1971), who notes that the regulatory process can be captured by small business industries as well, and uses Olson's theory of collective action as a building block to explain how "regulation is acquired by the industry and is designed and operated primarily for its benefit." Olson's theory implies that, for a given issue, the smaller the group, the higher the per-capita stake and therefore the incentive of its members to affect regulatory outcomes. Peltzman (1976), based on the emergence of some powerful consumer groups and the regulatory experience of the 1970s, took a broader view on Stigler's contribution that allows government officials to arbitrate among competing interests, and not always in favor of business.[8]

The main aspects of Peltzman's model are presented as follows. In the broadest sense, Peltzman's model aims at developing a theory of the optimum size of effective political coalitions. The regulator's objective is to maximize a majority M, generated by $M = nf - (N - n)h$, where n is the number of potential voters in a beneficiary group, f (net) probability that a beneficiary will grant support, N total number of potential voters, h (net) probability that he who is taxed (every non-n) opposes. The probability of support may now be specified as $f = f(g)$. Here, g is the per capita net benefit, and is: $g = \frac{T - K - C(n)}{n}$ with T total amount of money transferred to the beneficiary group, K amount of money spent on lobbying in order to weaken the opposition, C=C(n) cost of organizing a group of size n. There are the transaction costs that a group incurs during the process of forming and agreeing on its objectives. They increase progressively with increasing group size, i.e. $C_n > 0$ and $C_{nn} > 0$. It is assumed that the transfer is generated by a tax at the rate t on the wealth B of each member outside the benefited group, so that $T = tB(N - n)$ or $t = T/(B(N - n)$. The net probability of opposition generated by the tax is $h = h(t, z)$, with $z = K/(N - n)$ being the expenditures per capita for appeasing the opposition.

[7] Posner (1974, p. 341) divides all interest group theories of regulation in three main directions: (1) the Marxists and the muckrakers; (2) political scientists; (3) economic scientists. The first says that big business, the capitalists, controls the institutions of the society including regulation. Because of this, a great deal of economic regulation serves the interests of small-business. Concerning the second, one of the main useful statements of this theory is Marver H. Bernstein's "life-cycle" accounts, which suggested that agencies progress through various stages until lonely, frightened, and old, and over time they become the protectors of the regulated industry, rather than of the public interest. However, political scientists take the following untrue assumptions: pristine legislative purpose and possibility of capture by the regulated firm and not by the interest groups. The economic theory of regulation, on which we will concentrate in this section, provides more systematic explanation of regulatory capture and focuses on regulation as the outcome of the forces of demand and supply.

[8] The positive models developed in the last two decades by the Chicago school (Stigler, Peltzman, Becker) and the Virginia School (Tollison, Tullock) suffer from two methodological limitations: ignoring of informational asymmetries and a focus on the demand side (Laffont and Tirole 1993, p.475).

The following plausible assumptions are made: $f_g > 0$ and $f_{gg} < 0$, i.e. decreasing marginal returns of support. Analogous assumptions are made for the per-capita expenditure z: $h_z < 0$ and $h_{zz} > 0$.

$h_t > 0$ and $h_{tt} > 0$, i.e., increasing marginal costs of raising the tax rate. The problem faced by the regulatory authority is to choose size n of the group of beneficiaries, amount K spent on lobbying activities, and amount T which will be transferred to the group of beneficiaries.

To sum up, as C (n) rises progressively $C_{nn} > 0$, the group of beneficiaries should be relatively small. It is not profitable to spread the benefits over a large group, while it is profitable to spread losses over a large group (as $h_{tt} > 0$). Posner (1971, 1974) compared to Stigler and Peltzman, took into account not only interests of the groups but also their possibility to use financial resources and achieve a level of influence.

In the regulatory process, on the one hand, the relationships between the regulators and the regulated might tend to become too close and lead to capture, i.e. the pursuit of the regulated enterprises' interests rather than those of the public, which would affect the industry and the consumer's welfare respectively.[9] Regulators require a good deal of information in order to carry out their functions. The primary, and best, source of such information will often be the industry. Accordingly, in order to make regulation work, the regulator requires some assistance from the regulated firms. This gives the regulated firms a degree of leverage over regulatory procedures and objectives, a leverage that, over time, produces capture (Baldwin and Cave 1999, p. 36).

On the other hand, as an opposite to the regulatory capture situation, the regulator can be too harsh on the firm and might not adequately compensate the firm for its investments and efficiency improvements. Laffont and Tirole (2000, p. 5) call this situation "regulatory taking".

In practice, interest groups may influence public decision makers through the following methods (Laffont and Tirole 1993, p. 476): (1) monetary bribes are feasible, although not common due to their illegality; (2) more pervasive is the hoped-for future employment for commissioners and agency staff with the regulated firms or their law firms or with public-interest law firms; (3) personal relationships provide incentives for government officials to treat their industry partners kindly; (4) the industry may cater to the agency's concern for tranquility by refraining from criticizing publicly the agency's management; (5) the industry can also operate indirect transfers through a few key elected officials who have influence over the agency.

In telecommunications, the process of political influence is realized by the many interest groups with different power and end results. This has a special importance

[9] Mitnick (1980, p. 45) speaks about Marver H. Bernstein's "life-cycle" accounts, suggesting progress of agencies through various stages until lonely, frightened, and old, where they become the protectors of the regulated industry, rather than of the public interest.

in the deregulation and privatization processes of the telecommunications sector and will be considered here in detail. Figure 4.11 presents the main interest groups on deregulation and privatization processes in the telecommunications sector, based on Welfens and Graack (1997, p. 220).

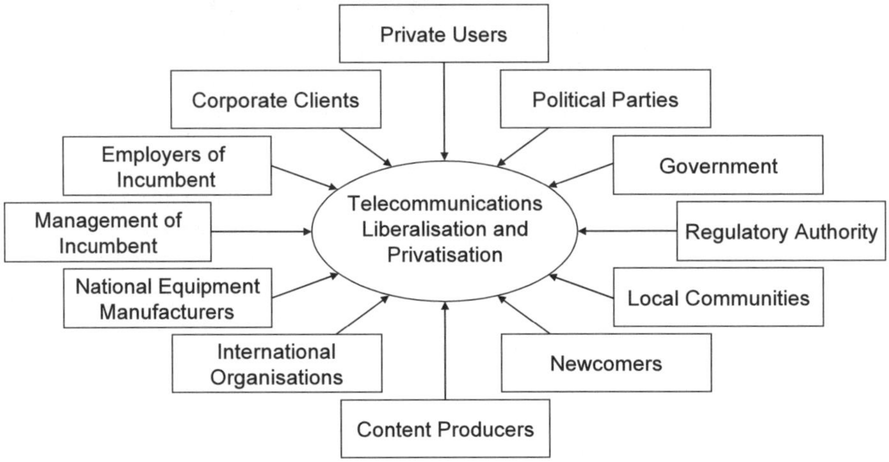

Source: Based on Welfens and Graack (1997, p. 220)

Fig. 4.11. Interest groups influencing deregulation and privatization processes in the telecommunications sector

Firstly, the influence and deregulation barriers could come from the groups relating to the monopolist telecommunications company. These are the management of the telecommunications monopolist (ex-monopolist) or employers of the telecommunications monopolist. However, the interests of these groups are quite different from each other. Moreover, corporate and private users of the telecommunications services could be influencing interest groups and can influence deregulation and privatization in the telecommunication sector but often to a very different extent.

Government interests are often present in the deregulation and privatization processes through fiscal and allocative interests, e.g. increasing of budget revenues or allocation of financial sources to the government departments. Interests of political parties are often determined by the program of political parties and new voting processes in the near future. The political parties opine the interests which will give them the biggest chance to win the next election. The regulatory authority has an enormous impact on the deregulation and privatization process in a country. Their results are often connected to the status of the regulatory authority and possibility of regulatory capture. The next interest groups among the state actors are regional communities. They may hope for additional revenue opportunities through liberalization and privatization processes.

National deregulation pressure on the telecommunications sector comes, as a rule, from two main groups: (1) newcomers which are interested in entering profitable markets and making profits; (2) telecommunication equipment suppliers and content suppliers interested in market liberalization due to increasing sales volumes. This could not be the case for the national telecommunications equipment suppliers if they had a monopoly status in this country that is very seldom seen in the real world and (3) international organizations like World Bank, ITU, OECD, EBRD and others are presented with the liberalization and privatization point of view and support the government of the countries to develop a reliable liberalization plan.

4.7 Design of Regulatory Institutions

The options for regulatory institution structure, competences and responsibilities, as a key element for positive as well as for normative regulation, are investigated in the final chapter of this section. Until recently, in many countries, a single Ministry or other government administrative unit performed the roles of telecommunications policy maker as well as owner and operator of the national telecommunications network. No need for a regulator was perceived in this environment, because the policy decisions, policy implementation and operation were developed by the same government officials. As mentioned above, privatization and market liberalization has led to a re-organization of the government institutions involved in the telecommunications sector. The most common gruff institutional model in the market economies around the world is illustrated in Fig. 4.12. This is compatible with the market-based supply of telecommunications services and facilitates compliance with the WTO Regulation Reference Paper.

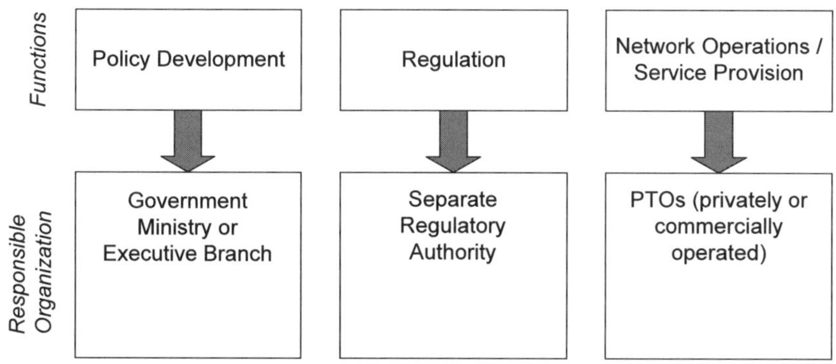

Source: Hank (2000, pp. 1–5)

Fig. 4.12. Standard institutional structure in developed market economies

However, the list of regulators can be extended and, in practice, the following regulator categories have played or still play a role: self-regulators, local authorities, parliament, courts and tribunals, central government departments, regulatory agencies, directors general.

Self-regulation typically involves an organization regulating the standards of behavior of its membership. This may be entirely voluntary and quite informal or subject to degrees of governmental supervision and legislative structuring. Local authorities have been regulators at a local level in countries such as Britain for centuries. This system provides the democratic control by those with detailed knowledge of an area, control that is likely to be more responsive to particular regional concerns than a regime run by a central government department or agency. In developed countries, in the eighteenth and nineteenth centuries, parliament imposed direct control over a number of industries to lay down in considerable detail the limits of allowable conduct; however, transition economies do not usually have this tradition. Experience points to a number of weaknesses in parliamentary regulation, such as no coherence. There has been some experience of regulation by judicial bodies in the past, e.g. in Britain. However, trial-type procedures as operated by courts and tribunals have generally not lead to good decision- or policy-making in the complex, shifting, and politically sensitive world of economic regulation. Due to the perceived inadequacies of such judicial bodies, regulatory (specialist, expert) agencies have developed in some instances.

Regulation through ministerial departments became the norm in developed countries in the middle of the last century. Accountability to parliament may be strength of the ministerial department but there are a number of reasons why ministerial schemes of control have tended to give way to agencies in twentieth century regulation. The perceived need to take issues "out of party policies" to either give continuity of policy development and longer-term planning to a sector or to achieve fairness in adjudication is one of the reasons for moving towards agencies.

Regulatory agencies are bodies that act on behalf of central government but are not a central state department. The advantages of this institution over ministerial departments are the possibilities to offer a greater degree of continuity of policy, to combine a wider range of functions successfully, to adjudicate free from political taint, and to be able to develop a high level of special expertise.

Directors general are single individuals or single independent regulators for their industries. The strength of a director general is that the public could identify regulation with an individual protector of their interests. However, there are some weaknesses such as the narrow experience of individuals compared to a board, great pressure on the individual, the fear of capriciousness and "rule of man", the lack of continuity of policy change of a director general, and limited accountability.

To sum up the world practice, it is well accepted that a country should have independent regulatory bodies following transparent procedures, subject to oversight by a strong and independent judiciary. Especially in transition and developing countries, each of these requirements is difficult to establish. Furthermore, without checks and balances, bureaucratic inefficiencies may be replaced by private corruption. Human capital is a scarce resource in many developing and transition countries. All these factors call for the modification of institutional design.

The following attributes are necessary for a regulatory body to function effectively in transition and developing countries (World Bank 2002, p. 168f):

1. Courts versus regulatory tribunals: The objectives of regulatory agencies are designing rules, monitoring compliance with rules, and enforcing compliance with rules. While many regulatory agencies achieve the first two well, they may still need court enforcement. The courts play an important role for hearing appeals after a regulatory decision. In many transition and developing countries, based on the fact that the courts are overburdened, the regulator needs to be given strong enforcement authority in the first instance. The question is whether courts relying on competition laws provide sufficient oversight for service providers. The experience of New Zealand serves here as a good example, which demonstrates, at least at the current stage of technological development, specialized regulatory tribunals are an important part of an effective regulatory regime.
2. Scope of regulators: Should such bodies operate at the national level, or should local regulatory bodies control local infrastructure enterprises? Should there be a different regulatory body for each principal infrastructure sector or for a particular function? There are some arguments in favor of localized regulation of infrastructure enterprises: (a) better knowledge of local conditions of a local regulator; (b) more direct political accountability under which a local regulator is likely to work, with the resulting greater improvement of the affected population in regulatory decision-making; (c) more effective monitoring of the regulated enterprise that proximity is likely to provide; and (d) frequent difficulties faced by national- or federal level regulators in coordinating with local governments, especially in matters as politically sensitive as access to infrastructure. The opposite factors in favor of centralization of regulation at the national level are: (a) the technical sophistication required of regulators, at least in some sectors, leading to economies of scale in regulation; (b) the shortage of local experts; (c) the presence of external effects among users at different locations in a single country, which may require both a single set of rules and a single agency; and (d) the more limited the agency's jurisdictional scope, the increased likelihood of industry "capture" of an agency.[10]

Generally, the smaller a country, the weaker the arguments in favor of local regulatory agencies and the stronger the first three arguments in favor of national regulation. Decentralized regulatory functions may be preferable within larger countries. In some cases, even though regulatory rules may be set at a national level, monitoring compliance with rules may be performed at a local level, e.g. by non-governmental organizations or communities. The decentralization argument for a large country is based on the fact that central governments in larger countries have sometimes lacked the power to impose regulation on local and regional enterprises without the agreement of the local and regional governments. In practice, the design of effective regulatory structures depends on political realities, e.g. France, with a very centralized political system, has mostly adopted a centralized structure of utilities regulation; in the USA, however, the states, being large

[10] The other argument in favor of centralization is a perceived lower likelihood of corruption, but the evidence here is mixed.

and autonomous, have large regulatory powers. However, in the telecommunications sector, due to technological changes and globalization of telecommunications services, regulation on the local and regional levels make less and less sense. This trend can already be observed in the US, where the responsibilities of the Public Utilities Commissions (PUCs) are significantly decreasing, and also as in the European Union, where the discussion about an "EU Super Regulator" is take place.

Factors which play a significant role in the choice between local and national regulators are also important for the consideration of sectoral specialization of regulatory bodies. An argument in favor of a specialized agency for each broad sector is that different sectors have different characteristics. Furthermore, there are economies of specialization and no particular economies of aggregation; that more agencies diversify the risk of institutional failure; and that more agencies allow for more policy experimentation. On the other hand, there are of course some issues that cut across sectoral lines and that would benefit from a coherent policy framework. Especially in the telecommunications sector due to the convergence processes, sectoral lines are not always very clear and are probably becoming less so. Thus, some countries like Australia and the United Kingdom, for example, set up regulatory authorities, which deal either with the telecommunications sector or with the broadcast TV and radio sector. Moreover, as seen in the localization/centralization issues, many transition and developing countries face a shortage of qualified personnel and an agency with broader jurisdiction probably has a lower likelihood of "capture" by the industry. Again, many of these arguments are principally related to country size and capacity.

In several countries, there is a functional specialization of different agencies, i.e. they have responsibility for different functions. It is possible to have a division of responsibility regarding economic and technical aspects of the telecommunications sector, but there are costs for the creation of multiple agencies, and likely economies of coordination. In several countries, the strategy to contract out some aspects of regulation, such as the design of pricing schemes or the monitoring of compliance of private firms is applied. For example, Argentina has hired private consultants to assist in rate rebalancing between both commercial and business customers and long-distance as well as local rates.

With the increasing introduction of competition into utilities, however, the interface between competition authorities and regulators is gaining increasing attention. In some countries (Venezuela, Poland), competition authorities act as effective "competition advocates" in the regulatory arena without assuming the regulatory portfolio themselves. In other countries (Australia, Bolivia), the competition authority has at least overall coordination and management authority over the regulatory bodies.

5 Telecommunications Role in the Economic Development and Sector Encouraging Policy Options

5.1 Modeling the Linkages Between the Economic Development and the Telecommunications Infrastructure in Transition Countries

In this section, the author investigates empirically the relationship between economic development and telecommunications in transition countries. After an introduction in the main hypotheses, explaining the role of telecommunications in economic development, main directions in economic growth theory as well as recent empirical studies on the link between economic growth and telecommunications (including studies dealing with infrastructure and ICTs) are reviewed. The data correlations and analysis of the main statistics are followed in Sect. 5.1.2. In Sect. 5.1.3, the model, investigating the causal relationship between economic development and telecommunications in transition economies, is built. Finally, the results of estimations are presented and the main conclusions are drawn.

It is widely accepted that telecommunications as a part of infrastructure as well as a component of information communications technologies (ICTs) are essential to countries' economic development. Obviously, investing in telecommunications infrastructure does itself stimulate economic growth because its products (like cable, switches) lead to increases in the demand for the goods and services used in their production. However, the economic returns on telecommunications infrastructure investment are much greater than the returns on just the telecommunications investment itself, because telecommunications are connected to other sectors of the economy through back-up and forward-linkages, having spillover effects on these sectors and creating externalities (Röller and Waverman 1996, p. 364; Welfens and Graack 1997, p. 208).

Transaction costs theory offers an explanation on this mechanism connecting telecommunications infrastructure and economic growth (Norton 1992, p. 177). Firstly, due to the poor state of telecommunications, there is a lack of readily available information. Decisions are not made or are made slowly because agents do not know the alternatives. Thus good telecommunications improve the efficiency of information markets. Secondly, a telecommunications infrastructure reduces transaction costs in numerous product and factor markets and leads in turn to higher aggregate output.

When the state of the telephone system is rudimentary, communications between firms is limited due to the fact that the transaction costs of ordering, gathering information and searching for services are high. With improving the telephone system, the costs of doing business fall, and output will increase for individual firms in individual sectors of the economy. Therefore, telecommunications infrastructure investment and the derived services provide significant benefits allowing firms to produce more efficiently. Firms can be able to engage in productive activities with greater flexibility, efficiency and innovation. With the intensified usage of information inputs in the production process, the importance of these effects is increasing, e.g. the proper functioning of multinational corporations, which at the beginning of the 21th century has a significant part of worldwide GDP, would not be possible without good telecommunications systems. To sum up, telecommunications investments lead also to benefits in other sectors.

In the transition and developing economies, a good telecommunications infrastructure is a very important location factor for foreign and domestic investors. In the process of investment decisions, a developed telecommunications infrastructure plays an important role in the locations' competition and systems' competition (Welfens and Graack 1997, p. 208).

The main challenge of this investigation is to examine the linkage between economic development and telecommunications infrastructure stocks in the transition countries. The fact that telecommunications decrease the transaction cost in the economy, suggests that telecommunications play a significant role in the economic development of transitions countries. It is to assume that this impact is higher compared to developed countries. Furthermore, it is of interest whether mobile telecommunications have a higher impact on the economic growth compared to traditional fixed telecommunications. Mobile telecommunications, which play a very significant role in the transition economies, require less investment and offer more mobility for the users. The validation of this hypothesis will depend on the availability and reliability of the necessary data.

5.1.1 Recent Literature Review

Generally, investigation of the economic growth sources is a very old topic in the economic theory. Adam Smith found in his famous "Inquiry to the Causes of the Wealth of Nations" several factors such as specialization that foster economic growth (Smith 1973). As reviewed by Grossman and Helpman (1994, p. 23ff), all empirical analyses, dealing with determinates of economic growth, can be divided in three different directions. One group of economists argues that capital accumulation is the driving force behind economic growth. The starting point here is the neoclassical growth model of Robert Solow, where accumulation of physical capital and labor are the main determinants of economic growth. At the same time technological progress, which according to Solow's estimation attributed to almost 90% of income per capita growth, is an exogenous variable and remains unexplained (Solow 1956, 1957). This aspect in Solow's model is criticized by many economists. Another critical issue of his theory is the view that per capita income of different countries will eventually converge. Diverse studies have examined empirically whether economic growth is converging relative to the USA and what factors force this convergence (Barro and Sala-I-Martin 1992; Mankiw et al. 1992; Aghion and Howitt 1998, p. 11) are more optimistic in respect to Solow's theory and insist that based on the decreasing marginal incomes from capital, the growth in income per capita will hold up. To have continuous growth rates, a permanent increase in knowledge is required.

The second group of economists casts external economies in a leading role in the growth process. The main idea here is when individuals or firms accumulated new capital, they inadvertently contribute to the productivity of capital held by others, e.g. Lucas (1988) argues that such spillovers may occur by the investment in the human capital, Barro (1990) investigates such impact from state investment in the public goods.

The third group of economists argued that the improvements in technology have been real force behind increasing the living standard. Romer (1990), Aghion and Howitt (1992) as well as Grossman and Helpman (1994) follow the idea that industrial innovation is the engine of growth.

The debate on the link between infrastructure and economic growth was opened with a question of impact of public infrastructure investment on economic growth. Aschauer (1989) investigates the relationship between aggregate productivity and, among other indicators, public infrastructure investment. He finds a high explanatory power of infrastructure investment for productivity in the USA and other OECD countries. However, some other researchers criticize the robustness of his results (Holtz-Eakin 1994; Garcia-Mila et al. 1996). He does not account for the appropriate causalities and correlations. Taking into account e.g. country fixed effects, his results change significantly. Thus, the available evidence regarding the returns from public infrastructure appears to be such that the original high returns do not hold up once a number of econometric measures are employed.

There are not too many studies, which focus on the specific role of telecommunications in economic development. Hardy (1980) is one of the first studies, which investigates the potential impact of telecommunications on economic growth. His main conclusion is that telephone density has a significant impact on the GDP. However, in his work neither fixed effects nor the problem of reverse causality was addressed. Norton (1992), using data from 47 countries for the period of 1957–1977, estimates the effect of the average stock of telephones between 1957 and 1977 on the mean annual growth rate, controlling for the stock of telephones in 1957 and a number of macroeconomic variables. He finds that the telecommunications variable is positive and significant and concludes that telecommunications infrastructure reduces transactions costs due to the output rising when the infrastructure is present. Röller and Wavermann (1996, 2001) investigate the relation between telecommunications infrastructure investment and aggregate output for 21 OECD countries in the period of 1970–1990. They estimate a system of four equations: aggregate growth function, demand function of telecommunications infrastructure, supply function of telecommunications investment and telecommunications infrastructure production function. Taking into account the problem of reverse causality and cross-country fixed effect, they find a causal relationship between telecommunications infrastructure and aggregate output. Welfens and Jungmittag (2002) analyze the relation between telecommunications approximated by the number of phone minutes and economic growth for Germany in the period of 1960–1990. They apply the concept of a time series cointegration. The result of this study is that telecommunications have a significant positive impact on the growth rates in Germany during the investigated period. However, the causality issues are not included in their investigation. This was taken into account in their other study (Welfens et al. 2005), where they prove this relationship. Waverman et al. (2005) consider the impact of mobile telecommunications on economic growth, deploying two different growth models: neoclassical and endogenous technological change. They find poor performance of the first model, but insist that the second model provides more robust results, which indicate a significant positive impact of mobile telecommunications in developing world.

Empirical investigations of related questions in transition economies are very limited. Although some previous articles do not focus directly on telecommunications, their approaches may be very useful for this investigation. Piazolo (1999), mostly interested in the Central and Eastern European countries (CEECs), included 25 transition economies in his regression. He points out that institutional changes in these countries can enhance economic growth perspectives. He conducts the cross-countries analysis by expressing the production function in terms of relative changes of variables, which are based on Barro (1990) and can be written as following: $\hat{Y} = \gamma + \beta\hat{P} + \alpha\hat{K}$, where $\hat{Y}$ is the average annual change of GDP per capita at constant prices, γ is technical progress, $\hat{P}$ is the average annual change in quality of institution, $\hat{K}$ is the average annual change in capital stock. His investigation has an innovative approach in measurement of change in the capital stock for transition countries but his regression shows quite low explanation power. This point is noted by the author. The other variables should be included in the investigation such as human capital stock, which is quite challenging because of data availability. Von Hirschhausen et al. (2002) investigate the relation between infrastructure policies and economic development in 15 transition countries in 1993–2000.[1] They use an aggregate production function to test the impact of total capital, approximated by net electricity consumption, infrastructure capital, approximated by telephone mainlines, and the speed of liberalization in major infrastructure sectors, approximated by the infrastructure reform index from EBRD.[2] Their model shows that early liberalization (high EBRD index) is conductive to economic growth. They could not find any significance of the telecommunications variable. The authors conclude that institutional reform in the infrastructure sectors is at least as important as the modernization of physical capital.

As a part of the ICT sector, impact of telecommunications on economic growth is included by considering of impact of ICTs on economic development. However, one may assume that the ICT impact should be higher compared to telecommunications. The effects of ICT on the growth rates are the subject of research by many economists. ICT investment contributed to growth in most OECD countries in

---

[1] Von Hirschausen et al. (2002) investigate a production function, which included such explanatory variables as gross fixed capital formations, gross government expenditures (as an indicator for infrastructure investment) and an institutional reform indicator. The usage of some variables may be doubted. This study also indicates that institutional reform in infrastructure sectors is at least as important as the modernization of physical capital.

[2] Moreover, they use the second model based on a stochastic frontier production function. This model will be not considered here due to the other research interest.

the 1990s (OECD 2005b). There is a broad consensus in the literature that ICT production (including ICT-producing services like telecommunications services) – mainly due to high rates of process innovations – strongly contributes to aggregate productivity growth and as a result to economic growth. Moreover, there is also evidence that usage of ICT contributes to economic growth as well (van Ark 2001; Audretsch/Welfens 2002).

In terms of ICT contribution to the economic growth in transition economies, there are a couple of studies. Piatkowski (2004) investigates multi-channel contribution of ICT to output and productivity growth in eight transition countries including Russia from 1995 to 2001. He finds out that in five new EU member countries Czech Republic, Hungary, Poland, Slovakia and Slovenia the impact of ICT on economic growth (between 1.29 and 0.54% points) was higher than the average for the EU-15 (0.73% points). In opposite, ICT contribution to economic growth in Russia (0.09% points) was lower than in the EU-15 and led to income deconvergence. Van Ark and Piatkowski (2004) compare contribution of the ICT-producing, ICT-using and non-ICT industries to labor productivity growth and found out that only in Hungary ICT-producing industries have contributed significantly higher than in EU-15 to the productivity growth. ICT-using manufacturing has exploited a large catch-up effect. Evidence in productivity improvements in ICT-using services is mixed.

5.1.2 Data and Main Patterns

In this investigation, 21 out of the 27 transition countries are being taken into account. Six countries are missing due to the low data availability. The list of all countries (included and not included) is presented in Table 5.1. The period of investigation is from 1996 to 2003. Despite the fact that much data is available starting from 1992, the results of the 12-year estimation (from 1992 to 2003) have to be considered with caution because of strong transition processes during this period and related high data fluctuations.

The data sources, which are used here, are the International Telecommunication Union's Database 2006 (ITU 2006a) as well as the World Development Indicators Database 2006 (WDI 2005) of the World Bank. EBRD's Transition Reports (EBRD 1998, 2002, 2004, 2005) are used to quantify the institutional variable based on the EBRD reform index.

As illustrated in Fig. 5.1, the simple correlation between the real GDP and the number of total phone connections is very strong.[3] This may be partly related to the country size as well as to the different degree of development across of the transition countries.[4]

---

[3] In the period from 1996 to 2003, R^2 between these two variables is 0.86.

[4] The correlation between the number of total phone connections per 100 inhabitants and the real GDP per capita in 2003 is 0.8. In this case, the impact of the country size is lower. However, the penetration rates are a bounded function. Thus, the interpretation of the result is more difficult. In this work, the decision is taken to investigate the relationship between the real GDP and the number of total phone connections controlling for the differences in the countries' sizes and development levels.

Table 5.1. List of investigated and not investigated countries

Included in the investigation	Not included in the investigation
Central Eastern European Countries	
Hungary (HUN)	
Latvia (LVA)	
Lithuania (LTU)	
Poland (POL)	
Slovakia (SVK)	
Czech Republic (CZE)	
Estonia (EST)	
Slovenia (SVN)	
South Eastern European Countries	
Albania (ALB)	Bosnia and Herzegovina (BIH)
Bulgaria (BGR)	Serbia and Montenegro (YUG)
Romania (ROM)	T.F.Y.R. Macedonia (MKD)
Croatia (HRV)	
Common Independent States	
Azerbaijan (AZE)	Tajikistan (TJK)
Armenia (ARM)	Turkmenistan (TKM)
Belarus (BLR)	Uzbekistan (UZB)
Georgia (GEO)	
Kazakhstan (KAZ)	
Kyrgyzstan (KGZ)	
Moldova (MDA)	
Russian Federation (RUS)	
Ukraine (UKR)	

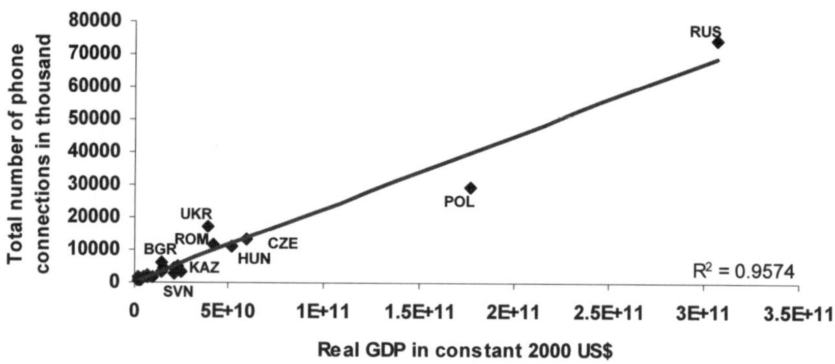

Source: WDI (2005) and ITU (2006a)

Fig. 5.1. Total number of phone connections vs. GDP in constant 2000 US$

The compound annual growth rates (CAGRs) of GDP and phone connections are presented in Table 5.2. This indicates that from 1996 to 2003, the CAGRs of GDP in the transition countries amount to 3.72% on average. At the same time, the CAGRs of the number of total phone connections are about 16.67%.

Table 5.2. Compound annual growth rates (CAGRs) of GDP and phone connections

	GDP million constant 2000 US$		CAGR 1996–2003 (in %)	Number of total phone connections (in thousand)		CAGR 1996–2003 (in %)	$a_4 = 0.08$* Impact of telecom (in %)
	1996	*2003*		*1996*	*2003*		
ALB	3,090	4,411	5.22	67	1,397	54.50	4.36
ARM	1,574	2,700	8.01	502	544	1.16	0.09
AZE	3,797	7,123	9.41	679	1,996	16.67	1.33
BGR	11,25	14,356	2.69	2,673	5,875	11.91	0.95
BLR	9,41	14,951	6.47	2,138	4,193	10.10	0.81
CZE	53,997	59,844	1.48	3,017	13,517	23.89	1.91
EST	4,359	6,550	5.99	490	1,513	17.48	1.40
GEO	2,549	3,737	5.62	560	1,229	11.87	0.95
HRV	16,504	21,115	3.58	1,453	4,519	17.60	1.41
HUN	38,841	51,687	4.17	3,119	11,317	20.22	1.62
KAZ	16,259	24,893	6.27	1,855	3,586	9.87	0.79
KGZ	1,116	1,539	4.69	348	519	5.86	0.47
LTU	9,705	14,084	5.46	1,015	3,175	17.70	1.42
LVA	6,176	9,553	6.43	764	1,885	13.76	1.10
MDA	1,375	1,566	1.88	594	1,489	14.04	1.12
POL	137,508	177,016	3.67	6,749	29,398	23.39	1.87
ROM	41,699	42,688	0.34	3,193	11,600	20.24	1.62
RUS	231,081	306,690	4.13	26,180	74,480	16.11	1.29
SVK	17,913	22,829	3.53	1,274	4,985	21.52	1.72
SVN	16,098	20,771	3.71	706	2,549	20.12	1.61
UKR	31,095	39,289	3.40	9,275	17,401	9.41	0.75
Average	31,253	40,352	3.72	3,174	9,389	16.76	1.36

*The meaning of this column is explained in Sect. 5.1.5.

5.1.3 The Model and its Empirical Implementation

As presented in the literature overview, the studies, investigated the relationship between telecommunications and economic development in transition economies, do not pay attention to a possible causal relation between these two parameters. In the author's view, it is a crucial issue to consider such a link. The investigation is based on the following approach: (1) causal relation between economic growth and telecommunications are proven through the estimation of two separated regressions, where national aggregate economic output and telecommunications are dependent and independent variables respectively; (2) the fixed effects in the panel analysis are used to take into account the above mentioned differences between the transition countries.

The first equation is constructed based on the modified model of the neoclassical growth theory, used, e.g. by Barro (1990). Instead of the public capital used by Barro (1990), the telecommunications capital approximated by telecommunications stocks is deployed. The first equation can be written as follows:

$$gdp = f(capital; hcapital; reform; telecom), \tag{5.1}$$

wherein the national aggregate economic activities (*gdp*) in transition countries can be explained through capital stock variable (*capital*), stock of human capital (*hcapital*), institutional variable (*reform*), which indicate the state of reforming process in each country, as well as stock of telecommunications infrastructure (*telecom*). Thinking deeper about the relationship between parameters in this equation, it is logical to suggest that stock of telecommunications influence national aggregate economic output with a lag of at least one year. The above equation is taking the following form:

$$gdp = f(capital_t\ ; hcapital_t; reform_t; telecom_{t-1}). \tag{5.2}$$

The second equation, modeling the demand on the telecommunication, can be written as follows:

$$telecom = f(tel\_price; gdp), \tag{5.3}$$

whereof stock of telecommunications infrastructure is explained through telecommunications price indicator *(tel_price)* as well as national aggregate economic output *(gdp)*. Thinking about this relationship in the real world, it is logical to suggest that national aggregate economic output has a lagged impact on telecommunications stock with at least one year.

$$telecom = f(tel\_price_t; gdp_{t-1}). \tag{5.4}$$

Both investigated regressions are panel data estimations with two dimensions, namely a cross-section/country dimension *i* and a time dimension *t.* If *y* stands for depended variable, and various purely exogenous/independent variables are denoted by *X*, the general form of both estimations is the following:

$$y_{i,t} = c + \delta X_{i,t} + \upsilon_{i,t}. \tag{5.5}$$

In the panel models, it is to assume that the error components have the following structure:

$$\upsilon_{i,t} = \mu_i + \eta_{i,t}, \tag{5.6}$$

whereof μ_i stands for the unobservable, time-invariant, individual specific effect, capturing any individual-specific effect that is not included in the regression, and $\eta_{i,t}$ denotes the remainder (white-noise) disturbance. The individual effects μ_i, can have a different structure. It allows estimating such a panel model either as fixed effects or as random effects model.

$$y_{i,t} = c + \delta X_{i,t} + \theta \mu_i + \eta_{i,t}. \tag{5.7}$$

If it is assumed that μ_i are fixed parameters, which should be estimated, and $\eta_{i,t}$ are the remainder disturbances, which are stochastically independent and identically distributed IID (0, σ^2_η), the appropriate specification is a fixed effects model. Moreover, $X_{i,t}$ must be independent of $\eta_{i,t}$ for all *i* and *t*.

Assuming that μ_i are random and distributed IID (0, σ^2_μ) as well as that additionally $\eta_{i,t}$ are distributed IID (0, σ^2_η), and μ_i and $\eta_{i,t}$ are independent from each other, this is the model with random effects. This model specification can be expressed also by (5.5) and (5.6). The further condition is that $X_{i,t}$ must be independent of $\eta_{i,t}$ and $\mu_{i,t}$ for all *i* and *t*. In respect to the investigated models, the question is whether to deploy the model with fixed or random effects.

The Hausman specification test compares the fixed versus random effects under the null hypothesis that the individual effects are uncorrelated with the other regressors in the model (Hausman 1978). If correlated (H_0 is rejected), a random effect model produces biased estimators, so a fixed effect model is preferred. In both investigated equations, the H_0 is rejected. As a result, in both regressions, the fixed effects have to be controlled.

Empirically, two estimations can be written as follows:

$$\log(gdp_{it}) = a_1 \log(capital_{it}) + a_2 \log(lf\_emp_i) + \\ + a_3 \log(reform_{it}) + a_4 \log(telecom_{it-1}) + \mu_i + v_{it}, \tag{5.8}$$

$$\log(telecom_{it}) = b_1 \log(tel\_price_{it}) + b_2 \log(gdp_{it-1}) + \eta_i + \gamma_{it}, \tag{5.9}$$

whereof *gdp* is the real gross domestic product, *capital* is approximated through *net electricity consumption* variable,[5] which may serve as a proxy for capital stocks in transition countries, *lf_emp* is the proxy for human capital. It is equal to the difference between total labor force and unemployment rates and may serve as a proxy for the human capital in transition countries;[6] institutional variable *reform* is approximated by the sum of six main EBRD subindexes: large-scale privatization, enterprise reform, competition policy, infrastructure reform, banking sector reform, reform of non-bank financial institutions, measuring the progress

[5] Accessing the capital stock in transition economies is very challenging. In the developed economies, the Perpetual-Inventory-Method is used for this purpose (Krüger 2000, p. 155 ff). This method is required to find out the initial capital stock in these countries that is very challenging based on the fact that at the beginning of the 1990s, in the transition countries many depreciation processes took place, and values of the capital stocks were strongly fluctuating. Due to this fact, following Von Hirschhausen et al. (2002), a net electricity consumption variable is deployed. For more details on the use of such approximation in different investigations, see the review in Von Hirschhausen et al. (2002).

[6] Of course the author recognizes that the rates of unemployment, especially in such countries, may be higher than reported due to non-reported unemployment.

in the long-term reforms (EBRD 2005, p. 203); *telecom* is the number of fixed and mobile phone connections (total). The separate investigation on mobile and fixed telecommunications is not possible due to the poor price data on fixed and especially on mobile telecommunications sector in transition countries. This is also the reason why *tel_price* variable – stands for telecommunications price – is approximated by real fixed phone connection fees.

The main parameters of each variable are presented in Table 5.3. The expected signs are identified here as well. Generally, it is to expect that in the national aggregated output equations, all variables have positive influence on the gdp variable. In the telecommunications equation, one may suggest that the telecommunications price has a negative impact on the number of phone lines, at the same time, the gdp influences the number of phone lines positively.

Use of the lagged variables in (5.8) and (5.9), which are describing the relationships closer to reality, helps as well to overcome the simultaneous causality bias in these estimations (Stock and Watson 2007, p. 325). The number of phone connections in the previous year may influence the gdp in this year, but the gdp of this year can not influence the number of phone connections in the previous year. This allows the conclusion that the lagged telecommunications variable and the error term are not correlated. Considering the relationship between price and number of telephone lines in the second equation, one can suggest endogeneity between with variable and residuals, but this is not the case due to the regulation of such kind of tariffs in all countries.[7]

Both equations are estimated as separated panel regressions, controlling for fixed effects through including the dummy variables for i and t dimensions. Such an estimator is called a Fixed Effect least squares estimator, also known as least squares dummy variables (LSDV) or the Within-estimator. The LSDV estimator and Within-estimator, describing the variation within the individuals or in deviation from the individual averages, lead to the same estimate for β. The LSDV is the best unbiased estimator (BLUE), if $X_{i,t}$ must be independent of $\eta_{i,t}$ for all i and t is achieved. However, due to the fact that the number of time observation in both regressions is only 12 and not unlimited, the consistency of the LSDV estimator is not achieved in the investigated panel regressions (Baltagi 2001, p. 14).

In order to ensure that autocorrelation in the residuals does not result in inconsistent and inefficient Within-estimator, White-period standard errors are computed (Arellano 1987), which are robust to arbitrary within cross-section residual autocorrelation. The existence of first-order serial autocorrelation is tested by regressing the within regression residuals against their one-period lag. The results are presented in the next section.

[7] As suggested by Von Hirschausen C, Sugolov P, Dodonov B (2002) endogeneity of net electricity consumption variable is tested using the Durbin Wu Hausman test, modified by Davidson/MacKinnon. An auxiliary regression is run. The lagged value of the net electricity consumption is used as instrumental variable. The resulting coefficient of the residual in the auxiliary regression is not significantly different from zero, which indicates the absence of endogeneity in the model.

Table 5.3. Variable description, expected relationships as well as summary statistics

Variable	Description	Expected sign	Mean	Median	Max.	Min.
GDP	Gross domestic product in constant 2000 US$ (in million)	To be explained	35,492.5	12,877.4	313,172.3	1,042.6
NET-ELECTRICITY	Net electricity consumption (in billion kilowatt hours)	+	104.42	16.91	881.50	2.62
LF	Labor force (in thousand people)	+	9,081	2,963	78,375	755
LF-EMP	Employed labor force (in thousand people)	+	8,215	2,542	73,294	653
REFORM	Sum of the six main EBRD subindexes: large-scale privatization, enterprise reform, competition policy, infrastructure reform, banking sector reform, reform of non-bank financial institutions	+	14	13.9	21.7	6.3
TELECOM	Number of fixed and mobile phone connections (in thousand lines)	+	4,420.6	1,669	74,480	42.8
TELECOM	Number of fixed and mobile phone connections (in thousand lines)	To be explained	See above			
GDP	Gross domestic product in constant 2000 US$ (in million)	+	See above			
TEL-PRICE	Telecommunications prices are approximated by the residential telephone connection charge (in constant 2000 US$)	–	16,672.65	99.96	3,437,776	5.97

Sources: ITU (2006a); WDI (2005); EBRD (1996–2005), Energy Information Administration Web site.

Table 5.4. Estimation results: economic development and telecommunications in transitions countries

	(1) Simple regression 1996–2003	(2) Simple regression 1992–2003	(3) Balanced panel regression with fixed effects (within) 1996–2003	(4) Balanced panel regression with fixed effects (within) 1992–2003	(5) Balanced panel regression with fixed effects (within) 1996–2003	(6) Balanced panel regression with fixed effects (within) 1992–2003
Output equation/dependent variable: log(gdp)*						
Const.	5.9308***	6.2677***	2.1254	6.3757	–4.0765	8.5145
	(2.4981)	(2.3182)	(4.6236)	(5.3024)	(6.3267)	(6.0143)
log(*net_electricity*)	0.1827	0.1930	0.1391	0.1327	0.2396**	0.3295**
	(0.1262)	(0.1306)	(0.1461)	(0.1260)	(0.1196)	(0.1417)
log(*employed labor force*)	0.3998**	0.4438**	1.1207***	0.8819***	—	—
	(0.1948)	(0.1915)	(0.3167)	(0.3568)		
log(*labor force*)	—	—	—	—	1.5218***	0.7276*
					(0.4324)	(0.4077)
log(*reform*)	1.5730***	1.5650***	0.8879***	0.5349***	0.8635***	0.3935***
	(0.4568)	(0.3153)	(0.2092)	(0.1822)	(0.2026)	(0.1464)
log($telecom_{t-1}$)	0.4546***	0.3890***	0.1010***	0.1228***	0.0826***	0.1123***
	(0.1721)	(0.1610)	(0.0253)	(0.0342)	(0.0254)	(0.0390)
R^2	0.846	0.829	0.998	0.996	0.998	0.995
SER	0.559	0.591	0.067	0.083	0.068	0.101
N	168	210	168	210	168	210

Telecom equation/dependent variable log(telecom)*				
Const.	−3.7348***	−3.6533***	−40.212***	40.4580***
	(1.9145)	(2.0401)	(13.4863)	(0.0072)
log(*price*)	−0.1752***	−0.1535***	−0.1811***	−0.1755***
	(0.0768)	(0.0665)	(0.06851)	(0.0601)
$\log(gdp_{t-1})$	0.8160***	0.8067***	2.3879***	2.3966***
	(0.0892)	(0.0930)	(0.5812)	(0.6369)
R^2	0.797	0.753	0.9583	0.9507
SER	0.565	0.6282	0.276	0.299
N	147	168	147	168

Standard errors are given in parentheses under coefficients. They are calculated based on White-period standard errors and variance (degrees of freedom corrected). Individual coefficients are statistically significant at the 10%***, at the 5%**, or 1%*** significance level.

5.1.4 Results and Interpretation

Both equations are estimated for two periods from 1992 to 2003 as well as from 1996 to 2003. The data inconsistency in the early stage of the transition process may cause less robustness in the results from 1996 to 2003.

In the output equation, the net electricity consumption variable is positive, but in modifications (1)–(4) not significant. However, if the labor force variable is deployed (without correction for unemployment rates), the situation is changing. One may assume that through strong fluctuation of the unemployment rates as well as possible distortions through "official" and "non-official" figures, the resulting numbers are not reliable. The sum of capital and labor force coefficients is about one in the long time period (see specification 6). The reform variable is positive and highly significant, which provides evidence for the importance of reforming processes in transition countries. The telecommunications variable is positive and significant in all modifications, that means that an increase in the number of lines has a positive impact on aggregate national output. For example, for balanced panel with fixed effects in the period from 1992 to 2003 (see specification 5), this amounts to 0.08%. This means that an increase in 1% in the number of lines last year is resulting in an increase of the aggregate national output by 0.08%. To avoid the possible shortage in this conclusion, the magnitude of this coefficient has to be assessed. If the CAGRs of the total phone connections in the investigated sample from 1996 to 2003 is about 17% per year, the total growth rates per year, caused only by increase of the telecommunications lines in a year before, account to 1.36%. At the same time, the CAGRs of GDP in these countries are 3.72%. As a result, the stock of telecommunications infrastructure ensures a significant part of the economic growth in transition countries and is significantly important.

On the other hand, the assumption of the causal relationship between telecommunications infrastructure and aggregate national output is proven as well. The telecommunications demand equation suggests that a 1% increase of the gdp in the year before has a positive impact on the telecommunications phone lines, amounting to 2.4%. Given the fact that a number of the phone lines was increasing from 1996 to 2003 by 17%, about 8.9% can be explained through the increase in national aggregated output a year before. The telecommunications price, approximated by the real residential telephone connection charge, indicates significant negative influence on the number of telephones lines (the higher price results in the lower number of lines). However, this outcome should be interpreted cautiously because this variable captures only some changes in the fixed telecommunications pricing and does not provide any indications for the mobile pricing. The consistent pricing data was not collected systematically in these countries, especially not in the early transition stages.

Generally, empirical investigation in transition countries is a big challenge due to very poor data state such as capital stocks or human capital. The transition period, followed by economic crises (e.g. the Russian financial crisis in 1998), is resulting in strong data volatilities during short time periods. Because of these reasons, the results of this investigation should be interpreted very cautiously. The author considers this study as the first step to learn about the relationship between economic growth and telecommunications in transition countries.

To sum it up, controlling for the country-fixed effects as well as keeping in check the possible causal relationship, this investigation finds out a positive, significant impact of the telecommunications infrastructure on the gross domestic product in transition countries as well as an opposite direction relationship: the gross domestic product has a significant und positive influence on the number of telecommunications lines. This provides the evidence that the development of telecommunications infrastructure in the transition countries fosters economic development. The still open questions are whether there are any differences in impacts of fixed and mobile telecommunications infrastructure, or whether the governments should invest in telecommunications infrastructure, and how high should be such investment to increase economic growth, employment, and the country's competitiveness.

5.2 Modernization of the Fixed Telecommunications Sector

Fixed telecommunications is the most traditional sector of the telecommunications industry. In this chapter, the Russian fixed telecommunications market will be considered, focusing on such issues as the differences between fixed telecommunications sector in the developed parts of the world and Russia; challenging privatization and liberalization; adequate universal service policy (whether Russia needs universal service program financing fixed infrastructure or is it only subsidising of too expensive technology); increase of fixed penetration rates; access regulation as an alternative for the Russian fixed sector; importance of VoIP as well as NGN deployment in Russia.

In the following, the country-specific trends in the development of the fixed telecommunications sector in Russia are investigated. Table 5.5 summarizes the main differences of the Russian fixed telecom in comparison to Western Europe:

Table 5.5. Comparison of the Russian and Western European fixed telecommunications

	Western Europe	Russia
Fixed penetration rates	High	Low
Upgrade required to introduced DSL	Low	High
Fixed network extension needs	Low	High
Competition from mobile networks	Middle	Strong
Competition from cable networks	Dependent on country: from very strong e.g. NL to very low, e.g. DE	Very low
Competition from other technologies	Limited	Strong in such technologies as Ethernet LAN as well as starting in WiFi/WiMAX
Regulatory impact	Strong access regulation	No access regulation at least for the next two years; Regulation of end-prices using rate of return method

Source: Own description

As mentioned in the Chap. 2 and presented in Fig. 5.2, fixed telecommunications penetration in Russia as well as in transition countries is usually significant lower in comparison to developed economies such as EU 15. Moreover, the main trend of declining of fixed penetration rates is observable. At the same time, many of the transition countries did not come close at all to the level of the developed countries.

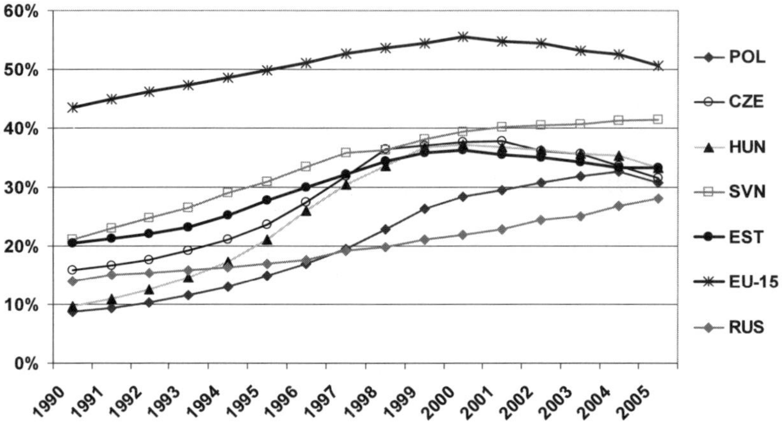

Source: ITU (2006a)

Fig. 5.2. Development of fixed penetration rates in Russia, EU-15 as well as in selected Eastern European EU countries

The quality of the deployed networks in Russia is insufficient and its upgrade in comparison to the developed countries needs higher investments. To sum up, the fixed operators in Russia (mostly regional companies of Svyazinvest) have to fulfil two aims at the same time: they have to introduce advanced services and extend their networks.

At the same time, the competitive situation is important. Mobile telephony is a very strong competitor, especially in the Russian voice market.[66] The population prefers to obtain mobile phones because it is simple, without waiting time and give more flexibility.

In terms of broadband, the fixed networks have strong competition from Ethernet LAN as well as from Fiber to the X technologies. The other growing competitors are wireless broadband access networks, which are gaining a significant market share. There are only few cable networks in Russia, which enable broadband access, due to the fact that high investment is required for the network upgrade.

[66] According to the IT research group ipsosinsight, only 7% of Russians access the Internet through wireless devices compared to 40% in Japan, 29% in the UK, 26% in the US. The reason is partly due to the fact that the 3G licenses are issued only at the beginning of 2007.

In terms of regulation, Russia has not had access unbundling regulations yet and the end price tariffs still contain rate-on-return. At the same time, in Europe all incumbents have to deal with very strong unbundling policy, which decrease their profits significantly.

To sum up, the fixed telecommunications in Russia is in a different position in comparison to e.g. Western European markets. More competition pressure from the other technologies can be identified. The current Svyazinvest's market share of the Russian broadband market is only about 30%. At the same time, some regulatory advantages are to observe. It is often argued that fixed telecommunications is one of the most reliable possibilities to access the Internet. As a result, low fixed penetration rates are the reason for low broadband development. It is expected that in the near future, wireless technologies: 3G and WiFi/WiMAX will be a reliable substitute for broadband at a competitive price level. The proper vision in regards to the regulatory policy of fixed infrastructure in Russia should focus on the one hand on consumer surplus and increasing competition. On the other hand, it should consider investment incentives. In both cases, the above mentioned country-specific developments should be taken into account.

5.2.1 Privatization as an Instrument to Raise Sector Efficiency

In retrospect, the privatization of the Russian telecom sector was conducted the wrong way around. Until 1992, the telecommunications infrastructure was state-owned. Between 1992 and 1995 the infrastructure was broken into pieces, some of which were rather small and meaningless on their own, such as the telegraph operators. Furthermore, the pieces were incorporated and privatized. Only then did the government create a holding Svyazinvest, with the aim of consolidating its stakes in the underlying operating companies[67] and later selling a non controlling interest in the holding.

Svyazinvest was created with the intention that the government would retain a controlling 51% stake in the holding and offer 49% to strategic investors and/or the public. After an unsuccessful first attempt, in July 1997, 25% plus one share in Svyazinvest was sold to a foreign consortium, Mustcom, led by George Soros, for $1.875 billion. In 2004, Soros sold his stake in Svyazinvest to Leonard Blavatnik from Access Industries for an estimated $700 million.

Due to high fragmentation, the consolidation of Svyazinvest was carried out in 2001 with the aim of improving the manageability of the companies (there would be seven subsidiaries instead of 89). It was also to create additional possibilities for cost cutting by centralizing and unifying capex and borrowing. Other goals included concentrating the main managerial functions, such as technical supervision, maintenance and procurement, marketing and operations of the central

[67] Svyazinvest consolidated the state stakes (typically 38% of the total stock, or 51% of the commons) in 76 regional operators, four providers of international and long distance services (including Rostelecom), four operators of telegraph services, and one R&D and two leasing subsidiaries.

companies. In 2001–03, the subsidiaries were consolidated into seven super regional operators, which roughly corresponded to the seven Russian federal districts.[68] As result, Svyazinvest holding owns in each subsidiaries (excluding MGTS) as well as in Rostelecom 38% of total or 51% of voting stock.

At the end of 2006, Leonard Blavatnik sold his stake of 25% + 1 share to the Sistema. As results, at the beginning of 2007, the Svyazinvest Holding has the following structure (Fig. 5.3):

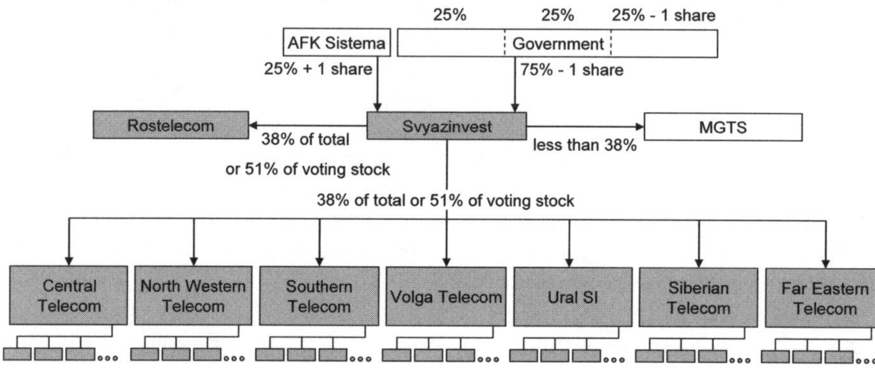

Source: Based on Troika-Dialog, 2006, p. 5

Fig. 5.3. Structure of the Svyazinvest Holding

Further privatization of Svyazinvest is still questionable. Svyazinvest is not on the list to be privatized in 2008. The Russian government said that the decision has not been made yet but must be made in one or two years.[69] Otherwise, the loss of company competitiveness due to the high investment needs for network upgrade is not avoidable. The Russian Minister for Economic Development left all possible options open: "If the state owns 75% of the company's shares, there must be either an initial public offering on the exchange, sale of a package to a private investor, or an injection of budget money."[70]

From the sale of 25% plus one share in 1997, there are many speculations how the state will proceed with the further privatization. The following major issues are on the privatization agenda:

1. what percentage should be privatized? 25% or all 75%? Should the government maintain some control in Svyazinvest? For example, in Germany and France, the state still has control shares in the incumbent companies. There is little clarity at this stage as to what will happen to Svyazinvest following the sale, i.e. whether the government will insist on it remaining

[68] for more on business challenges of the seven super regional operators see Kuznetsova et al. (2006).

[69] It is speculated that the reason is the presidential election in 2008.

[70] ITER-TASS, Russian leading News Agency, 19. April 2007.

intact or whether the buyers will be able to split it up into its various component assets. It does not look like that in Russia, the American experience in terms of government's splitting of AT&T into regional bells will be implemented. On the contrary, at the end of 2006, the Ministry for Economic Development planed to consolidate the activities of macro-regional seven companies into one holding. But this plan was not supported by the Minsvyaz due to the listing of each of the seven regional companies on the stock exchange. Minsvyaz expects that such plans would lead to a monopolisation of the market and result in increasing prices.

2. should it be an IPO or a private investor? For example, in many Eastern European EU countries, the strategic investors have control over the incumbent holdings, e.g. Deutsche Telekom in Matev Hungary, or France Telecom in TPSA in Poland. However, from the Russian discussion in 2005–2006 it is clear that the Russian government does not want Svyazinvest to go to foreigners. The company controls more than 70% of the Russian telecommunications infrastructure and is a strategic asset. Restrictions on ownership of telecommunications companies are not uncommon in the US, Western Europe and the rest of the world. The Kremlin will want Svyazinvest to remain in the hands of a Russian group that would itself be more manageable.

Sistema is more likely than other participants to get the government's Svyazinvest stake during a possible auction because Comstar UTS already has a blocking stake. However, after 6 months there are already many conflict points between Sistema and Svyazinvest's management. Sistema officials said that Comstar UTS would now focus on creating joint ventures with interregional operators rather than on acquiring independent companies in Russia's regions, RBC Daily reported. "Taking into account that Svyazinvest subsidiaries are the strongest players on the majority of local markets, it makes no sense (for Comstar UTS) to buy weaker operators."

In the 90s, the Russian government did not want to sell Svyazinvest because the prices in the market were not stable. Moreover, after the voucher privatization, when a lot of companies were privatized at very low prices, the government wanted to proceed more cautiously. Svyazinvest has been on the list of the strategic companies for a long time. At the beginning of 2007, the Russian government spoke publicly about needed privatization due to high investment. However, no future steps in this respect have taken place.

The market players have already been waiting a long time for this event. According to the analyst's options, the Svyazinvest privatization, more than any other event, can unlock the full value of the Russian regional operators. This would enable investment that is required to reduce opex and debt, optimize the workforce as well as increase revenues.

If the attention is turned back on efficiency as the aim of the whole privatization process, it is important to take into account the fact that privatization alone brings no significant efficiency advantages. This is clear when considering the experiences in the countries around the world which were mentioned in Sect. 3.3.3. Privatization only together with an independent regulator has proven a rise in efficiency. Russia has a lot of do in this respect.

5.2.2 Liberalization Through Tariff Rebalancing

The OECD distinguishes two main strategies of telecommunications liberalization (OECD 2002). The first is the "European style" liberalization, which includes fast opening-up to the competition process, trying to extend coverage and reduce the prices. Local loop unbundling is a part of this liberalization strategy. The second liberalization way is gradual and controlled competition, allowing e.g. duopolies in small regions.

In terms of the Russian telecommunications sector, the OECD recommended to open all telecommunications markets to competition, which could be deepened and broadened through a stronger and more effective system of access to the remaining non-competitive services such as local loops (OECD 2002).

The opponents of the "European style" of liberalization argue that such a rapid liberalization process increases the growth of the digital divide between the peripheral urban und rural areas in comparison to the central urban areas. It would also provide a negative motivation of the incumbent operators due to the narrowness of the profitable market as opposed to the rest. The reduced prices as a result of liberalization continue to be prohibitive for most of the population, while the advantages of the competition (greater offer, reduced prices, better quality) are accessible only to the most favored part of the population. As it could be seen at the beginning of 2007, Russia did not decide for the rapid liberalization policy and is rather on the more gradual introduction of competition.

In 2006, the liberalization of long-distance and international market had finally been started. Rostelecom lost its monopoly in the long distance market segment. Key regulatory developments have been completed with the liberalization of the long-distance market and the opening of this market is expected to see new alternative operators launch services, with competition expected to drive down tariffs. Numerous long-distance licenses have been awarded. Conditional to receiving the license is the requirement to offer services in all of Russia's 89 regions. Consequently, license holders have rolled out infrastructure.

At the beginning of 2007, Multiregional Transit Telecom (MTT) and Golden Telecom were competing with former monopolist Rostelecom in the Russian long-distance market. In total, 17 operators have received licenses to provide long-distance telephony in the country. TransTelecom is going to join this market in 2007.

Liberalization of the long-distance and international call market was a very important step in the sector reform. Further liberalization steps have to be pursued, such as the liberalization of the local calls market through the introduction of carrier selection and pre-selection, fixed number portability or wholesale product obligations in the cases where the copper local loops of the incumbent operator are still 'essential facilities'.[71] This will foster competition in the local markets, where the Svyazinvest still has the monopoly position especially in the residential market segment.

The monopoly position in the long-distance and international segments was justified based on the argument of the necessity to provide universal service obligations. Different kinds of cross-subsidization have been used in the Russian incumbent company for many years. The historical aspects of tariff rebalancing as well as the state of this process at the beginning of 2007 are described below.

On the way to the liberalization of the long-distance and international calls market, in 2001 tariff rebalancing reforms had been started. The monthly subscription fee and installation fee were increasingly outstripping inflation rates, e.g. the average monthly subscription fee for the urban subscribers has increased from 29 RUB ($ 1.18) in 1999 to 123 RUB ($ 4.01) in the third quarter 2003.[72] Figures 5.4 and 5.5 present the situation for the end of 2004. The high cross-subsidisation can be observed, e.g. between residential and budget/business subscribers. Both figures demonstrate that there is still a difference for residential subscribers between urban and rural areas in installation charges and monthly subscription fees. These differences are lower for the budget and business subscribers between the urban and rural areas in relation to installation charges as well as monthly subscription fees. The residential fees are often more expensive. Nevertheless, the costs in the rural areas are significantly higher than in urban areas.

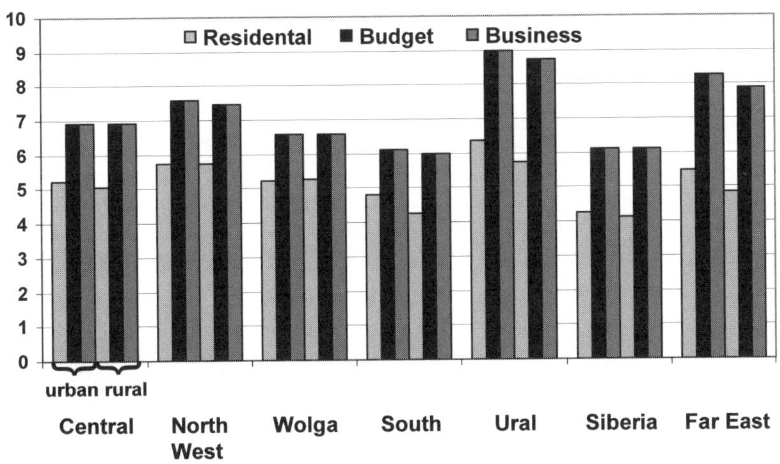

Source: www.svyazinvest.ru and own calculations

Fig. 5.4. Monthly subscription fee of the incumbent (in US$) in the different Russian macro-regions (December 2004)

[71] The similar policy approach is adopted e.g. in Hong Kong and Canada. The Canadian Radio-television and Telecommunications Commission (CRTC) set out criteria for what it called a "local forbearance framework" on deregulation, although incumbent telcos still must provide network access to competitors (Telecom Policy Report, 2006).

[72] www.svyazinvest.ru

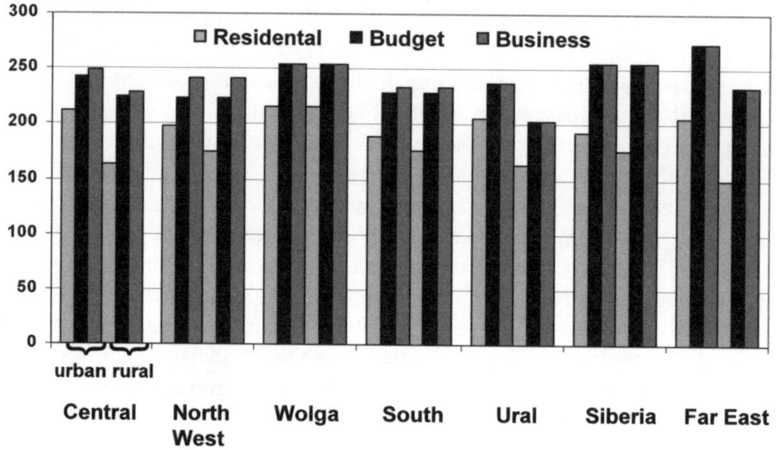

Source: www.svyazinvest.ru and own calculations

Fig. 5.5. Installation fee of the incumbent (in US$) in the different Russian macro-regions (December 2004)[73]

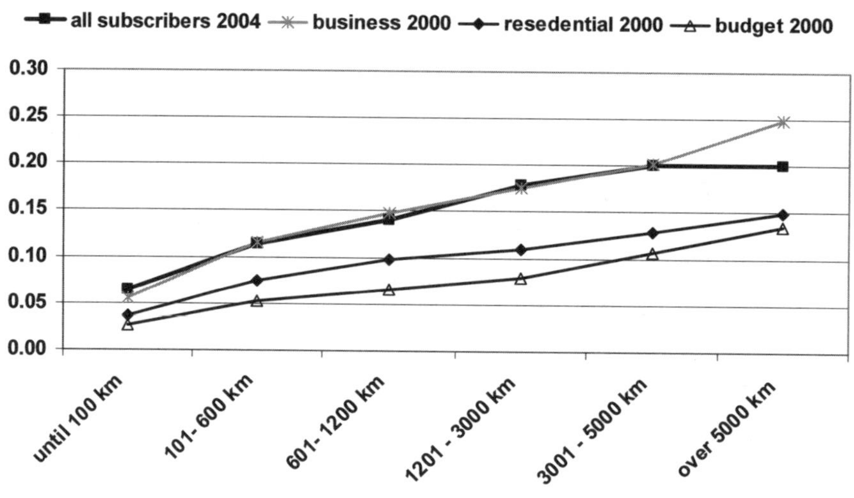

Source: Central Telecom (Moscow region) and Rostelecom [74] and own calculations

Fig. 5.6. Long-distance call charges (in US$) of the incumbent in the Moscow region[75]

[73] The dates are only on the installation fees. The connection fees exist and often amount to a certain proportion of the installation charges depending on the case.

[74] http://www.esmr.ru/index.html?id=16; http://www.hella.ru/rostelecom/tarif.htm (17.01.05)

[75] The long-distance charges are averaged between peak and off-peak charges.

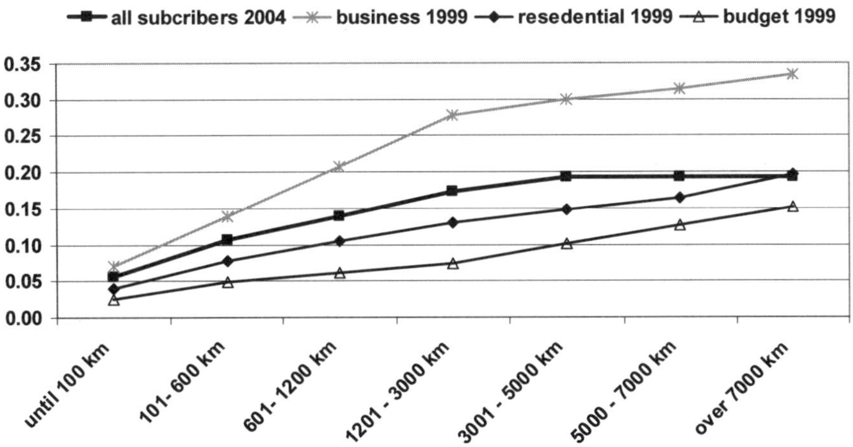

Source: South Telecom (Volgograd region)[76] and own calculations

Fig. 5.7. Long-distance call charges (in US$) of the incumbent in the Volgograd region

In general, the prices for long-distance and international calls have been decreasing during the last years. However, in many cases it can be expected that increasing the access charges "will still leave long distance and international call prices above cost, and where it occurs, competitive entry would tend to lower these prices further" (Cullen International/WIK 2001, p. 30). With rebalancing in this area a revaluation of distance-dependent charges is required. This has partly happened in Russia. Figures 5.6 and 5.7 present the current state of long-distance tariffs of the incumbent company compared to 1999–2000 in two different regions.[77] In addition, it can be seen that the cross-subsidizing between residential/budget and business subscribers was abolished.

At the end of 2004, the situation on the international calls market required some rebalancing as well. At this time, the competition from IP technology had already started to aggravate the situation. The cost of a 10 min call from the incumbent company in Russia to the USA costs about €6.7 (EU-25 average is €2.4); to Japan €8.2 (EU-25 average about €7).[78]

According to the press release of the incumbent company in 2003, the tariffs should be rebalanced until their marginal costs are covered and until 2005–2007 should include a certain rate of return for network development.[79] The marginal costs accounting method was planned to start in 2008. At the end of 2006, the situation in the tariff rebalancing was still a challenge and the authorities were

[76] http://www.vlz.ru/Tarif/Inter-gorod-telefon1/htm; http://www.volgatel.ru/fs_tarif_l.htm, 20.12.04

[77] The regions are picked freely and show the whole picture of the state of long-distance tariffs only partly.

[78] The data are for the Central region in Russia in 2004.

[79] http://www.svyazinvest.ru/press/?id=1848, 01.07.2003

speaking of another 3–4 years to finish the rebalancing process between local and national calls. At the moment, the tariffs include rate on returns.

One of the major rebalancing challenges is the social acceptance. Traditionally, in the Russian telecommunications there was wide range of the privileged groups, such as disabled people, war invalids, veterans, fascist camp victims, victims of the Leningrad blockade, families of Chernobyl and so on. The incumbent had to provide telecommunications services to these groups with a high discount. The amount of subsidies had to be paid back by the government to the incumbent. In 2005, the incumbent provided service to about 2.9 million disabled people and 7.7 million war invalids, which accounts for 25% of all Svyazinvest fixed phone connections. Not all of these subsidies were paid back to the incumbent from the government, e.g. state debt for 6 months of 2004 amounts to 7.7 billion Rub (or 214 million US$). The Russian government ensures in the Federal Law on Communications (2003), provision of telecommunications services to the groups of people which have special rights according to international Law, federal Law and local legislative documents.[80] Since 2005 a new charging system was required for these customer groups. The subsidies will be provided by the government budget directly in opposition to the system of 50% monthly subscription fees. From the economic point of view, the decision to change the system concerning disabled people was required. The same decision concerning war veterans, fascist camp victims, victims of the Leningrad blockade, families of Chernobyl and so on was quite a sensitive political question. Taking into account the income perspective, the privileges of these groups have mostly moral and political reasons. These parts of the population certainly must be supported, but a more neutral way should be found to ensure that competition is working and consumer surplus is passed to all customers including these privileged groups.

5.2.3 Universality Policy and Other Instruments Increasing Penetration Rates

Preceding liberalization of the long-distance and international calls market, requiring tariff rebalancing was on the agenda of fixed regulation for many past years. Consequently, the issues related to universal service policy, especially on the background of low fixed penetration rates, were and are still hot topics.

The universality in the Russian telecommunications sector is especially challenged because of the country's size, its harsh climate conditions as well as the ongoing transition process. The high digital divide between urban und rural areas is a challenging issue in Russia. 1/3 of all Russian population locations or 46 thousand do not have a phone box. According to the Russian Ministry on telecommunications, among these locations there are some with populations close to 3 thousand people. In 2002, the waiting list for a fixed phone in Russia totaled around 5.8 million people or 16% of all fixed network subscribers (in comparison Poland 4%, Hungary 0.2%). There were 1.27 public pay phones per 1,000 people (in comparison Poland 2.49, Hungary 3.99) and the digitalization grade in 2003 in

[80] Federal Law on Communications (2003), Art. 47

the urban areas totaled 54%, and in the rural areas 16% (in comparison Poland total digitalization rate is 86%, in Hungary 90%).

The policy of tariff rebalancing, declining profits of the incumbent company from more and more technological competition in the reserved segments, the opening of the long-distance market as well as often high net cost of universal services require implementation of a proper universality mechanism. Russia has opted for the universality fund option and declared this in the Federal Law on Communications (2003).

The Russian telecommunications law defined "universal access" for the first time. It includes the following services: (1) voice phone services for public access, which has to be located within 1 h walking distance; at least one phone box in every location must have free access to emergency calls; (2) by more than 500 people in a location, at least one point of public Internet access has to be provided.[81] According to the Federal Law on Communications (2003), the Russian telecommunications operators (not only universal service operators like often in many other countries) are required to ensure access to telecommunications services for disabled users as well as to provide free own directory enquiry services or to sell information at an economically adjustable cost to other telecommunications operators. In addition, each operator has to provide free emergency numbers for the emergency services.

The Russian government decided that these universal access aims are adequate and can be achieved by 2009. This decision was certainly based, on the one hand, on the low population distribution indicators and harsh climate conditions, on the other hand, on insufficient national income level and its distribution. About 80% of the Russian population is concentrated in the Central part of Russia. The average density of the Russian population is about 8.4 inhabitants per km sq (see Fig. 5.8).

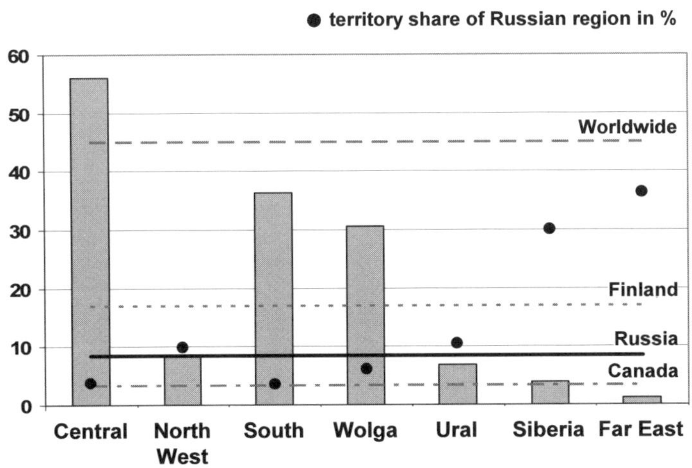

Source: Goskomstat (2004), WDI (2005)

Fig. 5.8. Russian population density compared to other countries

[81] Federal Law on Communications (2003), Art. 57

At the same time, the average worldwide population density is 45 inhabitants per km sq. In the EU-15, this indicator amounts to 154.6 inhabitants per km sq, in EU-10 84.5 inhabitants per km sq, in the USA 29 inhabitants per km sq, in Finland 17 inhabitants per km sq, and in Canada only 3 inhabitants per km sq. This highlights some of the difficulties involved in providing access to telecommunications in the many remote locations in Russia. In addition, national geography, topology and security matters often worsen the situation, especially in the North of Russia.

The important factors in achieving the universality aims are: (1) the level as well as (2) the distribution of national income. As reported by the Goskomstat, average disposable income of the Russians in 2001 is $1,200, which is lower than in the Eastern European EU member states as well as in Bulgaria, Romania and Turkey. However, the distribution of disposable average incomes between the different Russian regions is important in terms of the Russian universal service policy. As illustrated in Fig. 5.9, strong differences between the Russian regions are present. This is an obvious reason to suggest that a uniform universality policy on Russian territory is inappropriate. Different universality aims adjusted for the various Russian regions maybe a better economic policy option.

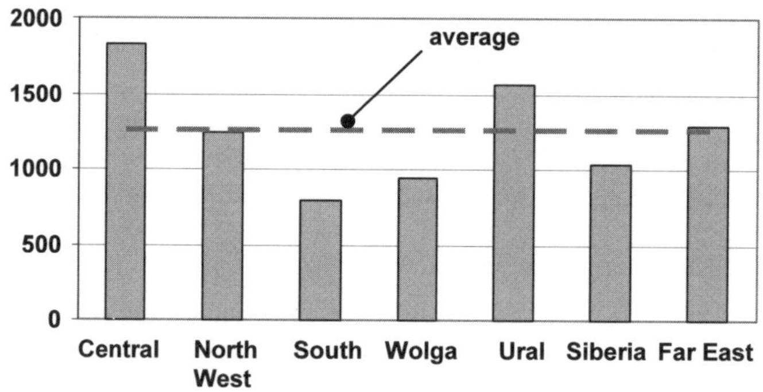

Source: Goskomstat (2004) and own calculations

Fig. 5.9. Disposable income in the Russian macro-regions (in US$) 2001

In respect to the level of national income, the relation between GDP per capita in PPP[82] and total penetration is considered to show how much Russia should or could invest in telecommunications by its GDP per capita based on the PPP. Fig. 5.10 presents the results for 2002, indicating that total penetration rates in Russia based on GDP per capita in PPP are lower than it could be based on this relation in other transition countries.

In respect to income distribution, the Russian GINI index measured to be 46 in 2000 shows that it is quite irregular. The value of the Russian GINI index in 2000 is one of the highest in the region, for example for Romania this amounts to 30, for Turkey 40, for Estonia 37, and for Finland 27.

[82] GDP per capita in PPP gives the possibility by the cross-countries comparison to take into account the purchasing power of different currencies by eliminating the differences in price levels between countries.

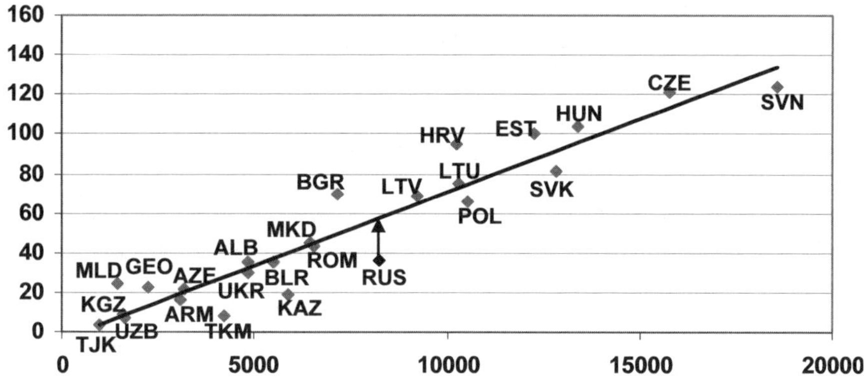

Source: ITU (2005), WDI (2005) and own calculations

Fig. 5.10. Total penetration rates to the GDP pro capita in PPP

According to the Federal Law on Communications (2003)[83] and its amendment, the Russian government established the universal services fund in July 2005 at the request of the Mininformsvyaz. Russian fixed-line and mobile operators are required to contribute to the fund 1.2% of their revenues, excluding those from interconnection and traffic routing services. A universal operator could be an operator of a public telecommunications network, which won a bidding process. If no applications are submitted or the winner could not be found, then universality obligations will be transferred to an operator with significant market share in the region (25% of the regional numbering resource or traffic units).[84]

The technological neutrality principle is often discussed in respect to universal service policy. Fixed and satellite technologies are deployed in Russia to provide universal service access. Mobile and broadband wireless access technology have not been used to provide universal services in Russia yet. There are some views that investing in the fixed infrastructure is a too cost intensive way to promote universal access. In the authors view, the investment in fixed technology is still reasonable at the moment. The main reason is the fact that through this universal service program, high capability backbone infrastructure is built. All other technologies such as wireless broadband technologies or mobile technologies send their traffic from the base stations through the backbone infrastructure, which is one of most expensive network components. According to the Russian universal service aims, the UA fixed lines should be used to install phone booths as well as Internet cafes. As a result, the population, which often has very low income in the locations without phones, does not need to carry additional costs for the phone devices.

The law determines the size of subsidy as an amount in the bidding process or as a maximum subsidy based on the difference between revenues and LRIC.[85]

[83] Federal Law on Communications (2003), Art. 59–60

[84] Federal Law on Communications (2003), Art. 58

[85] Federal Law on Communications (2003), Art. 61(1)

Each municipality defines by the bidding process a universal service operator for 5 years. This does not allow, e.g. bundling of the projects, resulting in the decline of the subsidy volumes. Moreover, the universality fund should be managed by the Agency, which is a part of the Russian Telecommunications Ministry. There is no independent management of universal service funds in Russia. A system of penalties in terms of universal service obligations is also unclear. Such a system has to be realized in order to put pressure on universal service operators to fulfill their obligations. Finally, there are often negative opinions about the role of universality fund as opposed to a tax or similar mechanism, and discussion about its redundancy is taking place.

The universal services policy found high popularity in Russia. In April 2007, there were about 600 contracts on universal service. The biggest part of tenders was won by the Svyazinvest. However, some other alternative operators as well as satellite operators (e.g. Web Media Services) or Russian Post received some universal service contracts too. For comparison, in 2006 investments in universal services of the Svyazinvest were about 6% of all investments; in 2007 this share will be about 24%.

An obvious question is, whether the universality policy should be the main instrument to promote high phone penetration in Russia. Or what are the other instruments to increase the phone penetration. Figure 5.11 summarizes the main instruments besides the universal services, which help to increase phone density. In the following, a closer look is taken on the other three mechanisms.

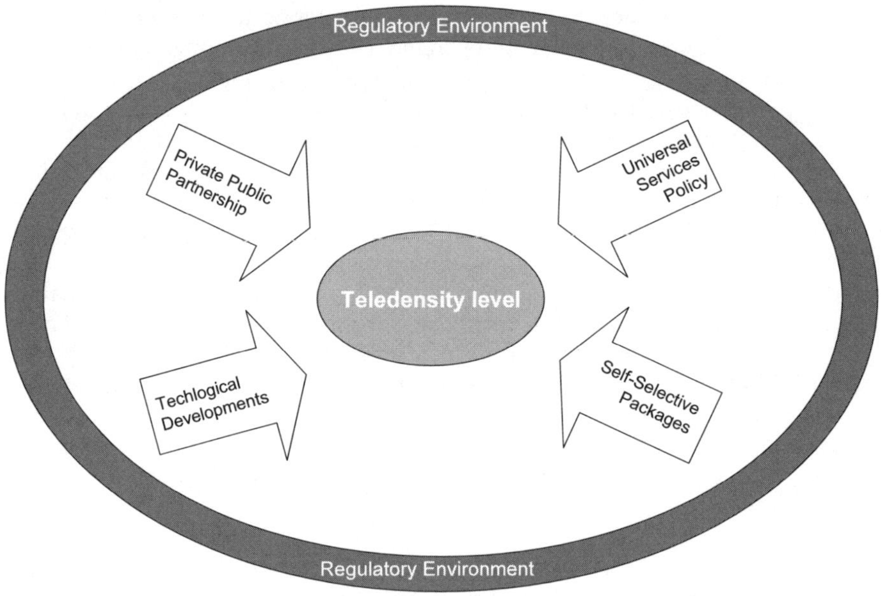

Source: Own description

Fig. 5.11. Instruments to increase the teledensity level

The introduction of self-selective package schemes is an important instrument to increase fixed penetration rates and can partly resolve social challenges of rebalancing discussed above. The subscribers (including the privileged groups) can choose a suitable tariff package. This price system stimulates the incumbents to increase output and, as result, improve economic welfare.

Originally, the self-selective package schemes had been planed to provide a choice between (1) the fixed monthly fee and free local calls and (2) lower fixed monthly fee and chargeable local calls. This was introduced by the Federal Law on Communications (2003)[86] but until February 2007 was not available to most customers based on technical reasons. In some Russian regions up until 2005 only the option (2) was introduced.

According to amendments to Russia's communications law, beginning February 1, 2007, fixed-line operators must provide residential clients a choice of three tariff plans instead of charging one fixed-rate tariff with unlimited minutes, which was practically the only option in most Russian regions. One tariff plan must offer subscribers unlimited traffic for a fixed monthly fee; another tariff plan must be based on a per-minute fee (users pay only a fee for line usage); and a third plan must be a combination of the first two, according to the amendments.

The new tariff plans offer some choice for the users, however, at the same time they are used as an instrument for further tariff rebalancing. The tariffs on the local market have increased by 11%. The Russian price regulatory commission speaks about real 6.5% due to the decline in the tariffs on long-distance market. Svyazinvest expects that new tariff plans will boost revenue by 2–5% within 12 months. Due to the fact that most of the holding's fixed-line operators set their tariffs lower than the maximum price-caps approved by the Federal Tariff Service, Svyazinvest does not expect a larger increase in revenues. The incumbent says that it has to deal with highly penetrated mobile market, which has seen many residential subscribers switch to prepaid mobile use for their voice telephony needs. The number of mobile subscribers in Russia at the beginning of 2006 was three time higher than the number of fixed subscribers.

Besides the self-selected price packages, the Federal Law on Communications in the case of providing services on regulated prices requires to ensure telecommunications services in credit for 6 months; and the first rate should amount to not more than 30% of the subscription charges.[87] Such a payment method may have an impact on the level of the disconnection rates and, as a result, on the fixed penetration rates. Furthermore, paired and parallel telephones lines and night telephones, remaining from Soviet times, may also influence the fixed penetration rates. These can be used after the work day by the residential subscribers. The share of these phone types is, however, very limited, and accounts to about 0.3%.[88]

All measures mentioned above have a limited impact. The Russian sector needs high impact instruments. One possible instrument could be stimulation of Private Public Partnership or third party infrastructure provision (e.g. by local authority)

---

[86] Federal Law on Communications (2003), Art. 54

[87] Federal Law on Communications (2003), Art. 54

[88] These figures in June 2003 are e.g. in Slovenia 0.5%, in Slovakia 0.9%, Hungary 1.4%

that constructs and manages telecommunications infrastructure to be leased to several operators on a cost-oriented basis. The role of the third party infrastructure providers has to be limited to the very basic elements of telecommunications infrastructure. As experiences of the European countries show, it leaves plenty of room for competition among operators on technological solutions, applications and services (Cullen International 2002, p. 2). Such measures do not seek to replace the private sector. On the contrary, all countries seek to involve the private sector in these projects and keep the public involvement to the minimum. The aim of this method is not to establish a state monopoly. It is important to set up in advance that which will happen after this infrastructure is established. If this company remains in the state/municipal ownership and will be continually subsidized by the state, then this can be a disruptive force for the competition in the market. If, however, this should function as a private company, the privatizations will be a method to improve its efficiency.

Finally, the developments of the different technologies in the field of telecommunications raise a question if the attention should be paid to promotion of the fixed telecommunications or can the other technologies take over this role. The experiences with deployment of the main competitive technologies are summarized below, providing examples for the fixed technology substitution. Due to the low initial capital cost, mobile telecommunications help to overcome, to some extent, the problem of low phone penetration in Russia, especially in terms of voice substitution. The deployment of 3G technologies is especially important in terms of the increase in mobile data. However, the licenses of mobile operators in Russia do not have very restrictive coverage requirements. Relative high costs of mobile services, low capability as well as security issues make the mobile technology less attractive in terms of broadband access. The deployment of CDMA mobile technology in the mobile fixed telecommunications networks (sometimes called WLL) at lower frequencies e.g. 450 or 850 MHz seems very promising. This technology will allow a viable solution for universal services in terms of support of both, voice and broadband, wireless access, coverage advantages as well as cost efficiency.[89] A couple of projects based on CDMA have already been realized in some Russian regions, e.g. Uralsvyazinform deployed CDMA on 450 MHz as mobile technology. The problem is that WLL, based on CDMA, was deployed in Russia on 800 MHz and is allowed by the Ministry to be used until 2010. Due to the Ministry's plans, this frequency range will be used in the future by the digital TV networks.

WiMAX networks, as broadband wireless access technology, are a real issue in Russia, giving a highly urbanized population a viable replacement for the aging infrastructure. The broadband wireless access technology provides high network capability comparable with fixed telecommunications. Many companies, known market players and newcomers, try to get licenses, to find investments and build WiMAX networks. Some examples of the latest announcements: (1) Summa Telecom received Russia-wide licenses for the 2.5–2.7 gigahertz frequency range to provide WiMAX services in late 2006 and is going to invest over U.S. $200 million

[89] http://www.cdg.org/resources/white_papers/files/Universal_Services_10-28-04.pdf

in Russia in 2007. (2) Synterra has received over U.S. $2.5 million in revenue from its WiMAX network since it launched the network a year ago. Synterra now has more than 1,700 WiMAX subscribers and the company's monthly average revenue per user (ARPU) is about $170. Synterra's WiMAX wireless broadband access network includes 60 base stations and a 2,000-kilometer optic fiber network, which covers 80% of Moscow. (3) Enforta announced that it will extend its wireless broadband network to an additional six cities during the second quarter of 2007. The additional six cities will include: Voronezh, Lipetsk, Penza, Samara, Tula, and Yaroslavl. The company also plans entry into eight cities during the second half of 2007 and will cover 32 cities of Russia. (4) Centertelecom (subsidiary of Svyazinvest) is also considering the roll-out of WiMAX.

Satellite is an expensive but highly reliable technology that plays one of the most important roles by promoting telecommunications services in remote areas. In Russia, satellite services are available from Globalstar (GlobalTel the Russian representation), Inmarsat (Morsvyazsputnik), and Thuraya (TM CAT). However, the clients of these companies are mostly fleet or big corporations. One alternative is Very Small Aperture Terminal (VSAT) systems which have been installed in remote Russian areas. The State company "Kosmisheskay svyaz" has been very active and installed VSAT. In 2003, the license process of VSAT was simplified and according to the vice minister, the number of these stations should increase: in 2003 there were only 2,500, in 2006 it increased to 75,000. Both GlobalTel and "Russian Post" are involved in the pilot project to install 100 satellite pay phones in the areas with only post communications.[90] Moreover, in 2006 the Russian President Vladimir Putin set a goal of providing Internet access to all Russian schools by 2008. From 53,000 Russian schools around 7,000 schools, located mostly in remote areas, were to be connected via VSAT satellites.

As a result, plenty of different standards are to be found in Russia, which are reasonable due to the country's size. Nevertheless, Russia still lies behind in the development of telecommunications, and strongly needs to promote higher telephone penetration. The most cost efficient and appropriate technologies should be deployed.

To sum up, the low teledensity level in Russia was often related to undersupply of telecommunications services. This was due to inadequate sector policies and partly to low demand stemming from relatively low disposable income. Teledensity can be increased using a strong consistent framework of universal services. However, the universal service policy is not a panacea. The other instruments such as self-selective packages, soft disconnection conditions, and primarily private public partnership should be broadly encouraged. Technological developments, as a basic element for the rapidly developing telecommunications sector, should be taken into account. Here the focus should be on finding the correct balance between cost efficient technology and network features, e.g. network capability.

[90] According to Vedomosty, a satellite call will cost about €0.5 depending on the call destination.

5.2.4 Far-Reaching Evolutionary Trends: VoIP and Next Generation Networks

All current market indications show that IP networks and services like VoIP will replace PSTN networks and services as well as influence developments in the mobile sector. The transition to VoIP is rapid and far-reaching, e.g. in 2007, in the USA 8% of all households have VoIP connections. The revenues of traditional operators are eroding strongly and they have to decide whether they will introduce VoIP by themselfs to retain customers, bundling e.g. naked DSL lines with mobile services or they do not introduce VoIP and refuse to offer naked DSL lines to alternative operators. Worldwide, VoIP technology is already offering significant cost reductions especially in national and international calls. However, in some countries, VoIP is strongly regulated or illegal and consumers can only use services from grey market operators.

As a result of IP developments, the operators have to update the old PSTN network to IP networks. The timescale of IP networks introduction has varied widely. Many national carries, mostly from developed countries, have committed themselves to make the transition to an IP network. As examples serve British Telecom (100% by 2009), MCI (100% of all traffic by the end of 2005), AT&T (100% by the end of 2010), Deutsche Telekom (100% by the end of 2012). As inevitable results of these technological developments, telecommunications operators have to cancel work contracts for many thousands of workers in the next a couple of years, for example, the DT AG announced that during 2006–2008 about 32,000 employers contracts will be cancelled.

Generally, in the IP telecommunications trends, it is important to differentiate between the short-term changes, which are largely evolutionary, and the long-term changes, which are more far-reaching. Table 5.6 summarizes the main short/middle term and long term developments in respect to technical concepts, market structure and regulatory models through the implementation of IP and later all IP networks. In the long term, PSTN networks will be fully replaced by IP, the market structure will be strongly influenced by the fact that transport network and services delivered on top of that network will be separated. As a result, different regulatory models are required.

- *Voice over Internet Protocol (VoIP)*

VoIP, the acronym for Voice over Internet Protocol (IP), is often called a "disruptive technology" due to the obvious trend to replacing of traditional PSTN network and services through IP networks and services like VoIP. Due to the ITU's forecast, by 2008 at least 50% of international minutes will be carried on IP networks and many carriers will be fully based on IP networks. According to Point Topic, the average growth of VoIP subscribers doubles every 9 months and the number of retail users at the end of March 2005 accounts for 11 million worldwide. Additionally, 6 million users use soft client user services and use VoIP over e.g. Skype. It is expected as well that much of mobile traffic will become IP-based and mobile VoIP will influence the shape of the mobile business globally. Mobile VoIP offers a great potential for cheaper voice calling, especially in the field of international roaming.

Table 5.6. VoIP and next generation networks

Short/middle term (from PSTN to IP networks)	Long term (towards all IP or NGNs)
Technical concepts	
PSTN phone services and VoIP services exist in parallel	IP/NGN networks and VoIP services are prevalent
PSTN-IP network gateways are needed in most cases	Subscribers and services are addressed manly by different types of Internet addresses
E.164 numbers are mainly used	E.164 numbers are likely to prevail at least in the global context
Terminals: Adapter + regular phone or a soft phone	New terminals e.g. combined GSM/UMTS/WLAN phones supporting IP/Internet telephony at home and other WLAN coverage areas
	VoIP is normally one service inside a large service set
Market structures	
New type of competition with possible advantages of cost structures and with new innovative services and possibly lower level charging models	Integrated, innovative and personalized services
	Nomadic use is important, increasing amount of cross border services
Voice traffic is shifting to IP based traffic and revenues from traditional phone services are decreasing	Cost and revenue model of services providers has changed radically
	The separation of the transport network and the services delivered on top of that network
Regulatory model	
Changes are required to the current regulatory regimes, need to take into account long-term influences	New legal framework/regulatory model is needed
Balance of basic main objectives: (1)To enable the development of new innovative services (2)To ensure acceptable social and consumer protection	

Source: Cohen et al. 2005, p. 11

Technically, VoIP refers to the use of IP transport technology for delivery of voice information. This means in general sending voice information in digital form in packets rather than in the traditional circuits of the public (circuit) switched telephone network (PSTN). The protocols used range from SIP and H.323 standardized by IETF and ITU to proprietary solutions like the Skype protocol. VoIP allows the transmission of voice information over IP networks, regardless of the network's dimension (local, regional or global) and general characteristics (closed network or public Internet).

There are the three following VoIP applications:

- VoIP services allowing calls to people using the same service (PC-to-PC)
- VoIP services allowing calls to any regular (PSTN) telephone numbers
- VoIP services allowing calls through an adaptor, at both the originating and terminating ends of a call and routing the call over an IP packet-switched, rather than traditional circuit switched network.

The VoIP technology is deployed unevenly around the world. Some countries provide legal framework to encourage many VoIP providers, others have blocked the provision of VoIP providers and others only have grey market operators. This means that in some countries VoIP is seen as an exciting technological development that offers cheaper calling opportunities, at the same time in the other countries it is seen as a threat to the existing order.

Emerging and developing VoIP technologies brought about many new challenges for regulators. In developing countries, where the position of the monopolist or ex-monopolist is still strongly protected, the main question is whether the VoIP technology should be legalized or some VoIP services have to be banned, e.g. in China. In developed markets, the main regulatory question is what aspects of the new services require regulation. Because VoIP is a relatively recent development even in developed countries, there is a little consensus about how best it should be regulated. As an example for different regulatory VoIP approaches serve the countries of the European Union (Popłońska 2007). Denmark defined VoIP services are treated in the same way as other voice services. The legislation claims to be technology neutral. In some European countries e.g. Austria Internet-only VoIP services are unregulated. VoIP services that enable access to the PSTN are regulated as telephony services. In some European countries e.g in Czech Republic, VoIP is not considered as a public telephone service, but as a data-transmission service – no regulatory initiative has yet been undertaken.

However, in Russia, VoIP is currently classified as a data-transmission service, but the VoIP regulatory policy is very contradictive. During the preparation of the Interconnection legislation amendment, the idea about banning the VoIP operators dominated. Nevertheless, in the interconnection legislation, the VoIP services were not banned but their provision requires some cardinal reorganizations. To provide VoIP services, an operator needs a license, which allows him to provide voice data. This is separate from a data transmitting service license. Moreover, to provide long-distance or international services (as well as local services), an operator needs a separate license. An operator cannot start providing e.g. long-distance services if it does not own telecommunications infrastructure in all Russian regions. This means that all VoIP operators can only be agents of the Rostelecom and in the future of MTT and a couple of others. The main advantage of this method is that the development of infrastructure based competition is forced in Russia. The disadvantages are the fact that the prices are rising and development of the VoIP technology is strongly slowing down.

- *Next Generation Networks* (NGNs)

Based on the definition of the ITU, an NGN[91] is a packet-based network able to provide telecommunications services and able to make use of multiple broadband, QoS-enabled transport technologies and in which service-related functions are independent from underlying transport-related technologies.[92] There are the following differences of the NGNs, some which were already mentioned in Table 5.6:

1. It enables unfettered access for users to networks and to competing service providers and/or services of their choice.
2. It supports generalized mobility which will allow consistent and ubiquitous provision of services to users.
3. It enables to provide a wide range of services including: data transmission, voice services and video services. As a result, convergence between different services will occur (see Fig. 5.12).
4. It is multilayer, where steering, management and service provision functions are independent from transport and access. The network has an open character, i.e. network layers will communicate through open interfaces enabling use of different equipment from diverse hardware producers.

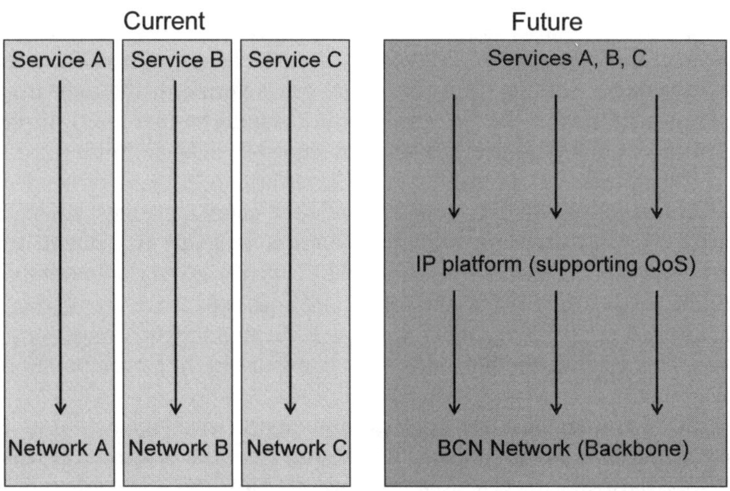

Source: Shaw (2006, p. 21)

Fig. 5.12. Convergence processes in telecommunications

Due to the above mentioned characteristics of NGN, migration from a vertical to a horizontal regulatory approach is required. The future regulation should be realized mostly on the level of access and applications. In terms of NGN, an often discussed question is the interconnection regime, whether existing Calling Party

[91] The general name is IP-enable Next Generation Networks.

[92] http://www.itu.int/ITU-T/studygroups/com13/ngn2004/working_definition.html

Network Pays principle should be keep, or Bill & Keep regime used in the Internet should be implemented or a mix of both is the most suitable option for NGN networks.

NGN networks updates in developed countries include two forms: access update or core network update. The actions are very investment intensive and are not often completed at the same time, e.g. Deutsche Telekom started with the update of access network to FTTC because the last mile of its network is relatively long. Its core network however is relatively new. In the UK, the last mile of network is relative short and core network is older. That's why BT started with the update of its core network.

The important question is, who drives NGN development. The following groups may influence the NGN implementation: telecommunications operators, ISPs, communications service providers, hardware providers, other ICT sector stakeholders, users and policy makers. In the countries, where the fixed networks are fully developed and investment sank, the telecommunications operators are often not interested in the implementation of the NGNs because of high depreciations on the existing networks.

In comparison to the developed economies, in transition countries with at least two times lower fixed penetration, the challenges in terms of NGN are very different. The update is required only for an existing fixed network. At the same time, investment in the extension of network is needed. In order to achieve the competitive advantages coming from the NGN characteristics, the new investment in transition countries in the IP infrastructure should be increased. In this way, the overall investments as well as operational costs may be minimized what in middle and long term will be expressed in lower prices. In terms of needed investment, telecommunications operators in developed economies have more financial resources from DSL services. DSL technologies will just roll out in transition countries. However, in the EU countries the relatively strong unbundling obligations are decreasing the profitability of incumbents, which are the market players who can afford so much investment. In Russia, the unbundling obligations are still underway. This ensures the profits of the incumbent in the development of infrastructure.

The head of Svyazinvest, the Russian ex-monopolist company, speaking publicly, has stated that in the holding, the strategic goal is a transition from traditional PSTN networks to IP-based networks.[93] However, officially, only from 2007 Svyazinvest plans to stop purchasing PSTN equipment. Some test networks were started around Russia, e.g. in Kaluga (Siemens), Novosibirsk (Alcatel), Ekaterinburg (Nortel), Magadan (Nuawei), Omsk (Siemens).

According to Marder (2007) and Evdokimenko (2005), besides the discussions about NGNs in Russia, there are no real options for their development. In the Law on Interconnections, which went into power in January of 2006, all telecommunications networks are divided in two groups: phone networks like fixed and mobile and based on certain technology networks such as data, telegraph and

[93] In Russia, these networks are already called as NGNs.

TV networks. The NGNs are not mentioned at all as a kind of network that shows the old principle of these rules: "One service – one network".

Moreover, the same source mentions that the principle of open network architecture could not be achieved in the Russian reality as well. Due to the Interconnections Rules, there is a certain hierarchy in the interconnections: international and long-distance networks are allowed to interconnect other international and long-distance networks and regional networks; regional networks are allowed to interconnect with local networks. Direct interconnection of international/long-distance and local networks and the latter with mobile networks are not allowed. To sum up, the new Interconnection Rules are "very traditional phone oriented" and require many important corrections as soon as possible. Therefore, the future of NGNs in Russia should be reconsidered and hopefully corrected in the proper way.

5.3 Mobile Telecommunications: Instruments Stimulating Diffusion

Mobile telecommunications, as the most rapid developing telecommunications sector at least from 1995 to 2005, is the main focus of this chapter. The role of mobile telecommunications in the narrowing the digital divide is investigated in Sect. 5.3.1. In the next section, the attention is turned to diffusion factors and instruments stimulating the mobile diffusion. In the middle of 2006, due to significant improvements in economic development, especially increasing income, as well as strong price wars in most Russian mobile markets, mobile penetration rates achieved 100% However, in terms of active sim-cards, the picture looks slightly different. In 2Q06, the sim-card activity degree was only 66%. Based on this fact, there is still room for increase in the mobile penetration. The instruments such as introduction of MNP and MVNOs as well as deployment of new technologies (e.g. WiMAX) can still be effective in stimulation of mobile telecommunications diffusion. Mobile broadband services are the next challenge in this sector.

5.3.1 Mobile Telecommunications Role in Narrowing the Digital Divide

Transition economies are characterized by the significant digital divide. However, this digital divide gap is gradually narrowing, e.g. Fig. 5.13 illustrates the narrowing of digital divide in mobile telecommunications. According to the WTO's Report (WTO 2004), the narrowing of digital divide in the world is even faster than the narrowing of the income gap between rich and poor countries. In the following, the statement on faster digital divide narrowing in comparison to income narrowing is proved empirically for transition economies. Moreover, the contribution of mobile telecommunications to narrowing of digital divide from 1996 to 2002 in comparison to the contribution of fixed telecommunications and Internet is investigated.

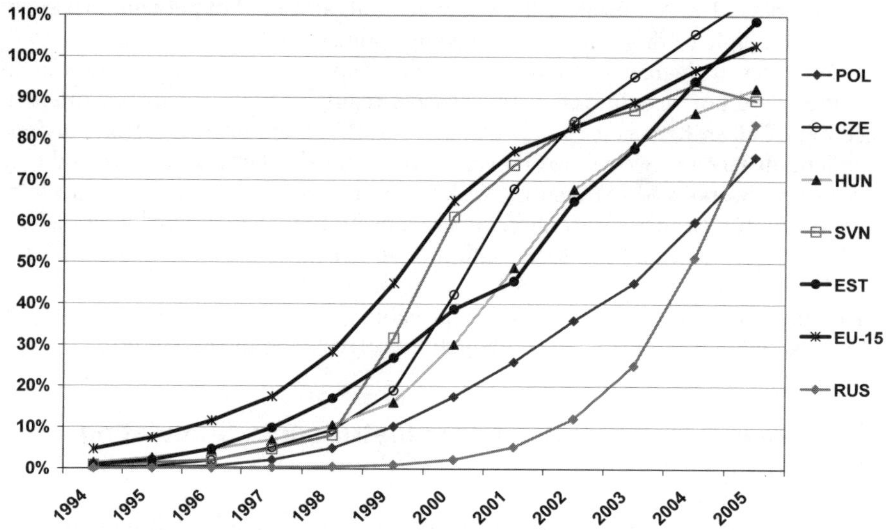

Source: ITU (2006a)

Fig. 5.13. Development of mobile penetration rates in Russia, EU-15 as well as selected Eastern European EU countries

To prove the statement that the digital divide is narrowing faster than the income gap between transition and industrialized countries we apply the concept of β -convergence on cross-countries data (e.g. Jungmittag 2002). Absolute β -convergence exists if countries, which show a lower level of a certain parameter in the initial starting point of time, grow faster than a country with a higher parameter in the initial time period. To estimate absolute convergence one has to calculate the average growth rates of a parameter y for all countries $n = 1,\ldots, N$ during a certain fixed time period from 0 to T as $g_n = (\ln y_{nT} - \ln y_{n0}) / T$ and estimate the regression

$$g_n = \alpha + \beta \ln y_{n0} + \varepsilon_n \tag{5.10}$$

using the OLS method. If the regression coefficient β is significant and smaller than zero then there is convergence of the parameter y . For the purpose of proving the statement mentioned at the beginning, the four equations using as parameters growth rates of GDP per capita, mainlines, mobile telecommunications, and Internet users from 1996 to 2002 are estimated. The used data are from the International Telecommunication Union (ITU 2005) and the World Bank (WDI 2004). The group of industrialized countries includes EU-15, USA and Japan; the group of transition countries includes all transition countries, except Bosnia and Herzegovina and Serbia and Montenegro due to the poor state of the data. For Kyrgyzstan, Tajikistan, and Turkmenistan the data on mobile telecommunications and Internet are zero or not available at the early time periods. To retain this data in the estimation, to each observation a 0.01% point is added. The estimation results are presented in Table 5.7.

Table 5.7. Estimation results on narrowing the digital divide in Eastern Europe

Variable	MODEL(1) Dep. var.: average growth rates of GDP pc	MODEL(2) Dep. var.: average growth rates of mainlines	MODEL(3) Dep. var.: average growth rates of Internet users	MODEL(4) Dep. var.: average growth rates of mobile telecoms
Constant	0.033387*** (5.707501)[a]			
LOG_GDPPC1996	−0.005354*** (−3.395610)			
Constant		0.032901*** (4.113432)		
LOG_MAINLINES1996		−0.016014*** (−2.875301)		
Constant			0.166381*** (22.76711)	
LOG_INTERNET1996			−0.051773*** (−7.181107)	
Constant				0.202828*** (24.99271)
LOG_MOBILE1996				−0.060634*** (−8.087048)
R-squared	0.223756	0.171283	0.563168	0.620495
DW stat	1.615694	1.828221	1.627415	0.860964

[a]t-statistics in brackets

Based on these estimation results, absolute β -convergence for all four parameters is to be observed. Moreover, it is possible to conclude that the convergence processes between transition and industrialized countries are faster in the telecommunications sector compared to income convergence in the time period considered. The fastest growth rates during the investigated time period demonstrate mobile telecommunications that proves the statement about the special role of mobile telecommunication in bridging of digital divide.[94]

Due to the fact that the test on absolute convergence is only sufficient to prove whether all countries demonstrate convergence, to find out if some country groups or even a single country are converging, conditional convergence has to be tested. For this purpose, all countries are divided into different groups and their convergence is checked in terms of the mobile telecommunications variable. Due to short time period investigated, it should be emphasized that some difficulties may arise with the robustness of the following result: in Russia and FSU mobile telecommunications demonstrate convergence to the EU15 level; in CEE and SEE country

[94] Based on the Durbin-Watson test values, especially for mobile telecommunications, the results need some cautious in the interpretation.

groups one can expect in the long-term the penetration levels to be 4 and 7.5% higher than the EU15 level respectively.

5.3.2 Diffusion Factors of Mobile Telecommunications

As found in Sect. 5.1, the real GDP and price level are significant factors, which influence the telecommunications diffusion in the transition countries. However, changes in GDP require a long-term prospective. In contrast, price level is a short -and middle-term issue. Demand for mobile telecommunications can be increased by lowering prices. For the improvement in the mobile technology diffusion, it is crucial to foster effective competition in the market place leading to a drastic reduction in prices. The instruments that can be used for this are considered in the next section. In this section, the attention is directed to price levels in the transition countries.

As it was already mentioned in Sect. 5.1, the historical data on the mobile telecommunications services in transition countries are missing altogether for too many transition countries. Figures 5.14 and 5.15. illustrate the results for a low usage mobile telecommunications basket. Figure 5.14 presents the nominal price of the basket. Figure 5.15 shows the basket price levels in PPP. The nominal price for the Russian mobile telecommunications basket is low in international comparison. The price in PPP is, however, relatively high. This should be a reason why the penetration rates in terms of active sim-cards are still lagging behind. Similar results can be found for middle and high usage baskets.

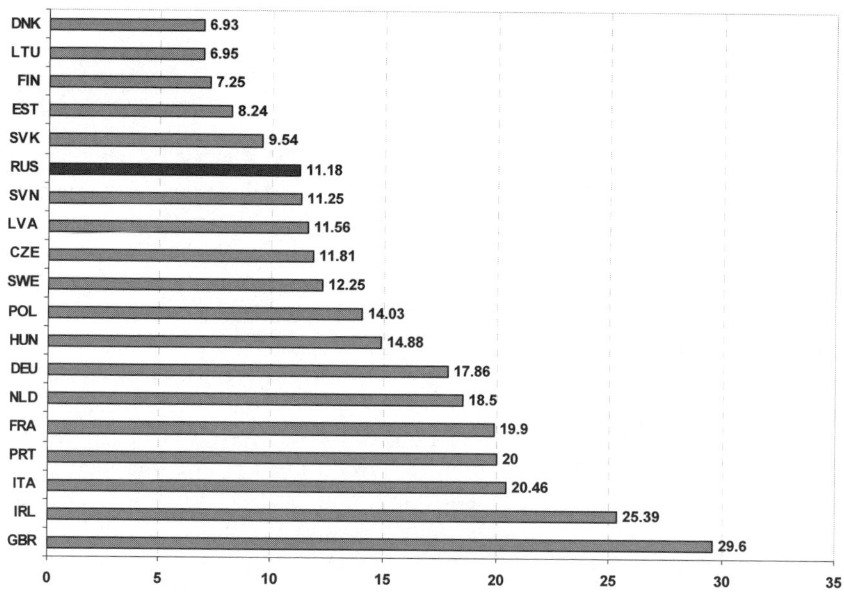

Source: EC (2007), own calculations for Russia

Fig. 5.14. Low usage mobile telecommunications basket (in US$) per month 2006

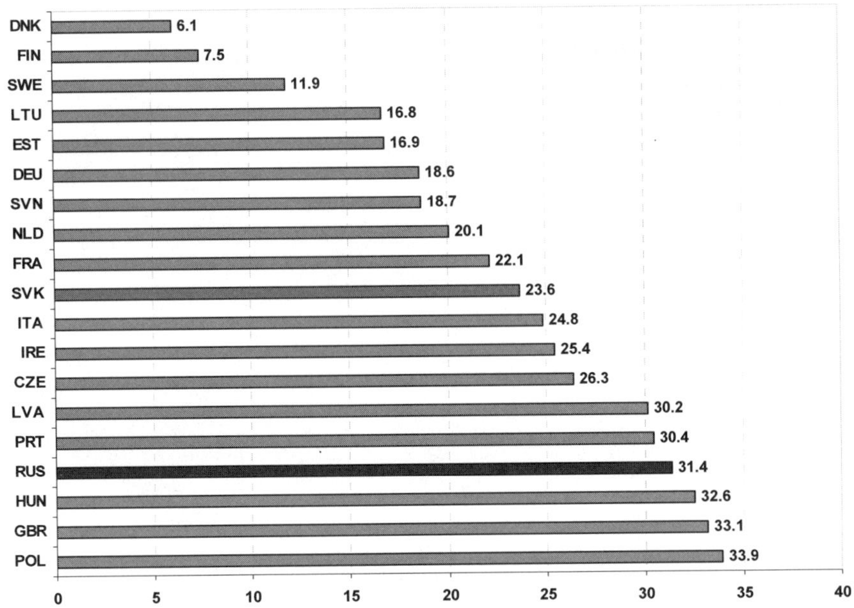

Source: EC (2007), OECD (2005c), own calculations for Russia

Fig. 5.15. Low usage mobile telecommunications basket in PPP (in US$) per month 2006

Some other diffusion factors, like institutional parameters or fixed telecommunications developments, relating to fixed-mobile substitution,[95] are expected to be important in transition economies. These factors are not considered here but they should be of interest in further research.

5.3.3 Instruments Stimulating the Diffusion of Mobile Telecommunications

As illustrated in Fig. 5.16, the following factors are identified as having an impact on the diffusion process through an increase of competition: pricing schemes and interconnection regimes, MNP, national roaming obligations and MVNOs as well as technological dynamics and standards.

[95] Due to the fact that transition countries have a relatively low penetration of fixed telecommunications compared e.g. to the EU-15, one speaks about technological substitution in these countries (Ros and Banerjee 2004). There are still a very limited number of studies concerning fixed to mobile substitution in transition economies. Vagliasindi and Taubman (2004) investigate the substitution effect in Eastern Europe and the former Soviet Union, and find some substitution effect at the county level and a complementary effect at the enterprise level.

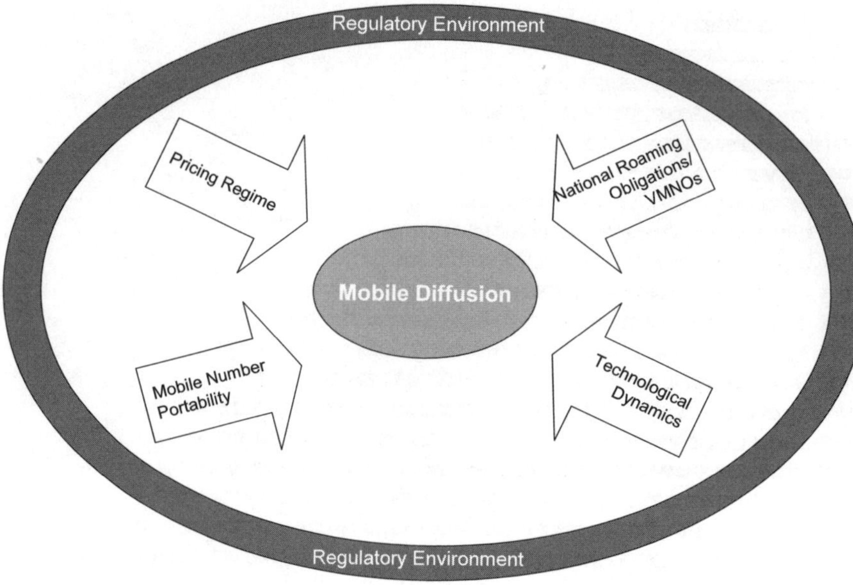

Source: Own description

Fig. 5.16. Instruments to facilitate the diffusion process

The next table (Table 5.8) summarizes the state of art (mid. 2007) in terms of these factors in Russia and EU-15.

Table 5.8. Instruments to facilitate the diffusion process in international comparison

	EU-15	Russia
Pricing Regime	CPP	CPP[a]
MNP	Yes	No
National Roaming Obligations	Yes	No
MVNO	Yes	No
Setting of standards	Yes	Yes[b]

[a]In July 2006 CPP regime is finally implemented; [b]However, the standard is set in Russia: the licenses in the other standards are granted

Source: Own description

In the following, each instrument is considered in detail as well as advantages and disadvantages of their implementation in terms of the mobile diffusion process are described.

5.3.3.1 Pricing Schemes (CPP vs. RPP) and Interconnection Issues

In Russia until July 2006, as in the US, Canada and a couple of other countries, calls received on a mobile handset originating from a wire line are usually were paid by the mobile customer. This policy regime is called receiver party pays (RPP). In most other Eastern European countries, the regime of the calling party pays (CPP) has been adopted, whereby the customer who originated the call is charged for the service. The pricing regime is fundamental for the interconnections issue. The interconnection rates significantly influence the process of diffusion, because they are reflected in the end prices of services.

In the countries with CPP, there is a very wide discussion about the optimal level of termination charges, and it is often accepted that a CPP regime is associated with higher rates for mobile termination charges, because each network operator has a "bottleneck" monopoly for the termination of calls made to subscribers on its own network (Armstrong 1997). On the other hand, Wright (1999) and Thompson et al. (2005) provide examples to show that with partial mobile penetration, the socially optimal termination charge could exceed the actual costs.

The RPP regime is considered as an alternative approach for dealing with the monopoly call termination problem. Doyle and Smith (1998) were the first who showed that if the receiver were to pay for some or all of a call, prices of calls to mobiles would be lower and usage would increase. Later several studies deal with the question of how RPP may help with the internalization of the call externalities when subscribers derive utility from receiving calls (e.g. DeGraba 2000). The main idea here is that if both parties benefit from a call, they should both bear its costs in proportion to the benefit they receive. Therefore, imposing all of the costs of a call on the calling party's network can be inefficient if these costs are reflected in the calling party's usage rates.

In the early stages of mobile telecommunications development, the markets with the RPP regime demonstrate faster growth; in the later stages of diffusion, countries with CPP are the growth leaders (OECD 2000, p. 39). The OECD study provides evidence that with the changing structure of calling opportunities[96] and the introduction of prepaid cards, the CPP has become a more significant factor over time. Since 1991, at least 27 countries have changed from RPP to CPP. It was argued that RPP does restrict mobile traffic and growth, particularly inbound calls, and that changing from RPP to CPP will generally increase traffic. The studies on these countries indicate a significant impact from these changes, for example in Mexico. The same trend is assumed for the developed countries based on a market trial by one US operator. Littlechild (2004), however, argues that in all these countries other factors play a part in development (e.g. introduction of prepaid services, variety of mobile telecommunications networks standards, numbering system of the fixed telecommunications network, economic development, regulation and so forth).

The RPP policy presents the following advantages compared to the CPP (OECD 2000, p. 36): (1) independence of the mobile telecommunications pricing

[96] The share of calls involving mobile networks is rapidly increasing.

structure from the fixed network regulation, especially if a fixed network monopoly exists; (2) constraining the charges for call termination by the competition because charges for both incoming and outgoing calls are paid by the same subscriber, resulting in a lower price level (this aspect was mentioned above). However there are the following concerns about RPP: (1) it may reduce the accessibility of mobile subscribers; (2) users have to budget airtime for receiving calls; prepaid cards are not so attractive; and (3) the competitiveness of the mobile network is lower compared to the fixed network with CPP. The last point is connected to the fact that in the CPP regime, high termination charges drive mobile operators to set low mobile charges, so as to attract subscribers to their network and thereby collect more termination revenues. These revenues may be largely passed back to mobile consumers and as a result, more people can get mobile phones, which provides positive spillovers both to fixed-line users and other phone users (Thompson et al. 2005).

During the discussion about RPP versus CPP regimes in the USA, there are beliefs from the CTIA[97] that wireless phone providers should be able to offer the CPP option and allow the market place to determine its value. However, one should mention that the other question is if there is a framework to introduce such policy by a single mobile operator (OECD 2000, p. 39).

In Russia, the discussion about changing from the RPP to the CPP pricing regime took place very intensely. At the beginning of 2005, the Russian Ministry of Information Technologies and Communications announced a change from RPP to the CPP pricing regime effective from July 2005. After a couple of months, the introduction of CPP was delayed for about one year, because a number of supporting regulations had to be established. In July 2006 CPP policy was finally introduced. This required a fundamental interconnection paradigm shift and saw many technical and regulatory obstacles (e.g. about 6% of the "big three" mobile subscribers have a phone number of the fixed telecommunications network). From July 2006, a fixed network subscriber has to pay 1.5 Rub. for the call from fixed to mobile, 0.95 Rub from this amount are paid back by the fixed operator to the mobile operator.

In the past, there were some mobile operators which implemented CPP regime or its single elements on its own. One of the Russian regional mobile operators, "Sibirskay Sotovaja", implemented the CPP regime in the form of a special tariff option. This was very popular among the subscribers (about 60% of all subscribers used this tariff option). On the other hand, it caused many conflicts with other mobile operators as well as subscribers. The reason for this lies primarily in the weakness of the Russian interconnection law which does not provide the possibility for effective implementation of a CPP regime.

In the RPP environment the Russian mobile companies – when compared to mobile operators in the countries with CPP – did not receive additional revenues from call termination[98] and could not be so flexible in the pricing of services. This is a reason why the Russian mobile operators did not use subsidies of mobile

---

[97] Cellular Telecommunications and Internet Association

[98] This accounts e.g. in France for about one-third of the incoming calls revenues (OECD 2000).

handsets as a method to attract subscribers. Tele2 started to use this strategy on the Russian market. In spite of strong interest on the customer side, the other operators were not convinced to follow suit. In 2007, introducing of the CPP regime shows that the ARPUs of the Russian "big three" have increased significantly more than MOU. This is directly related to implementation of the CPP regime, where termination charges are an additional revenue source.

The policy option of changing from RPP to CPP in Russia was quite promising from the prospective of accelerating mobile telecommunication diffusion and closing the digital divide. Successful examples of this policy option were demonstrated by the Czech Republic in 1996 and by Mexico in 1999. However, a different impact from this measure in Russia was expected due to the relatively high current penetration rates compared to the above mentioned countries. The disadvantage of this change is aggravating the problem of termination charges regulation which is a controversial issue in many countries with a CPP regime. Russia now has to deal with the regulation of termination charges. In this respect, the old RPP regime could be more efficient in order to ensure fair competition in the market.

Interconnections in Russian mobile telecommunications are quite an ambiguous issue. The interconnections were defined only in the Federal Law on Communications. Until then, interconnection prices were set in line with bilateral negotiations between the operators, taking into account a recommendation concerning the terms and conditions of the interconnections between fixed and mobile public networks, issued by the Ministry only at the beginning of 2003. As a result, interconnections in Russia are very problematic and have brought about many court cases, especially concerning the Russian specific mobile network structure[99] and the pricing system of the Russian fixed telecommunications network.[100]

According to the Russian Federal Law on Communications, the significant market power (SMP) positions in the Russian regional mobile telecommunications markets are prevalent, but the Ministry has not intervened thus far. Frequently the mobile operators that occupy dominant market positions behave in an anti-competitive manner in the regional markets, and regulatory interventions may be required. The abolishment of the monopoly on the long-distance and international telecommunications market in Russia would have significant implications for the

[99]According to Minsvyaz (2003), the mobile operators are obliged to pass traffic from one region to the other (domestic long-distance calls) and abroad (international calls) through the channels of special transit companies. Within one region, the different mobile telecommunications companies can be interconnected directly. Very often direct connection of the newcomers was refused by established operators. As a result, they have to transfer their traffic via a regionally-fixed network or transit company channels that decrease their competitiveness in terms of the price level. Blurred definition of the interconnection regime allowed the established operator to argue that they do not have to connect a newcomer company.

[100] Some of the fixed operators in the different Russian regions decided to charge long-distance prices for calls to federal mobile phones, which are used in the same region but the main switching centre is placed in another city. They argued that this is connected to the Ministry's recommendation mentioned above. According to this document, the fixed operator used its network for the traffic transfer of the mobile operators on the long-distance. The mobile operators held that they have a special agreement with Minsvyaz RF.

mobile operators. Emerging competition would cause the prices for long-distance and international traffic transfers to gradually fall, and this could be reflected in lower rates for long-distance and international mobile telecommunications services.

5.3.3.2 Mobile Number Portability (MNP)

MNP is the ability for customers to retain their assigned mobile telephone numbers when changing the subscription from one mobile network operator to another. This reduces switching costs of mobile users creating a more competitive environment. Newcomers can enter the market more easily, and competition among all mobile operators is intensified. Nevertheless, MNP can be a source of many disadvantages like relatively high costs of implementation and reduction in tariff transparency as a result of the fact that the prefix of a mobile telephone number no longer indicates its network assignment (Buehler and Haucap 2003, p. 3). It is very often discussed as to which financing model should be adopted: the state carries the cost of implementation, mobile operators or consumers. Gans et al. (2001, p. 172) argue that mobile operators have to implement and pick up the overall costs of MNP. Haucap (2003, p. 92) comes to another conclusion and says that the state should carry the cost, and buys out implementation of MNP from mobile operators. Although some welfare analysis of portability demonstrated that the widespread presumption in favor of number portability is not necessarily in the interests of society in general, or even of consumers,[101] in many countries MNP was implemented, aiming to reduce customers' switching costs and attempting to make mobile telecommunications more competitive.

One should note that the main decision parties (operators) responsible for the success of MNP are not interested in implementing the system stating that implementation costs can influence their performance significantly. In addition, MNP can trigger price wars between the operators who seek to win over new customers. From this point of view, one should expect a higher churn rate, especially in the first months after the system is introduced. Such developments were observed in Australia and Hong Kong. Moreover, it is to be expected that the tariffs might have to be unified, especially thc differences between on-net and off-net calls which will have to disappear, as the calling party will not be able to identify the users from the same network based on their number.

The Russian Ministry is planning to make a decision concerning the implementation of MNP in near future and began a discussion on this issue in spring 2005. A detailed study about the impact of MNP for the Russian telecommunications market, like in many other countries, has not yet been conducted. According to the new regulation concerning mobile telecommunications from May 2005, MNP was not to be implemented in Russia and until the end of 2007 there is no progress on this issue.

[101] Small and Aoki (1999) found out that in developing telephony markets, from the reductions in the cost of switching benefit consumers and the entrant, and have no effect on the incumbent. In well-developed telephony markets, it is possible for consumers to receive less surplus following a reduction in the cost of switching between carriers.

5.3.3.3 National Roaming Obligations and Mobile Virtual Network Operators (MVNOs)

In order to increase competition and enforce price reductions national roaming obligations[102] and the market entry for the MVNOs[103] may be quite important issues. Due to the fact that mobile operators have different network coverage, the incentives for concluding roaming agreements with new operators and for letting MVNO into the market are quite low. The main concern here is that investments carried out by one firm can increase the value of the service provided by other firms when there is a roaming agreement between the firms.

Valletti (2003) considers the case of two mobile operators with different coverage (full and small coverage) and concludes from his model that in this case, no one operator is interested in roaming, unless they are colluding. Competition over coverage would result in that firms looking for some coverage differentiation in order to relax price competition.

Foros et al. (2002) contemplate a situation in which one mobile operator benefits from a free roaming agreement with another operator. For example, one network benefits from national roaming agreements because this also allows his own customers to place more calls. They conclude that operators will always have incentives to voluntarily enter into roaming agreements in this case. Foros et al. (2002) investigate the case of two symmetric operators focusing on the question as to whether it is welfare improving to let firms semi-collude by choosing their investment cooperatively before they compete in the downstream market. They discover that if the investments are set non-cooperatively, the firms agree on too high a level of roaming quality compared to the social optimum. In contrast, if the investments are set cooperatively, the firm's choices on roaming quality coincide with the regulator's interest. In the second part of their study, the authors investigate the case of two symmetric facility-based operators and VMNO. Here they find there is little scope for regulation of roaming quality if a virtual operator is present, both under cooperative and non-cooperative investments.

Haucap and Wey (2003) consider the situation if there is already more than one mobile operator with full network coverage in a market. In this case, operators have incentives to sell or lease free capacities because it is still more advantageous to profit from leasing capacities to third parties rather than having others leasing their capacities. They also assert that the collusive denial of market entry in order to exclude VMNOs and to refuse the conclusion of national roaming agreements may be dynamically efficient, as it makes infrastructure investment more attractive.

The Russian regulator has not officially issued licenses to MVNOs. The existing MVNOs entered the market without any clear rules. According to the Russian Telecommunications Law, each operator should have own infrastructure. Due to

[102] Agreements on sharing infrastructure are called roaming in mobile markets (Foros et al. 2002).

[103] VMNOs are radioless operators that own and control at least some part of the mobile network, while contracting out to regular radio-based mobile network operators (MNOs) the radio part along with all the remaining complementary network facilities and service applications that are necessary to provide mobile services to end users (Ulset 2002, p. 537).

this fact their activities could be seen as illegal as has already happened to Corbina Telecom, which had been providing telecommunications services in the Moscow license area using the D-AMPS mobile technology standard. The license, however, belongs to VimpelCom. Taking into consideration that the biggest Russian mobile operators very often have SMP positions in the different regional markets, the establishment of a well-defined legislative framework for the MVNOs would bring positive effects in terms of accelerating the diffusion process.

The meaning of the national roaming obligations can differ due to institutional conditions and market developments. In Russia, the mobile telecommunications licenses are mostly regional and in the course of time only a few federal operators with country wide coverage emerged. It is very difficult for the regional operators to compete due to the limited geographic area in which telecommunications services can be provided. The obligation of the dominant operators to provide national roaming to other regional operators would definitely help to foster fair competition in the regional markets. On the other hand, one should take into consideration that imposing such obligations on the big operators may decrease the overall investment dynamics, as no market player would have the incentive to develop network infrastructure with full coverage. This decrease may be slowed down with the appropriate level of roaming charges. The Russian institutional framework does not foresee national roaming obligations, while market-based agreements among the regional operators are nevertheless often the norm.

5.3.3.4 Technological Dynamics

Due to high innovation dynamics, competition between the mobile telecommunications technologies as well as competition of mobile technologies with other technologies such as WiMAX/WiFi has intensified. This has significant implications in terms of standardization determining the speed of the diffusion process. In particular for the countries with scarce financial resources and relatively poor market potential, the choice of optimal technology in terms of sustainable development, fast modernization, and high rates of return on invested capital is very important. It is often argued that one single standard boosts investment concentration, leads to substantial network coverage, enhances quality of infrastructure due to economies of scale, and intensifies network effects accelerating the diffusion process. Moreover from the international point of view, the choice of the proper standard has implications in terms of interoperability contributing to the internationalization process. On the other hand, the deployment of different standards can lead to enhanced technological competition and foster efficiency in terms of spectrum management. Due to all these facts, policy makers have a great responsibility when selecting certain standards that have direct implications on the diffusion process.

There are not many studies dealing with how and when standards are chosen. Hausman (2002), based on the example of the USA, argues that regulatory delays are extremely costly in terms of technological diffusion and are associated with high welfare losses. Toivanen (2004) analyzes governments' choice of first generation mobile telephony empirically and finds out that larger and richer countries are faster to adopt 1G; that indirect network effects are taken into account in countries' timing decisions, and political institutions affect the speed of adoption.

The regulators around the world consider the issues of spectrum management. On the one hand, a single standard has all advantages mentioned above and could be very effective. An example here is the GSM implementation in the European countries. On the other hand, to improve efficiency of the telecommunications sector spectrum the neutrality principle is promoted. At the beginning of 2007, the EU Commissar promotes the technological neutrality and spectrum trading in the next EU Regulatory Framework. At the same time, the EU Commissar said officially that the EU countries have to choose the DVB-H mobile TV standard in the next 2 years, otherwise the EU will obliged to do it in 2 years.

In Russia, technological developments have relatively strong influence on the process of mobile telecommunications diffusion. Firstly, the mobile operators in the GSM standard have to deal with operators in the CDMA standard. The fixed wireless networks in the CDMA standard[104] are often deployed in the big cities, where the traditional mobile telecommunications operators generate most of their revenues. These are, for example, the IS-95A/B networks based CDMA technology of 2G (800 MHz). At the beginning of 2007, in Russia, there were about 20 fixed wireless networks based on this technology.[105] The position of the Russian Ministry concerning this standard is less comprehensible. Mininformsvyaz allowed use the 800 MHz until 2010.

Furthermore, the mobile networks are also deployed in the CDMA standard. They have quite a limited number of subscribers. These networks were developed through the move of the operators of NMT-450 analogue networks towards converting their network to the digital standard IMT–MC-450 based on CDMA. The biggest part of assets is operated under the brand Sky Link and belongs to Sistema holding. Sky Link is currently testing a 3G network, and governmental officials indicated earlier that these 3G frequencies would also have to be put up for tender. However, whether the Sky Link will receive this license is still unclear. The Russian Ministry said that Sky Link will be able to build the UMTS network if it finds it more attractive.

Secondly, the mobile operators, moving to upgrade their network to 3G, have to deal with emerging wireless broadband access technologies like WiFi and WiMAX. However, often the mobile operators obtain WiFi or WiMAX licenses in order to either deploy these technologies as part of their network and increase its capability or efficiency, e.g. in the big cities or at the airports. In 2006, the deployment of WiMAX took concrete forms, overcoming the technical characteristics of the mobile technologies, e.g. relative low bandwidth, but showing still some shortage in the mobility as well as relative high prices. The WiMAX technology is deployed in Russia. The full substitution of these technologies to mobile

[104] Fixed wireless technologies limit the mobility to the cells covered by the contract antenna. In this way, each consumer buys access to specific cells. Besides limited mobility, the services provided by wireless local loop (WLL) telecommunications do not differ from mobile telecommunications. They can offer a wider telecommunications service range, e.g. internet access.

[105] http://www.cdg.org/worldwide/index.asp

networks is still restricted due to relatively limited mobility. However, in the urban areas, these are real competitors to both mobile and fixed broadband networks.

In 2007, the 3G licenses were issued in Russia. They contain relatively low coverage obligations. The operators as well as the Russian Ministry do not have high expectations that the 3G networks will be extended at the earlier stages beyond Moscow and St. Petersburg. The Russian mobile operators are already looking into the deployment of alternative technologies: VimpelCom launched a WiFi network in Moscow and received a WiMAX license; Megafon is also considering WiMAX to some extend as alternative to 3G.

To sum it up, the technological progress and relative saturation of the mobile market move the focus from the competition between different mobile technologies to the competition of mobile technologies with other technological platforms. To decrease this competition pressure, mobile operators obtain the WiFi/WiMAX licenses and integrate these technologies into their business models. Fixed mobile convergence (FMC) solutions are the next step in the development of the Russian telecommunications market (Sedix and Fadin 2007). The Russian regulatory policy with respect to technological developments should be aimed at the new wave of technologies such as mobile broadband. In the short-run period, MNP and MVNOs are the instruments, which will have an impact on "real" mobile penetration rates.

5.4 Broadband Infrastructure and Content: Demand- and Supply Sides

Broadband opportunities are emerging as waves of innovation reshape the information and communications technology sector. These innovations are occurring across all levels of the industry from technological developments and business models to regulatory and policy frameworks. These create broadband opportunities for end users, large-scale network operators, small entrepreneurs, local communities and government alike. As a result, a new vision by potential broadband providers, and a new paradigm by policy makers and regulators are required (Best and Pehrson 2005, p. 3).

ITU distinguishes the following positive impacts of broadband technologies (Best and Pehrson 2005, p. 3):

1. Eroding information differentials resulting from geographical constraints that prevent marginal communities from participating in regional, national and international processes.
2. Access to regional, national and international resources through broadband access technologies can substantially improve the living standards of marginal communities.
3. Enhancing the sustainability of marginal communities by supporting the transfer of knowledge and expertise to marginal communities.
4. Improvement of information flows, increase the range of options available to marginal communities.
5. Positive impact on the productivity of business.
6. Supporting the growth of regional and national IT industries.

During the last years the governments' aspiration is the participation of the whole population in the so called "Information Society". The broadband infrastructure is the very important foundation of any information society; more and more countries are working to ensure universal and affordable broadband access to their citizens. Broadband is not only about access to music and movies but to information in general. Broadband access is increasingly being seen as a catalyst for economic success in the information economy. Due to these facts, some economists argue that hand in hand with this political dimension of broadband, the degree of market intervention by governments is utmost important (Falch 2005, p. 15).

Falch (2005, p. 3) distinguishes three dimensions of the broadband decisive factors (see Table 5.9): (1) factors affecting supply of broadband services and factors affecting the demand on broadband services; (2) factors influencing content and factors influencing infrastructure; (3) Technological, economic as well as political/cultural factors affecting both supply and demand conditions for both content and infrastructure development.

Table 5.9. Factors affecting broadband penetration

	Supply	Demand
	Technology	Technology
Content	Economy/Culture	Economy/Culture
	Policy	Policy
	Technology	Technology
Infrastructure	Economy/Culture	Economy/Culture
	Policy	Policy

Source: Falch (2005, p. 3)

However, technology is an important factor in broadband development; it is also global in the sense that the market actors in various countries have access to the same technologies (see Sect. 2.1). This is the reason, why a study of national differences in broadband development must therefore focus on (1) economic/cultural and (2) policy factors, resulting in a deliberate policy towards stimulation of supply and demand growth. Three groups of policy factors are distinguished by Falch (2005, p. 12): facilitation, regulation and direct intervention. Facilitation includes improvement of general framework conditions, regulation includes measures stimulating competition and improving market transparency, while direct intervention includes direct support to infrastructure development and content production. This classification is used in the small benchmark below to find out the main drivers/factors for the broadband developments in these countries.

5.4.1 Successful Experiences in Broadband Development Around the World

Small and medium enterprises especially in rural areas or big corporations profit from broadband telecommunications infrastructure. Building broadband infrastructure requires high investment. The governments of many developed countries started exploring inventive solutions that would encourage the development of broadband. The developments of broadband infrastructure in transition and in developed countries have quite different backgrounds, e.g. low fixed penetration rates. Nevertheless, the understanding of the experiences in other countries is useful. Table 5.10 summarizes the main aspects of broadband experiences in South Korea, France and the US, which are considered below in detail.

Table 5.10. Broadband experiences in the different countries

Country Examples	BB household penetration 3Q06(%)	Economic/cultural factors	Facilitation and regulation factors	Direct interventions factors
South Korea	82	Significant economies of scale; High readiness of consumers to spending on BB services Useful BB content	Adoption of the government programs, forcing infrastructure based competition Late implementation of mandatory unbundling	Very strong state financial participation
France	47		Strong mandatory unbundling policy in DSL	Strong, especially though local authorities
USA	41	Leader in Internet content	Strong competition between fixed and cable Regulatory unbundling was stopped in 2005	Low, especially on the early stages

Source: Own illustration

5.4.1.1 South Korea

This country has the highest penetration in the world and the average bandwidth is also much higher than in Europe. Lee and Choudrie (2002) point out the following success factors:

1. Geography and demographics. Significant economies of scale for broadband network deployment are delivered by the fact that 80% of all Koreans live in densely populated urban areas and 49% live in large apartment complexes.
2. Government policy. The government of South Korea has established a set of national policies such as the Korean Information Infrastructure Plan (KII) and the cyber building certification system (to promote the broadband access platform in apartments and other buildings). In the framework of the KII plan, the key elements were the deregulation of the communications sector and encouragement of facility based competition. The KII plan involved three parts. Firstly, the Korean Information Infrastructure Government (KII-G) constructed a nation-wide backbone for broadband services. Secondly, the Korean Information Infrastructure-Public (KII-P) is intended for home and business and invested in by private carriers and building owners. KII-Ps first phase was completed to connect fiber to large buildings; KII-Ps second phase was also completed to connect 30% of all households with ADSL

and CATV. The third phase objective is to provide 80% of the Korean households with Mbps access. The Korean Information Infrastructure Testbed (KII-T) is utilized by research institutes and universities and was jointly invested in by the government and private carriers. The main goal of the KII-T was to test the validity of technologies and to confirm and evaluate their application potential. (Lee and Chan-Olmsted 2004, p. 659). The KII strategy also includes the provision of incentives to the private sector in the form of loans for the construction of the access network and the investment in R&D. Similarly, the government carried out actions targeting the adoption of broadband: free access in public institutions and organizations, subsidizing PCs for the households, support for e-commerce and the creation of innovative businesses and contents (high-quality educational content). Educational programs in IT involved about one third of the population who received training during 3 years. In contrast to Europe, the revenues generated as a result of 3G license issues has been recycled into the telecommunications sector, providing funds for research and networks investments.

3. Facility based competition: The Korean broadband access market is characterised by strong facilities based competition. Due to the fact that the landlord, not the incumbent, owns the block wiring in the apartment complexes eased the complexity of interconnection at the access level. As a result, absence of a local loop bottleneck has reduced the need for heavy regulation of the incumbent allowing the Korean Telecom to operate with relatively few regulatory rules. Subscriber LLU did not occur until 2000–2001, much later than the introduction of alternative platforms. At this time, Korea was already among the leaders in international Internet access.
4. Prices for broadband services measured per Mb are among the lowest. Furthermore, Koreans seem willing to pay a larger share of their income in order to have a high bandwidth available.
5. PC Rooms (PC bangs) are a major demand driver for broadband content and services especially in the early phase of broadband deployment.
6. Clear user benefits through available content: There is a vast amount of services available for users, not only entertainment services like on-line games, but also a wide range of educational services.

5.4.1.2 Europe

The greatest penetrations growth rates can be seen in those countries which have the greatest penetration rates. This shows the emerging of digital divide within the European Union. In the countries with greatest deployment of alternative technologies, the highest broadband penetration rates are observed. That can be considered a validation of the statement that there is a positive effect of intermodal competition in broadband development. If no viable alternative infrastructure exists, competition depends on the access to the facilities of the incumbent. This competition depends completely on the intervention of the market regulations to ensure non-discriminatory access to the new entrants (EC 2007, pp. 28–29 in Annex 1).

In Europe, there are countries which have strong government participation through infrastructure initiatives, e.g. Sweden, and there are some which have less government participation, e.g. Germany. Some governments e.g. in the UK argued on the first stage that "the government does not believe that there is a case for a general subsidy for broadband roll-out". However, later on there have been several cases of public funding of broadband projects.

a. France

The national broadband strategy of France sets up the following objectives: (1) 95% of population to be within reach of a broadband offer; (2) 90% of industrial areas to be connected by optical and have access to competitive broadband offers; (3) 60% of households to own a PC by 2010. The major policy initiative is the promotion of broadband access to rural areas.

The government supports the action of local authorities to develop infrastructures in scarcely populated areas. The infrastructure developed in this way will be available to all operators under transparent and non-discriminatory obligations. The local authorities can use finance from the Broadband Fund and make direct use of EU structural funds on such projects.

The French government supports alternative technologies by creating awareness, removing administrative obstacles and launching calls for projects. Two big projects of public funding of broadband networks in France were approved of in the last years. To speed up roll-out and reduce cost, Electricite de France will allow network operators to install fiber alongside existing electricity lines (Cullen International 2002).

b. Sweden

The Swedish government spent €1.1 billion by 2004 in an initiative to provide broadband networks to rural areas. The aim was to provide broadband network access to 98% of the country's towns and villages. The funding was expected to be matched by private investment of equal size. National broadband network policy is commitment of the state to build a national broadband network through a telecom subsidiary of the national electricity grid operator. This system is operated independently and opened to all ISPs that want to rent dark fiber. Furthermore, in Sweden, subscribers are offered tax reductions where the cost of a broadband connection exceeds €884. The funding is for 50% of the costs that exceed €884, up to a maximum €552 (Cullen International 2002).

5.4.1.3 USA

Although the USA is the leading country in development of the Internet, the penetration of broadband in the USA is lagging behind countries like Korea, Japan, Canada and the Nordic countries. Taking into account the fact that the USA is the cradle of the Internet and its total dominance in the development and provision of content indicates that the American policy in stimulating investments in and demand for broadband networks is not very successful. The US has not initiated any specific broadband certification procedures or government-led infrastructure building projects beyond the usual cheerleading role in encouraging of an information superhighway through the private sector (Lee and Chan-Olmsted 2004, p. 662). However, the general regulatory approach has encouraged the development of broadband. The relatively long delay and uncertainty on the open access issue was the reason for some confusion and impeded investment and innovation in the industry. The regulatory asymmetries of the United States may be the main contributors to the dissimilar growth rates of each of the broadband technologies. The deployment of own accesses by the CLECs has progressively fallen during the last years. At the end of 2004, the FCC has redefined its unbundling model: *"The new framework builds on actions by the Commission to limit unbundling to provide incentives for both incumbent carriers and new entrants to invest in the telecommunications market in a way that best allows for innovations and sustainable competition"* (FCC 2004, p. 1). In March 2005, unbundling obligations will essentially be limited to the local copper loop.[106]

Although the US government has the general cheerleading role in the infrastructure stimulation policy, some government initiatives were realized. Some states such as Washington and Colorado have passed legislation and/or provided sponsorship to encourage the aggregation of public and private demand. Low interest loans were implemented to boost infrastructure roll-out to rural locations; provisions for telemedicine and distance learning are included here. Through the rural broadband loan and loan guarantee program in total amount to 1.302 billion USD in financial resources made available by the Rural Utilities Service (RUS) to provide services in rural communities with a population up to 20,000. Some findings are assessable for Schools and Libraries Programs. Most states offer some form of tax credit to telecommunications companies to provide services to disadvantaged areas. The more economically depressed the area, the greater the tax incentive (Analysis 2004, p. 30).

To sum up, the experiences in other regions often show strong government participation as well as strong regulatory measures in the market. On the one hand, this strong type of market interference conflicts in many respects with a liberal approach, where development mainly is left to the free market. Usually, it is argued that private companies are in a better position to provide the services. Moreover, economies of scale are "lost" if the state is providing its own infrastructure. Market intervention negatively affects the incentives to invest in broadband access points. On the other hand, the use of public sector activities to stimulate either demand or supply and as result, the economic growth does not conflict with this approach. The question here is, whether the benefits of the latter are higher in comparison with welfare loss through the market distortions. In respect to this, the question is how much broadband infrastructure has to be developed e.g. financed by the state or e.g. through regulatory holidays, to maximize this welfare effect.

[106] For more information on the unbundling in the USA see Bauer (2005)

5.4.2 Regulatory Policy Encouraging Broadband Penetration

Broadband stimulating policies in developed and transition/developing countries are quite different. In the developed countries, the universalization of fixed telephone lines is already mostly completed and the main aim is to achieve a degree of penetration similar in the availability of broadband infrastructures. As a result, policies are required for convincing those who have access to and do not find any advantages of connecting. With respect to broadband access, the goal is to bring infrastructure to rural or isolated areas. This could be achieved directly by subsidies or indirectly, by providing incentives for service-providing companies to serve certain communities (Gomez-Barroso and Feijoo 2005).

In transition countries and to larger extend in developing countries, a different situation is observed. On the one hand, they must continue to move forward expansion of basic networks. On the other hand, they need to start generalizing the access to advanced services, which are currently available only in the capitals and main cities. These countries have to deploy really ubiquitous networks and simultaneously promote their usage. Increasing layers of population should qualify in the usage of new technologies (Robles et al. 2005).

The rapid technological development, especially in wireless technologies, provides opportunities for the transition countries to plan beyond increasing basic teledensity and into broadband. However, the current perceived lack of local demand and available revenue streams could prevent the commercial deployment of broadband access networks in many areas of transition countries. This is especially evident in non-urban areas, at least by large-scale operators. Moreover, the low PC penetration rates in many transition countries could be an obstacle for positive impacts which may arise from the availability of broadband networks.

In the most advanced countries, households dominate demand. However, in the less advanced economies the use of broadband in businesses is important. Business applications may also stimulate demand from households. The structure of the economy is important for the overall demand. An economy dominated by informational activities must be expected to generate more demand for broadband services than an economy based on agricultural production (Falch 2004, p. 6).

In the following, the measures encouraging the broadband development will be discussed.[107] The all measures are summarized in Table 5.11:

(1) Investment promotions

The regulatory policy should be aimed at maximizing investment flows into the telecommunications industry. As it was discussed in Chap. 3.4, this could be achieved through market liberalization and permitting foreign ownership in the sector.

(2) Relaxing of licensing conditions and neutral licensing/authorization

The deployment of broadband can be encouraged through relaxing the licensing conditions for large-scale broadband access providers and by ensuring a consistent framework that clearly targets a set of defined policy objectives.

---

[107] This discussion is partly based on Lee et al. (2005)

Table 5.11. Measures, encouraging the broadband development

	Supply	Demand
	Aspiration through the government's program	
Content	Availability of useful content	PC availability Skills development
Infrastructure	Investment promotion Relaxing of licensing conditions and Neutral licensing/authorization Encouragement of large-scale and small scale providers State participation in network building	Dominant players and regulatory position. State support for the infrastructure demand State/Regulator's initiatives promoting price and quality transparency

Source: Own description

To encourage the deployment of broadband access networks, sector regulation should be neutral and the licensing or authorization regime should reflect this position. This means licensing/authorization frameworks focus on encouraging the provision of and investment in broadband access networks, rather than defining the specific method of delivery. In the field of licensing radio spectrum for the provision of broadband services, this is particularly important. But it is also potentially applicable in terms of fixed line deployment allowing the flexibility to use copper, fiber or satellite. Technology and service-neutral licenses/authorizations also enable broadband providers the flexibility to offer a full range of services (triple play) especially in rural areas, increasing revenues stream options. It is recognized that total technology neutrality in licensing framework may be quite difficult to achieve, but regulators are increasingly providing licensees with the maximum flexibility possible when selecting which technologies they wish to adopt in the provision of broadband access services, within existing standards and international frameworks. Generally, there is the risk that licensees may choose to deploy non-standard, unique and proprietary technologies, but given the substantial benefits of internationally recognized and adopted technologies, this is considered a relatively low risk possibility.

(3) Encouragement of large scale and small scale providers

The regulatory framework should encourage a full range of potential broadband providers from large scale and small scale network operators, to universities and local governments to deploy broadband access networks through the following measures:

- The regulatory environment should be tailored to give incentives to small broadband providers, local community providers, to deploy the local broadband access networks. This could be achieved through the lightening of licenses or general authorization requirements for operators and service providers in small, non-urban areas. Broadband providers in small, non-urban areas can test the business case on the small scale and decide in the future to commit to more large-scale deployment. A regulator could replace licensing requirements for commercial community broadband providers by a general authorization or registration framework, just as some countries have already established "open entry" policies for ISPs.[108] If the license requirement remains, it is particularly important that the license fees for very small broadband providers be kept as low as possible, if not eliminated altogether.

- Operators can be encouraged to extend their networks to rural areas through infrastructure sharing arrangements. These arrangements existed already in mobile networks in rural areas and could also apply to new broadband and wireless networks.
- Large scale operators can be given incentives to deploy non-commercially viable networks in return for appropriate rewards.
- Regulators could provide direct (targeted smart subsidies from universal access fund contribution/grants) or indirect (e.g. tax exemptions) financial support to the full range of broadband providers.

(4) Dominant players and regulatory position

The dominant operator (often ex-monopolist) should be prevented through an asymmetric regulatory regime to constrain the development of competition in the broadband market, resulting in a reasonable price level. Local loop unbundling policy is implemented e.g. in Europe with aims to promote competition and increasing of prices. Moreover, the regulator should allow broadband providers to offer a full range of services and applications, such as the triple play of voice, Internet access and broadcast.[109]

(5) State support for the infrastructure demand

The state could take initiatives and supports the demand side, for instance through tax exemptions for broadband users (as it is done in Denmark) or funding of broadband access to certain types of organizations (as it is done in the US, where grants are provided for instance to community oriented institutions). The public sector can also stimulate demand by provision of broadband connections to its own institutions such as schools, hospitals, ministries etc. For instance, in Japan indirect support is provided through the possibility for making use of public infrastructure facilities such as ducts on very favorable terms.

(6) State participation into backbone network building

The regulator can take a number of steps to encourage the expansion of fiber backbone networks to boost the capability of both wireline and wireless broadband

[108] Reducing or eliminating licensing requirements is not synonymous with not regulating service providers. Local commercial broadband providers could still be subject to government oversight through general business regulation in areas such as consumer protection.

[109] Many European regulators took a closer look at the bundling policies of incumbents. In the early state of this discussion, there were a couple of regulator's opinions, which would like to regulate unreasonable bundling. With the increasing of number of bundling offers (triple and quadruple plays), the regulators reviewed their decisions with the results of accepting the incumbents bundling with offering of each product separately on the wholesale level.

technologies. This is forging synergies with transport and energy infrastructure projects and providing incentives for 2G mobile operators to replace their microwave links with fiber networks and then make it possible for all owners of such communications resources to lease unused capacity to others for commercial deployment. An alternative is perhaps for governments to fund such networks directly and to oversee access to them by both incumbent and new service providers.

(7) Availability of useful content

Government agencies or ministries and the regulator can cooperate to develop initiatives such as e-government programmes that can be seen as a sort of direct intervention in content production as the public produces its own content. This can stimulate demand for content resulting in demand for infrastructure. A related kind of support is the financing of educational content. This is done for instance in South Korea.

(8) PC availability

Broadband infrastructure alone is not solution of the low broadband penetration issues. End-user terminals, primarily PCs, are important. One way here is setting up single access points, where users can access the Internet. The alternative ways include, for example the "no compromise PCs", which are mostly subsidized from the software vendors and chipmakers like in India. In some countries, there is some amount of subsidy in the purchasing of PCs.

(9) Skilled users

The government can also take a lead in facilitating broadband development through upgrading the competences and readiness to take up new technologies, for instance through the commission of extensive training programs. In South Korea, extensive training programs have contributed to an increase of the potential customer base for broadband connections.

(10) State/Regulator's initiatives promoting price and quality transparency

Regulatory bodies may also play an active role in increasing the market transparency inter alia by providing information on prices, on availability of products and on consumer rights. In many cases, operators are required by law to provide this information anyway. For instance, when a NRA decides to provide an information service which allows users to search for broadband access services by typing in their postal code, the NRA does not adopt a decision or order. Facilitation measures serve a very important function: They provide market information at no costs to the individual. Indeed, it is very cost-effective if an NRA uses the information provided to it by communication companies to increase market transparency – one of the core assumptions of perfect competition.

(11) Aspiration through the government programs

As experiences of the other countries show, one particular challenge of state industrial policy in regards to broadband developed as well as ICT in general is 'guideposting'. This is when a public institution takes the lead in the creation of a common vision with aspirational elements on future developments. Demonstration projects like those funded by eEurope and other EU programs may function in a similar way. Many national plans for the information society, e.g. the e-Japan plan, play this role. Common visions may include common standards. Although much of the standardization work is done at the international level, there are still important areas, for instance in digital signatures and EDIFACT messages, where development of national standards is necessary.

The main principle in the development of governmental broadband policy in particular and ICT policy in general is the principle of balance: "balance between demand and supply side". If the government boosts broadband access availability to the users, which do not see any advantages of broadband access (e.g. high prices or not so much useful content), it will not ensure successful development.

5.4.3 Development of the Russian Broadband Infrastructure

In the broadband deployment, Russia is still lagging behind. The comparison of growth rates of the different European countries versus broadband penetration rates in 3Q06 shows that the countries with low penetration have higher growth rates (see Fig. 5.17). However, Russia is still behind in terms of penetration rates, number of lines as well as growth rates. Based on this fact, the main aim should be to accelerate growth of the broadband segment like in the Czech Republic and Poland.

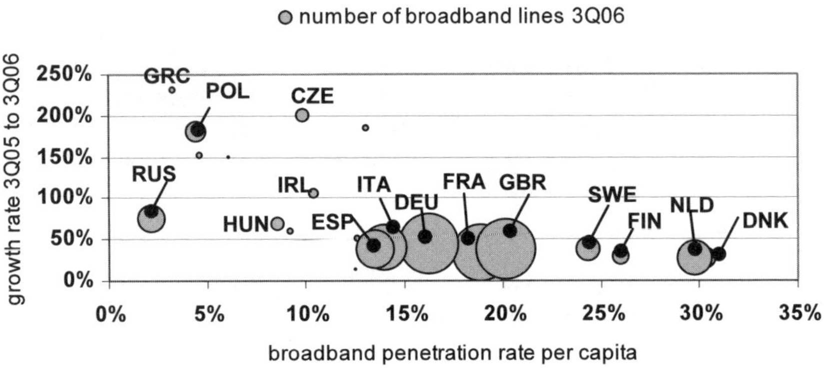

Source: ECTA (2007), Point Topic (2007) and own calculations

Fig. 5.17. Broadband penetration, broadband growth rates, number of broadband lines in comparison

Speaking to Russians over the Internet in 2007, First Deputy Prime Minister Dmitry Medvedev said that the government was supporting the development of broadband Internet. "Broadband Internet is our future and all technologies that are used including Wi-Fi and WiMAX are to help allow Internet access in many Russian regions, not just in Moscow and St. Petersburg," Medvedev said. However, until today the Russian government did not work out any comprehensive plan of broadband development. According to the Russian telecommunications source, in 2006, the Russian Ministry does not have development of broadband as a strategic aim. It sees its mission in the promoting of universal access in the areas where there are no phones at all.

Table 5.12 summarizes the state (beginning of 2007) of the Russian broadband infrastructure development on the supply and demand side in terms of all measures identified above.

Table 5.12. Development of the broadband infrastructure in Russia

	Infrastructure	Situation in Russia
Supply	Investment promotion	Liberalization has partially taken place, foreign investor participation is still limited; relative high regulatory risk
	Relaxing of licensing conditions and neutral licensing/authorization	Strong spectrum deficit, chaos in the spectrum assigning especially for wireless broadband technologies, no serious plans to implement authorization or neutral licensing yet
	Encouragement of large scale and small scale providers	Very limited, broadband is not supported by the universal service fond. mostly not at all municipalities initiatives
	State participation in network building	Limited state activities
Demand	Dominant players and regulatory position.	Still in very developing stage
	State support for the infrastructure demand	Partially implemented, very good example, Internet at schools
	State/Regulator's initiatives promoting price and quality transparency	Very limited

Source: Own description

In terms of broadband infrastructure development, all technologies should be used. An advantage of Russia in this context is the fact that 80% of the population lives in the cities. Believing the quotation at the beginning of this section, the Russian government has an adequate position in respect to technological neutrality. The promotion of the competition between different platforms will certainly foster deployment of broadband infrastructure through infrastructure competition. Hopefully, the problems in regards to proper authorization/licensing of "home networks" operators as well as clear frequencies assignments for WiMAX networks, which exist at the end of 2006, will be overcome soon. In respect to the fixed broadband, many countries successfully used the regulatory access unbundling policy. This is still an open question in Russia. The implementation of this policy could drive broadband penetration in Russia. In the regions, where only one network infrastructure exists, this regulatory policy can be justified.[110]

[110] see e.g. example of Canada in Telecom Policy Report (2006).

One could notice very positive developments with respect to provision of Internet access through the post offices in the rural areas, as well as the President's program related to Internet promotion at Russian schools.

Taking the experiences around the world, governments are highly prioritizing broadband in economic development and encouraging broadband subsidizing. The advantages and disadvantages of this method are discussed above. In the author's view it is important to increase the competitiveness of the country by supporting such projects or taking a lead in them. The important issue here is how the ownership rights will be divided after the projects are built and no new state monopolies will be established. Such form of participation as Private Public Partnership should certainly be deployed e.g. between regional authorities and private partners to deliver broadband access in the markets with market failures.

5.4.4 Development of the Russian Broadband Content

The encouragement of the demand side is taking a concrete form (see Table 5.13). The program "PC in each house", mentioned in Sect. 2.4.7, started in February 2007, will increase PC penetration in the Russian regions. As a result, this program will be certainly of advantage for Russia. The outcome of the program sounds certainly very promising. However, the balance between demand and supply side should be always kept in mind. Stimulating the demand side could of course give some improvements in PC availability, but it will not really give "real" benefits to the people or encourage PC usage strongly. An end aim should be always to bring people onto the Net, where they will certainly find advantages (as well as material advantages). These range from the bus plan, e-government services, and legal information to the possibility to work from home, which are important for increasing productivity in the economy and better life quality. This point of view is as well supported by the comparison of gaps in computer penetration and Internet usage with other transition countries. Russia compared with Poland and Hungary does not have such a large gap in computer penetration but a larger gap in Internet usage.

Table 5.13. Development of the broadband content in Russia

	Content	Situation in Russia
Supply	Availability of useful content	Limited
Demand	PC availability	"PC in each house"
	Skills development	High qualifications of human capital, limited state initiatives

Source: Own description

The promotion of the skills to use broadband is another important measure. An obvious advantage of Russia is its high qualification of human capital. However, broad state initiatives in this direction are not to be observed.

In terms of content supply, Russia has one obvious advantage: the Russian language belongs to the top 10 world languages, which significantly helps provide useful content. As discussed above, one of the direct measures to promote useful content is encouraging broadband applications and usage in the fields: e-government, e-commerce, e-learning, e-health. There are no unique concepts and recommendations in this field. Many countries and regions have developed their own ways of success. To compare the results of the different policies is very challenging. There is no unique definition, how these could be measured. To give an idea of which indicators are important to measure the progress in information society, the system of the European Union is summarized. In the European Union, the member countries are compared in the field of broadband applications based on online supply and functionality of 20 basic public services as well as the number of enterprises with Web sites. To reflect the broadband usage, the following indicators are used in the EU: in the field of e-government: private, corporations, state (e-procurement), in the field of e-commerce: product availability on the Internet, share of Internet sales, in the field of e-learning: private use and corporate use and in the field e-health: online use of health related activities/information

Until the beginning of 2006, the Russian government was working in the field of encouraging development of an information society mostly based on the program "Electronic Russia 2010". Any other broader programs, such as ICT Master Plan, which are promoting broadband infrastructure and broadband applications, were not implemented by the Russian government. In this situation, some Russian regions often took their own initiative and have started some regional programs.

Officially, the Russian Ministry speaks about the following main directions of broadband applications and usage: e-government, e-commerce, e-education and e-health. The main difference of e-government in Russia compared to other e.g. European countries consists in that in the European context, e-government is primarily on-line services to households and enterprises from the government. In the Russian context, the marking point is improving government efficiency through implementation of ICT in terms of processes automation and regimentation of relationship inside of the government authority itself and between different authorities. Due to the fact that administrative and institutional structures are still in the reforming process, the challenges of the transition process and heritage of Soviet times are still remarkable. At the same time, through digitalization processes radical organizational changes in administrations have occurred. Thus the accent of the Russian government is not reasonless. However, in the middle-term prospective, the online supply and functionality of basic public services to citizens should be prioritized. This will give to the population impulses for content demand.

The other important aspect of workable e-government is ICT accessibility. In transition economies, the problem of the accessibility belongs to the core limitations of development of e-government. How the development of broadband can be encouraged, was discussed above. In terms of e-government, the poor accessibility to broadband, the too fast implementation of e-government can lead to the extension and duplication of tasks of the public institutions, because the public services have to be provided in off-line and on-line ways. On-line programs require enormous initial investments that might be never paid back. Even the advanced economies claim e-governments as inefficient due to high costs. This may be a reason for additional budget constraints. The workable e-government assumes no duplication of the tasks; the public institutions should be able to fulfill their goals based on the new system and should not be a disadvantage for anybody (Ponder 2005; Golubeva et al. 2005, p. 3).

One of the main challenges in the development of e-Russia is the digital divide between Russian's different regions. According to the studies "E-Readiness of the Russian regions 2004–2005" of the Institute for Information Society Development, the degree of the digital divide between the Russian regions can be presented in Fig. 5.18 Moscow and St. Petersburg resource rich regions such as are the leaders of this ranking.

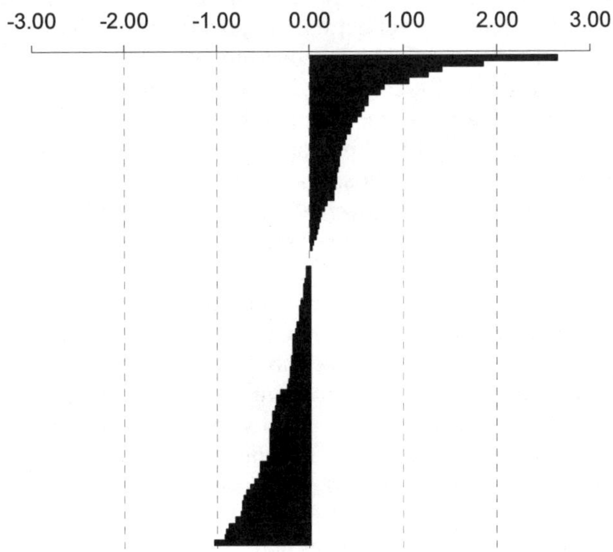

Source: IDIS (2005), own interpretations

Fig. 5.18. E-Readiness of the Russian regions

A deeper view into this ranking shows that the digital divide between the Russian regions is higher in terms of ICT usage and lower in terms of ICT factors (see Fig. 5.19). A differentiated approach to the different Russian regions is needed to close this gap.

In Russia, the regions can win the awards "The best region in ICTs" for improving government efficiency through the implementation of ICT. However, one has to expect that such awards will be issued for promotion of ICT by the population, e.g. best broadband connectivity region or best e-health region. However, the initiative of some regions could be considered very positive[111]; the general framework must be set up. As it states at the beginning of chapter, Russia is

[111] e.g. laptop for each student in Cheboksari.

still missing a guiding role of government in the ICT action plan. Only aspirations and a clear understanding of the challenges will foster the Russian regions to move towards an information society. This move will be more smooth and promising if all regions are moving in the same general direction made by the Russian government.

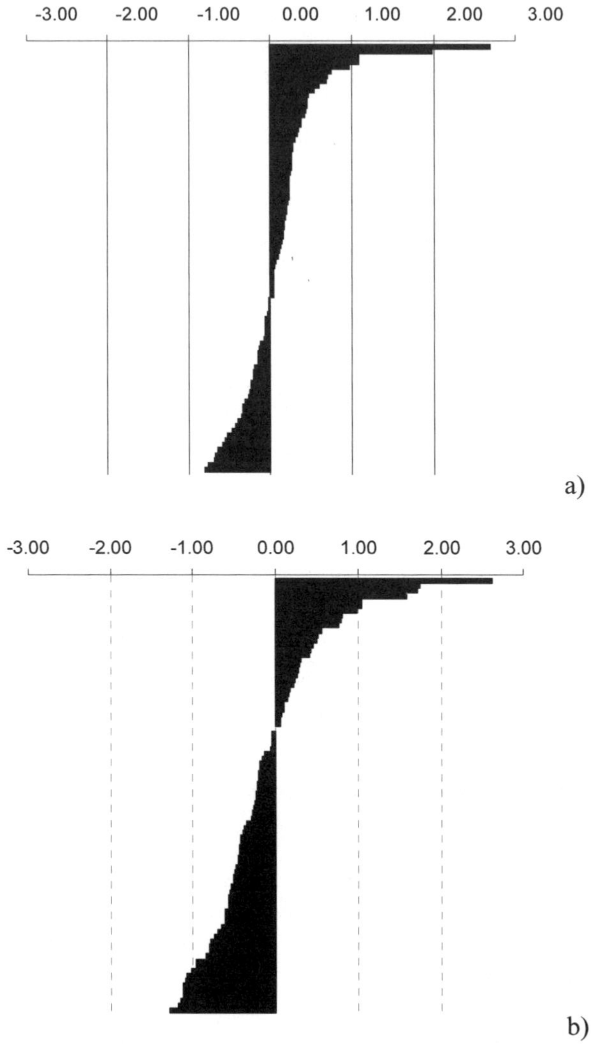

Source: IDIS (2005) and own interpretations

Fig. 5.19. Subindexes of the E-Readiness index in the Russian regions: (a) ICT factors and (b) ICT usage

5.5 Reform Processes Under the Impact of Politics and Institutional Modernization in Russia

All above described instruments and mechanisms in the field of telecommunications privatization, liberalization and regulation are normative. In praxis, there is strong political influence. In the following section, the outcome of the reforming processes under pressure from the different interest groups is analyzed.

Due to the low efficiency of markets and institutions in Russia, which is confirmed in many raking studies (see section 2.4), one has to suggest that the real outcome of positive telecommunications regulation will be quite different from the normative concept presented above. To assess this difference between normative and positive regulation outcome, the schema from Section 4.6 adapted to Russia is analyzed. The next figure (Fig. 5.20) presents interest groups influencing deregulation and privatization processes in the Russian telecommunications.

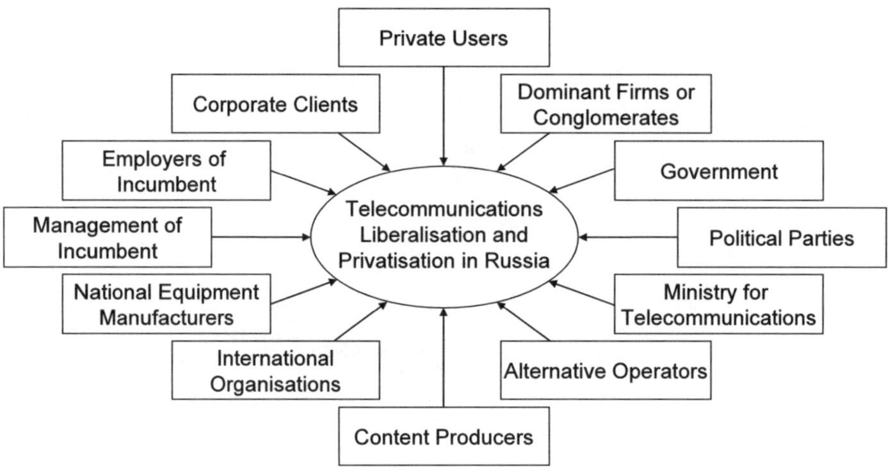

Source: Based on Welfens and Graack (1997, p. 171)

Fig. 5.20. Interest groups influencing deregulation and privatization processes in the Russian telecommunications sector

As in the many other network industries, where incumbents are still partly or fully owned by the state, the major privatization and deregulation barriers may come from the groups related to the incumbent company, e.g. management or employers. But more often the barriers come from the state itself, which may appear to be a major opponent of the privatization and liberalization process. In Russia, where privatization has been prepared for at least the last 10 years, 75% of Svyazinvest is still owned by the state. It is obvious that due to high investment needs, this company should be either privatized or highly subsidized by the state. However, the incumbent is still not on the list of companies to be privatized in 2008. Since the government owns the incumbent company and simultaneously introduces the regulatory framework, it is very difficult to expect that this regulatory rule will be favorable towards any other companies. An example here is the long-distance and international call market liberalization, which officially happened in Russia only at the beginning of 2006 after many years of discussions. It was one of the requirements for the country's WTO accession. This liberalization document allows provision of long-distance and international services only for the operators with their own country-wide network. Due to the fact that only a few companies fulfill this condition, the biggest part of extra profits was accumulated by the state-owned companies for a certain time.[112]

Furthermore, government interests present in the deregulation and privatization processes through the fiscal and allocative interests, e.g. increasing in budgeted revenues or reallocation of financial resources. The latter was the conflict of many months in Russia, where the approval of the Military Ministry of the Svyazinvest privatization was needed. The Military Ministry did not sign this decision until the government guarantied certain prices on the telecommunications services for the military after privatization.

The degree of influence of the employees of the ex-monopolist company as an interest group is quite low in Russia. In all sectors of the Russian economy, one cannot find a strong culture of trade unions. This is the case for the telecommunications ex-monopolist as well.

The next interest group, who may influence the privatization and liberalization process in telecommunications, are corporate and private users of the telecommunications services. The influence of the corporate users on the direction of privatization and liberalization is partly limited because most all corporate users use the services of alternative operators, which have relatively high quality. The private users firstly are looking at the price level. Because of this, the measures like rebalancing, which are directly connected to liberalization, found mostly no support. However, looking the developed countries, most private users are quite supportive if they have to pay many times less for national or international calls.

In key sectors of the Russian economy, dominant firms and conglomerates have strong influence on recently enacted national laws and regulations. Considering the fact that 80% of the telecommunications revenues in Russia are concentrated by the four holdings which are mostly subsidiaries of the biggest financial-industrial groups of the country, it could be expected that this interest group has special influence on the deregulation and privatization processes in Russia.

The role of political parties in Russian practice is not too strong. However, one can see more and more state officials, which at the same time have a position on the board of the biggest Russian companies. Due to this fact, one can expect a strong connection between business and state, e.g. Minister of Mininformsvyaz is on the boards of Svyazinvest. In this condition, it is difficult to expect independent regulatory actions.

Like in other countries, national liberalization pressure is exerted on the telecommunication sector generally from three main groups: (1) Newcomers which

---

[112] However, if the duplication of networks is considered to be positive because it has fostered infrastructure competition, this obligation may have long-term positive impact.

are interested to enter the profitable markets and make profits; (2) Telecommunications equipment suppliers and content suppliers, which are interested in the market liberalization in order to increase sale volumes. Russia, which mostly imports its telecommunications equipment, has in this respect relatively moderate pressure. (3) International organizations like WTO, World Bank, ITU, OECD, EBRD and some others pursue the liberalization and privatization point of view and encourage the governments of the countries to move towards liberalization.

To sum up, it is obvious that the privatization, as well as liberalization processes in Russia have very strong influenced by politics and the country's biggest financial-industrial groups.

In the institutional modernization, there is a lot of room for improvement in Russia. Russia does not have an independent regulator. That makes the process of regulation very political. The Russian Ministry regulates the fields of broadcasting TV and radio, which seems quite adequate in terms of convergence processes. Despite the fact that Russia is a large country, a centralized regulation system is implemented. That is mostly connected to the Russian mentality, but in terms of rapid technological development and strong globalization of the telecommunications services, can be considered very positive. The regional competences in such fields as regional initiatives in the increasing regional e-readiness or private public partnership projects should be strongly encouraged.

The price regulation in telecommunications is implemented by the Federal Energy Services that is also not an authority independent of the Russian government. In the field of competition policy, which is gaining more and more importance with the liberalization process in the telecommunications sector, there is obviously the need for improvement. The Federal Antimonopoly Service (the reorganized Ministry for Antimonopoly Policy) should narrow its tasks and concentrate more on the competition issues and not on e.g. the telecommunications tariff regulation, that was practiced until 2004 (OECD 2004, p. 8).

The court system plays an important role in an efficient regulation policy. Judiciary and law enforcement in Russia in comparison to the other transition countries Czech Republic, Poland and Hungary is relatively weak. On the questions "How often do you associate the descriptions "Fair and impartial" (Fig. 5.21A), "Honest/Uncorrupted" (Fig. 5.21B) with the court system in resolving business disputes, the highest share of respondents in Russia answer negative (never or seldom). Most of respondents in Russia, as in the other three transition countries, are also not sure that the court systems of these countries are able to enforce their decisions (Fig. 5.21C).

Furthermore, self-regulating institutions in the form of organized interests and public-private initiatives are quite important for the rapid telecommunications development. There are some self-regulatory institutions in the Russian market, for example PRIOR for the development of an information society in Russia, ICU and the association of the Russian 3G operators,[113] which coordinates the Russian 3G networks.

[113] www.3gassociation.ru

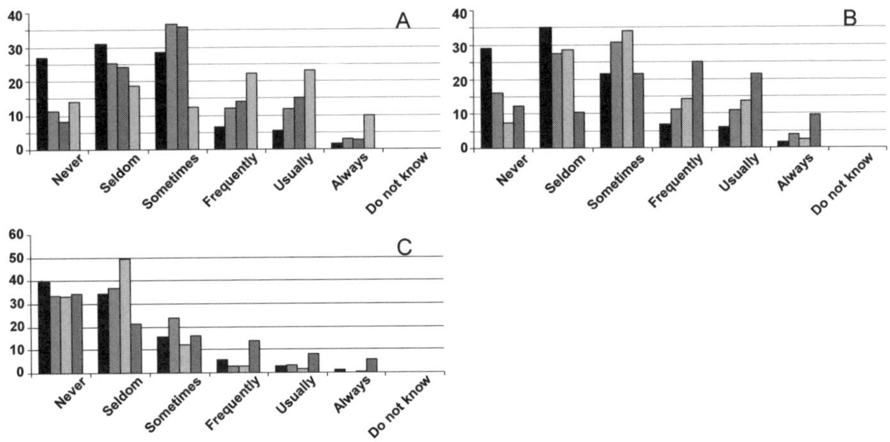

Source: BEEPS (2002) and own calculations

Fig. 5.21. Judiciary and law enforcement in Russia in comparison to the other transition countries

As a result, taking into account the strong political impact on reforming processes in Russia, it is expected that the outcome will be different in comparison to the normative findings. However, to become a world economy, Russia must properly develop the telecommunications sector. This is especially important in terms of globalization around the world and increasing the role of the telecommunications sector.

6 Conclusion

The aim of this research was to investigate the role of telecommunications sector in transition countries, to find out its special features and based on these, to suggest adequate strategies for the future development of this sector. The empirical investigations focus on the whole group of transition countries. With respect to key policy issues, Russia has been a special focus.

The main questions to answer were:

1. What role do telecommunications play in the economic development of transition countries? How strong are the linkages between economic development and telecommunications infrastructure in transition countries?
2. What are the main differences in the telecommunications sector of transition countries compared to the developed countries?
3. What are the main policy options for the development of the fixed, mobile and broadband infrastructure as well as Internet usage promotion in transition countries and especially in Russia?

In the first three sections, the quantitative and theoretical basis has been established. In Chap. 5, the answers to the questions above are provided, based on the investigation results from Chaps. 2, 3, and 4. The key insights of the study are summarized below.

Chapter 2 started with the presentation of the traditional structure of the telecommunications sector and with the description of the current technological developments. The telecommunications technologies are developing rapidly, giving strong impulses for industry reforms. Technological development is, however, only one factor for the reforming processes. The other sector-specific factors such as demand changes, changes in sector governance, and the countries' specific parameters related and unrelated to the telecommunications sector, play also an important role. Furthermore, international organizations or unions such as WTO, ITU, World Bank, or European Union can influence such sector reforms. To show the main historical developments and current state of the reform processes around the world, the US and Germany have been taken as examples. Starting 2005, in these countries, two different views on the telecommunications sector regulation are observed: the European view, where competition promotion should force investments, and the American view, where ensuring company profit gives incentives to invest.

The investigation of the telecommunications sector in transition countries cannot be considered without knowing the historical developments on the central-planned economy. Here telecommunications were considered as a non-profit-oriented production process aiming to support the socio-economic superstructures. The state-owned telecommunications industry was characterized by very poor performance and high access deficit. As result, the starting point for the reforming processes in transition countries was a public monopoly with quite poor performance but it was under other circumstances as in the market economy.

Based on the investigation of the international ranking studies, Russia, a special focus of this study, enjoys high economic growth and relatively stable macroeconomic indicators. However, quality of political institutions in Russia is low. In the field of ICTs, Russia has relatively well developed infrastructure and a high quality of human capital, which is often reflected by the indicators of individual ICT readiness and usage. This is certainly the strength of the Russian ICT sector. Despite this strength, the Russian ICT policy design and governmental ICT readiness/ usage are partly insufficient. In terms of these issues, Russia is very often ranked behind BRICS countries like China, India and Brazil. Special attention to these areas is required to better exploit the existing opportunities.

The Russian telecommunications sector showed significant growth rates in the last ten years. The biggest part of the telecommunications revenues is concentrated in the hands of four big holdings. The role of mobile telecommunications in Russia is especially prominent. The modernization of the fixed infrastructure and respectively the broadband infrastructure is, however, still a challenge for Russia. Due to the low broadband penetration, the development of an information society in Russia requires much attention. Given the regional diversity in terms of population density and per capita income, one must raise the issue to which extent there is sufficient room for differentiated regional development strategies and regulatory policies.

The Minsvyazinvest – the Russian telecommunications regulator – as well as the Federal Tariff Services are the main regulatory bodies in telecommunications. Their independence and impartiality are issues to work on in Russia. Due to the perspective of a future OECD membership of Russia and the pending WTO negotiations, one should indeed consider options to implement regulatory reforms which establish an independent authority.

In Chapter 3, the theory of privatization and liberalization are presented, which starts with the consideration of the special characteristics of the telecommunications sector. The most fundamental economic characteristic of the telecommunications sector is network effects. For a long time, it was argued that telecommunications is a natural monopoly characterized primarily by economies of scale and scope. The prices under the natural monopoly are significantly higher than average costs und cause a static and dynamic inefficiency in comparison to a competitive situation. This is the reason for permitting and encouraging as much competition as possible. Due to the fact that only some parts of the telecommunications sector can be characterized as a natural monopoly, the other part of the telecommunications sector can be open for competition. The disaggregated approach can be used for localizing market power of such monopolistic bottlenecks. Only a disaggregated regulation of the non-contestable parts of the network, characterized by natural monopoly features as well as irreversible costs, is justified.

Privatization, defined as the deliberate sale by a government of state-owned enterprises (SOEs) or assets to private economic agents. It is used in this study in its broader definition and includes any takeover of property rights (control over use, benefits from property, transfer or sell, exclusion rights) of a company or parts of a company by the private subject. The aims of privatization are usually efficiency, fiscal, and distributional objectives. These goals can sometimes be in clear conflict with each other. In this study existing literature on the privatization experiences in different countries was investigated. It was found that privatization ensures its positive impact on rates of phone penetration and efficiency only in conjunction with deregulation, liberalization and efficient regulation through an independent regulator. In transition economies, the privatization process is particularly challenging due to the changing institutional background, the creation of a domestic stock market as well as democratization of the state. Privatization can be carried out rapidly or be delayed due to incomplete information and institutional instability. A state-owned company can be restructured before or after its sale. It can also be sold all at once or in stages. There is not "a unique recipe" on these issues. Each approach has supporters and opponents. The decisions should be based on the assessment of the country specific situation and carried out on the case-by-case basis.

Privatization alone has, however, little immediate impact on the market structure. Allowing entry to and competition in the sector appears to bring far greater benefits. A monopolistic provider, whether state-owned or private, faces fewer incentives to improve service and lower prices than do firms operating in a competitive environment. Liberalization of the market can be carried out using three main instruments: restructuring, liberalization of market entry, and tariff rebalancing. Liberalization of the market entry and price liberalization are based primarily on the abolishment of cross-subsidizing mechanisms.

Chapter 4 is devoted to regulatory theory of the network industries with special focus on telecommunications industry. Telecommunications regulation is often associated with post-privatization and post-liberalization control of utilities. It can be divided into three phases: from strong regulatory interventions to ensure the first competition (phase 1) over the regulatory interventions only in monopoly network position (phase 2) to the abolishment of regulation and applications of general competition law (phase 3). As a result, the regulation should be a time-limited process.

After detailed analysis of the different regulatory schemes in terms of end-user price regulation as well as access and interconnection price regulation, the broad basis for the comparison between advantages and disadvantages of the different regulatory methods is established. On the one hand, it is obvious that high powered incentives schemes (price-cap) should be preferred to low powered schemes (rate of return regulation) to encourage short term efficiency. However, there is no clear consensuses on the impact of different regulatory schemes on long term investment, which very important, especially in respect to high investment need. The regulator's access to full information about the supply and demand is quite limited. Due to this fact, many theoretical models to achieve an economically efficient outcome can not be realized in practice.

Another important issue of regulatory theory is regulation in order to achieve universality aims. These are theoretically justified by such factors as network externalities, redistribution as the state's aim or promotion of economic development. There are two different regulatory instruments to finance universal service policy: access deficit charges and universality fund. A couple of disadvantages such as price inflation of subsidizing services, encouragement of service providers to bypass the PSTN as well as the development of new technologies undermine the viability of Access Deficit Charges (ADC). The universality fund mechanism is therefore often preferred to the ADC mechanism. The collection mechanism of such a universality fund should follow such principles as: collection revenues by minimizing economic efficiency losses through adequate distribution over the different products, an administrative efficiency through collection by the state, which already has the infrastructure, and sustainable revenues base as well as equity between different financing sources.

However, the universality aims in transition countries can be already partly achieved through the regulatory activities in terms of tariff rebalancing and de-averaging in accordance with rural and urban supply costs. The freedom in terms of the introduction of self selected packages should play a positive universality role, minimizing the level of disconnections caused by tariff rebalancing.

Considering regulatory theories, it is important to keep in mind that the outcomes of the regulatory models are quite different if the positive regulatory theory is taken into account. There are two explanations for governmental interventions. On the one hand, the government's role is the correction of market imperfections and maximizing of social welfare. Regulatory agencies should pursue this aim. On the other hand, the interest group may have influence on the formation of public policy with a negative effect on the social welfare maximization. Many economists have contemplated about who may achieve such regulatory capture: big business industries, small business industries or powerful consumer groups. The outcomes of privatization and liberalization plans can also be strongly influenced by, e.g. the incumbent companies, newcomers in the telecommunications sector, telecommunications equipment suppliers as well as international organizations.

In the final section of Chap. 4, the design of regulatory institutions is discussed. This is a key element in order to achieve regulatory efficiency. An independent regulatory authority is necessary to increase investment incentives. Besides this, convergence trends between media and telecommunications industries represent a special challenge to merge the separate authorities in the joined institutional body. Moreover, trends from a federal regulatory system to a centralistic one are observed, because the centralistic system of regulatory institutions seems to fit better within the context of the globalization of telecommunications services.

In Chap. 5, firstly, the link between economic development and telecommunications is investigated. Controlling for the country fixed effects as well as keeping in check the possible causal relationships, the conducted empirical investigation shows that the telecommunications infrastructure has a positive, significant impact on the gross domestic product in transition countries. An opposite direction relationship is also a case: the gross domestic product has a significant und positive influence on the number of telecommunications lines. As a result, this analysis evidences that the development of telecommunications infrastructure in the transition countries fosters their economic development. However, the open questions still are, whether there are any differences in impacts of fixed and mobile telecommunications infrastructure, or whether the governments should invest in telecommunications infrastructure, and what impact have such state investments in terms of economic growth, employment, and the country's competitiveness.

Secondly, different policy options in fixed, mobile and broadband infrastructure and content are considered. The Russian fixed telecommunications sector with low penetration rates is characterized, on the one hand, by stronger competition pressure from other technologies, and on the other hand, by some regulatory advantages in the form of rate-of-return regulation and no unbundling obligations. The privatization and liberalization process has started and still needs to be completed. Privatization aiming at the increase of efficiency gains is a very important challenge for Russia, especially in respect to broadband development. Svyazinvest owns access to the end users in Russia. Such a position in the fixed line network is a natural starting point for market expansion. Svyazinvest urgently needs investment to upgrade infrastructure in order not to lose in the competition process and to increase broadband penetration rates in the whole country. This will respectively increase the growth rates of the Russian economy in general. Whether privatization alone, without establishment of an independent regulatory authority, will increase efficiency gains is still questionable. The liberalization process, which opened the international and long-distance call markets for competition at the beginning of 2006, has to be rolled out into other parts of the sectors, e.g. the local calls market through the introduction of carrier selection and pre-selection, fixed number portability or wholesale product obligations in the cases where the copper local loops of the incumbent operator are still 'essential facilities'. The liberalization of the market is possible through tariff rebalancing, which is still on the way to be completed. At the moment, the tariffs are not fully rebalanced and contain the rate-on-return. Due the tariff rebalancing, the universal service policy is a high priority challenge and has been on the Russian agenda since the beginning of 2000. The main framework of the universal service program is being implemented at the moment and has already yielded the first positive results. The future development of such programs should be considered. The fact that the rates of development between the Russian regions are very different should result in differences in terms of universal service aims. However, in order to increase penetration teledensity rates, other instruments should be considered. The introduction of self-selected packages and flexible payment models are certainly very effective measures. Higher impact measures must be encouraged. These could be Private Public Partnership projects, which showed positive experiences in other countries. The rapidly developing telecommunications technologies are the engine of the sector. By promoting high teledensity through the fostering of other technologies, the trade-off balance should be found between cost efficient technology and network features, e.g. network capability. Upgrade of the fixed telecommunications networks to NGN or implementation of new NGN networks is very current topic. This allows the fixed telecommunications to remain attractive for the end-user and to be able to compete with other technologies. The Russian market players are starting to move in this direction but the Russian Telecommunications Law has not yet supported the NGN development. The law needs significant changes such as the definition of NGN networks in general or implementation of proper interconnections rules based on the open IP network infrastructure. In transition countries, NGN migration issues will play a different role in comparison to e.g. the Western European countries because the existing fixed telecommunications networks are significantly smaller. The operators often must continue the expansion of basic networks, deploying already new technologies.

Mobile telecommunications came into transition countries at the time, when they were suffering under low fixed phone penetration rates and phone services deficits. Thus the role of mobile telecommunications is crucial in narrowing the digital divide in these countries. On the one hand, the mobile telecommunications diffusion depends on the income per capita or respectively, country income. On the other hand, price of mobile telecommunications services is another significant diffusion factor, which can be influenced by the government in the short and middle term period more easily. Due to the fact that the penetration in terms of active SIM-cards may still be improved in Russia, implementation of measures to stimulate mobile diffusion is still reasonable. For example, implementation of MNP as well as MVNOs brought increased competition and penetration to the European markets, which were considered to be quite saturated. The details of the implementation of such measures are quite important. For example, reasonable prices on MNP can ensure the positive influence of MNP. Some countries have regulated prices on ported numbers e.g. Italy or some leave it up to the operators. As this investigation shows, not only the introduction of MVNOs is important but also national roaming obligations can play a role in the success of this measure. Some countries, however, do not use the mandatory obligations and rely on the mandatory negotiations in this respect. Experiences of some countries e.g. France show that expecting mandatory obligations, some market players may offer access for MVNOs on their own initiatives to avoid possible regulatory interventions.

The technological development discussion in Russian mobile telecommunications sector is now at the stage, when the decision should be made mostly in terms of mobile broadband as the next step in the technological development. This will enable the operators to retain subscribers and acquire new customers. In Western Europe, the 3G licenses were acquired by mobile operators at relatively high prices and operators have deployed the 3G networks aiming to get investment back. In Russia, the 3G license prices and coverage requirements are significantly lower. At the same time, new technologies like WiMAX have become available on the market. In some cases, it seems cheaper and more reliable to provide next generation services such as broadband access than traditional technologies.

Broadband development in Russia is lagging behind. The experts argue that the broadband development is crucial for the economical development. One differs between broadband content and broadband infrastructure as well as their demand and supply sides. All broadband influencing factors, which can be influenced by an individual country, are divided into the two following groups: economical/cultural factors und policy factors. To find out how important each factor group is, the broadband policies in three leading economies are compared: South Korea as the leader in broadband penetration, France as the country, which has successfully implemented the EU policy and promoting competition through unbundling as well as the USA as the country where the Internet was born. As a result of this benchmark, two main trends in these countries can be noticed: in South Korea and France the support of government plays a very important role in fostering broadband development. In France, regulatory policy, which supports competition through regulatory access unbundling, ensures high penetration rates. In opposite, such a country as the USA, where the governmental support is less often to happen, the penetration rates are lower. Based on the broader international experiences and expert options, the main instruments fostering broadband development can be structured in terms of support of the demand or supply sides of broadband content or broadband infrastructure. This overview is useful in investigating the status of the implementation of each instrument in Russia and to find out where Russia is relatively strong and where urgent efforts are needed. The broadband content in terms of both demand and supply may be seen as Russian strengths compared to the broadband infrastructure. The initiatives of the Russian government encouraging demand on content as well as partial supply of content in the form of "Electronic Russia 2010" are supported by high qualifications of the populations. In terms of broadband infrastructure, a clear weakness may be found. On the supply side, more transparent regulatory rules that encourage different market players to invest into the infrastructure are required. On the demand side, in the regions where only one kind of broadband infrastructure is available to the end customers, local loop unbundling may make sense in order to increase broadband penetration rates. The government subsidies into the broadband infrastructure are certainly useful in order to decrease the gap between Russia and other countries but must be viewed with some healthy skepticism.

Due to the strong political impact, it is expected that the outcome of the reforming processes will be different in comparison to the normative models. The Russian regulator fits well to the convergence processes, regulating telecommunications and broadcasting, as well as to rapid technological developments and has full central competences. However, it is still lacking independence. This makes the process of regulation very politically sensitive. For the successful integration into the world economy, which is characterized by the strong globalization processes, a developed telecommunications sector is required. If adequate regulatory reforms are implemented, this could have at least two benefits. Firstly, the FDI inflow could increase, stimulating employment and leading to higher incomes and more innovation in Russia. Secondly, the Russian ICT companies, which would be strong through competition and not through protection, could create more successful outflow of FDI from Russia to other countries. Outward FDI is becoming more and more important in the Russian economy, primarily enabling the Russian ICT companies and their domestic suppliers to expand into new markets. The internationalization of business through investment and trade has been one of the main value-enhancing influences in the global economy over the last decade (OECD, 2007b).

Future research in this field can be developed in two main directions. On the one hand, the empirical investigation of the impact of telecommunications infrastructure on the economic performance can be extended when more data becomes available. An interesting empirical question is whether there are differences in the impact on the economic development of the different telecommunications infrastructures. Is the impact of the mobile telecommunications in the transition countries higher in comparison to developed countries? With the development of broadband, the interesting empirical question is the impact of broadband on the economic development and factors influencing broadband penetration in transition economies.

On the other hand, an interesting group of research questions is new developments and respective regulatory policies in transition countries. Are the regulatory interventions required at all? If yes, what should they look like? For example, an exciting topic is convergence issues and how to regulate emerging market structure, where TV companies offer telecommunications services and telecommunications companies offer broadcasting content. What are the regulatory implications if the bundling offers provide significant market power to the market players? What are the essential regulatory implications of the NGN developments, when the concept of the networks has strongly changed? It has been more than 15 years since the transition to a market economy but market structures are still different in the countries that had centrally planned economies. This required different policy implementation in many areas including the telecommunications sector.

References

Aarnikoivu S, Winter J (2006) Mobile broadband wireless access. helsinki university of technology, research seminar on telecommunications business. http://www.tml.tkk.fi/Opinnot/T-109.7510/2006/reports/MBWA.ppt

Aghion P, Howitt P (1992) A model of growth through creative destruction. Econometrica 60:323–351

Aghion P, Howitt P (1998) Endogenous growth theory. MIT Press, Cambridge, MA

Alleman J, Rappoport P (2005) Regulatory failure: time for a new policy paradigm. In: Alleman J, Gassot Y (eds.) Dynamic solutions to policy failures. Communications and Strategies, No. 60, 4th quarter, pp 105–123

Ambrose W, Hennemeyer P, Chapon J-P (1990) Privatizing telecommunications systems: business opportunities in developing countries. IFC Discussion Paper, Washington, DC

Analysis (2004) International broadband market comparisons. Report for the Department of Trade and Industry, UK, Update April 2004

Arellano M (1987) Computing robust standard errors for within-groups estimators. Oxford Bull Econ Stat 49:431–434

Armstrong M (1997) Mobile telephony in the UK. Regulation Initiative Discussion Paper, No. 15, London Business School, UK

Armstrong M (2002) The theory of access pricing and interconnection. In: Cave M, Majumdar S, Vogelsang I (eds.) Handbook of telecommunications economics, vol. 1, Elsevier, Amsterdam, pp 297–386

Armstrong M, Vickers J (1996) Regulatory reform in telecommunications in central and eastern Europe. Econ Transit 4:295–318

Aschauer DA (1989) Is public expenditure productive? J Monet Econ 23:177–200

Audretsch D, Welfens PJJ (2002) The new economy and economic growth in the US and Europe. Springer, Heidelberg

Averch H, Johnson LL (1962) Behaviour of the firm under regulatory constraint. Am Econ Rev 52:1052–1069

Baldwin R, Cave M (1999) Understanding regulation: theory, strategy, and practise. Oxford University Press, New York

Baley EE (1973) Economic theory of regulatory constraint. Lexington Books, Toronto

Baltagi BH (2001) Econometric analysis of panel data, 2nd edn. Wiley, West Sussex

Baron DP, Myerson RB (1982) Regulating a monopolist with unknown costs. Econometrica 50(4):911–930

Barro RJ (1990) Government spending in a simple model of endogenous growth. J Polit Econ 98(5):103–125

Barro RJ, Sala-i-Martin X (1992) Public finance in models of economic growth. Rev Econ Stud 59(4):645–661

Bauer JM (2005) Unbundling policy in the United States: players, outcomes and effects. Presented at the ITS Regional Conference 2005, Porto

Baumgarten G, Markova E (2006) Investitionen und Innovationen durch Deregulierung. Ein Plädoyer für mehr Marktwirtschaft und weniger Regulierung. Computer und Recht. 22 Nr. 10, S. 659–665

Baumol WJ (1977) On the proper cost tests for natural monopolies in a multiproduct industry. Am Econ Rev 67:809–822

Baumol WJ (1982) Contestable markets: an uprising in the theory of industry structure. Am Econ Rev 72:1–15

Baumol WJ Panzar JC, Willing RD (1982) Contestable markets and the theory of industry structure. Harcourt Brace Jovanovich, San Diego

BEEPS (2002) Business environment and enterprise performance survey 2002. EBRD, London http://www.ebrd.com/country/sector/econo/surveys/beeps.htm
Belk JK (2004) Three topics that continue to be misunderstood by the wireless world. http://www.qualcomm.com/enterprise/pdf/3G_Myths_JBelk_5-12-04.pdf
Berndt A, Kunz M (2003) Immer öfter ab und an? Aktuelle Entwicklungen im Bahnsektor. In: Knieps G, Brunekreeft G (eds.) Zwischen Regulierung und Wettbewerb: Netzsektoren in Deutschland. zweite Auflage, Physica, Heidelberg
Best M, Pehrson B (2005) Broadband provisioning for developing countries. Global Symposium for Regulators, ITU, 5 December 2005, Tunisia
Boiteux M (1956) Sur la Gestion des Monopoles Publics Astreints à l'"Equilibre Budgétaire". Econometrica 24:22–40; trans. (1971) "On the management of public monopolies subject to budgetary constraints". Journal of Economic Theory 3:219–240
Borbély D (2005) EU export specialization patterns in selected accession and cohesion countries: tough competition on the EU15 market? Papeles del Este No.9.
Borrmann J, Finsinger J (1999) Markt und Regulierung. Franz Vahlen, München
Borrows J et al (1994) Universal service in the United States: dimensions of the debate. WIK, Diskussionsbeitrag Nr. 124
Bortolotti B et al (2002) Privatization and the sources of performance improvement in the global telecommunications industry. Telecommun Policy 26:243–268
Boutchkova M, Meggison W (2000) Privatization and the rise of global capital markets. Fin Manage 29(1):67–77
Braeutigam RR (1981) Regulation of multiproduct enterprises by rate of return, mark-up, and operation ration. Res Law Econ 3:15–38
Brunekreeft G (2003) Access pricing and Diskriminierung. In: Knieps G, Brunekreeft G (eds.) Zwischen Regulierung und Wettbewerb: Netzsektoren in Deutschland. zweite Auflage, Physica, Heidelberg
Buehler S, Haucap J (2003) Mobile number portability. Discussion Paper No. 17, University of the Federal Armed Forces, Hamburg
Cain P, MacDonald JM (1991) Telephone pricing structures: the effects on universal service. J Regul Econ 3:293–308
Campbell RW (1995) Soviet and Post-Soviet telecommunications: an industry under reform. Westview Press, Boulder
Cave M et al (1993) Measuring changes in the quality of public services. Sage publications, London
Cohen et al (2005) VoIP and regulation. Global Symposium for Regulators, ITU, 5 December 2005, Tunisia
Cullen International (2002) Broadband stimulation in France, Ireland and Sweden. Cullen International Study, September 2002
Cullen International/WIK (2001) Study on universal service in the accession countries. Main Report, June 30, 2001
De Bijl P, Peitz M (2003) Regulation and entry into telecommunications markets. Cambridge Press, Cambridge
DeGraba P (2000) Bill and keep at the central office as the efficient interconnection regime. OPP Working Paper Series, FCC
Dewenter K, Malatesta PH (2001) State-owned and privately-owned firms: an empirical analysis of profitability, leverage, and labour intensity. Am Econ Rev 91:320–334
Dewenter R, Haucap J (2004) Grundlagen und Auswirkungen der Liberalisierung in der deutschen Telekommunikationsbranche. In: Ragnitz J (ed.) Deregulierung in Deutschland – theoretische und empirische Analysen. Tagungsband, Institut für Wirtschaftsforschung Halle, Sonderheft, 2/2004

Dobrovolskaya N, Saluena A (2004) Development of Russian mobile communications. Publication 9, Lappeenranta University of Technology, Northern Dimension Research Centre, Finland Doyle C, Smith JC (1999) Market structure in mobile telecoms: qualified indirect access and the receiver pays principle. Regulation Initiative Discussion Paper Series, No.21

EBRD (1998) Transition report 1998: financial sector in transition. EBRD Publication, London

EBRD (2002) Transition report 2002: agriculture and rural transition. EBRD Publication, London

EBRD (2004) Transition report 2004: infrastructure. EBRD Publication, London

EBRD (2005) Transition report 2005: business in transition. EBRD Publication, London

EC (2005a) Annex to the review of the scope of universal service in accordance with article 15 of directive 2002/22/EC. Commission Staff Working Document

EC (2005b) European electronic communications regulation and markets 2004 (10th Report). 2 December 2004, European Commission, Europe

EC (2006) The challenges of convergence. i2010 High Level Group, Discussion paper, 12 December 2006, European Commission, Europe

EC (2007) European electronic communications regulation and markets 2006 (12th Report). 29 March 2007, European Commission, Europe

Economides N, White LJ (1994) Networks and compatibility: implications for antitrust. Eur Econ Rev 38:651–662

Economist Intelligence Unit (2005) The 2005 e-readiness rankings. White paper of Economist Intelligence Unit, The Economist http://graphics.eiu.com/files/ad_pdfs/2005Ereadiness_Ranking_WP.pdf

ECTA (2007) ECTA Broadband Scorecard 1Q07. European Competitive Telecommunications Association, www.ectaportal.org

EITO (2002) European information technology observatory report 2002, European Information Technology Observatory, Europe

EITO (2004) European information technology observatory report 2004, European Information Technology Observatory, Europe

EITO (2006) European information technology observatory report 2006, European Information Technology Observatory, Europe

Electronic Russia (2004a) Sovremenie telekommunikazii – credstva objedinenija otraslevix programm informatisazii. Infromazionnii Bjulleten 4(13), Prime-TASS

Electronic Russia (2004b) Dejatelnost OAO VolgaTelecom po sozdaniju edinnogo informazionnogo prostranstva PFO. Infromazionnii Bjulleten No. 4(13), Prime-TASS

Evdokimenko E (2005) Priznanie operatori i prespektivi NGN v Rossii. Setevoi Zhurnal, No. 10, 2005

Falch M (2005) Effectiveness of broadband policies. Presented at the ITS Conference 2005 in Porto. http://userpage.fu-berlin.de/~jmueller/its/conf/porto05/start.html

Faulhaber GR (1975) Cross-subsidization, pricing in public enterprises. Am Econ Rev 65(5):966–977

Faulhaber GR (1996) Voting on prices: the political economy of regulation. In: Rosston G, Waterman D, Lawrence Erlbaum Associates (eds.) Interconnection and The Internet. Selected Papers from the 1996 Telecommunications Policy Research Conference, 1997, Mahwah, NJ

FCC (2004) FCC adopts new rules for network unbundling obligations of incumbent local phone carriers. FCC News, December 15, 2004

FCC (2005) Chairman Kevin J.Martin comments on adoption of wireline broadband internet access order. FCC News, August 5, 2005
Federal Law on Communications (2003) Federal Law on Communications, Russian Federation, signed by the President on July 7, 2003 http://www.minsvyaz.ru/ministry/documents/768/2744.shtml
Finsinger J, Kraft K (1984) Mark-up pricing and firm decisions. Zeitschrift für die gesamte Staatswissenschaften, Bd. 140:500–509
Foros O, Hansen B, Sand JY (2002) Demand-side spillovers and semi-collusion in the mobile communications market. J Ind Competition Trade 2:259–278
Gans JS, King SP, Woodbridge G (2001) Numbers to the people: regulation, ownership, and local number portability. Inform Econ Policy 13:167–180
Garcia-Mila T, Mcquire TJ, Poter RH (1996) The effect of public capital in state-level production functions reconsidered. Rev Econ Stat 177–180
Golubeva et al (2005) Development of e-government in St. Petersburg: evaluation of web sites performance and usability. http://unpan1.un.org/intradoc/groups/public/documents/NISPAcee/UNPAN017777.pdf
Gomez-Barroso JL, Feijoo GC (2005) Public policies against the digital divide: a necessary adaptation to different degrees of development. Int J Inform Policy Law 1(2)
Goskomstat (2004) Rossiisky Statistichesky Eshegodnik (CD-Rom)
Grossman GM, Helpman E (1994) Endogenous innovation in the theory of growth. J Econ Persp Winter:23–44
Guislain P (1997) The privatization challenge: a strategic, legal, and institutional analysis of international experience. The World Bank, Washington, DC
Hank I (ed.) (2000) Telecommunications regulation handbook. McCarthy Tetrault, InfoDev, Toronto
Hardy A (1980) The role of the telephone in economic development. Telecommun Policy 4(4):278–286
Haucap J (2003) Telephone number allocation: a property rights approach. Eur J Law Econ 15:91–109
Haucap J, Wey C (2003) Licensing virtual mobile network operators: how (not) to ruin competition. Working Paper, Social Research Paper (WZB), Berlin
Hausman JA (1978) Specification tests in econometrics. Econometrica 46: 1251–1272
Hausman JA (2002) Mobile telephone. In: Cave M, Majumdar S, Vogelsang I (eds.) Handbook of telecommunications economics, vol. 1. Elsevier, Amsterdam, pp 564–605
Holtz-Eakin D (1994) Public-sector capital and the productivity puzzle. Rev Econ Stat 76:12–21
IBM (2003) Fourth report on monitoring of EU candidate countries: telecommunication services sector. IBM, 16 December 2003
IDIS (2005) E-readiness of the Russian regions 2004-2005. Institute for Information Society Development, Moscow
IEF (2006) 2006 index of economic freedom. In: Miles MA, O'Grady MA, Holmes KR (eds.) The link between economic opportunity and prosperity. The Heritage Foundation, Washington, DC
IKS (2005) iKS-Rating: Sotovaja Svyaz v Rossii. iKS, January 2005, http://www.iks-consulting.ru/iksrating_sot_jan_2005.php
ITU (2003) Deployment of IMT-2000 systems handbook. International Telecommunications Union, Geneva
ITU (2005) World telecommunication indicators database 2005, CD-Rom. International Telecommunications Union, Geneva
ITU (2006a) World telecommunication indicators database 2006, CD-Rom. International Telecommunications Union, Geneva

ITU (2006b) World information society report 2006. International Telecommunications Union, Geneva

Jasinski P, Yarrow G (1996) Privatization: an overview of the issues. In: Yarrow G, Jasinski P (eds.) Privatization: critical perspective on the world economy. Routledge, London

Jungmittag A (2002) Innovationsdynamik in der EU: Konvergenz oder Divergenz? Eine Zeitreihen-Querschnittsanalyse. Universität Potsdam, EIIW Diskussions-beitrag 92

Klemperer P (1995) Competition when consumers have switching costs: an overview. Rev Econ Stud 62:515–539

Knieps G, Blankart CB (1994) Das Konzept der Universaldienste im Bereich der Telekommunikation. In: Jahrbuch für Neue Politische Ökonomie, Bd. 13: 238–253

Knieps G (1987) Zur Problematik der internen Subventionierung in öffentlichen Unternehmen". Finanzarchiv 45, Heft 2:268–283

Knieps G (1997) Phasing out sector-specific regulation in competitive telecommunications. Kyklos 50:325–339

Knieps G (2001a) Wettbewerbsökonomie: Regulierungstheorie, Industrieökonomie, Wettbewerbspolitik. Springer, Heidelberg

Knieps G (2001b) The economics of network industries. In: Debreu G, Neuefeind W, Trockel W (eds.) Economic essays – a festschrift for werner hildenbrand. Springer, Heidelberg, pp 275–293

Knieps G (2004) Lecture materials in theory of regulation WS 2004/05. Institut für Verkehrswissenschaft und Regionalpolitik, Freiburg

Knieps G, Vogelsang I (1982) The sustainability concept under alternative behavioural assumptions. Bell J Econ 13:234–241

Krüger J (2000) Produktivität und Wachstum im internationalen Vergleich: Theoretische Modelle und empirische Analysen. Josef Eul Verlag, Reihe: Internationale Wirtschaft, Band 17, Lohmar/Köln

Kruse J (2001) Regulierungsbedarf in der deutschen Telekommunikation? In: Immenga U, Kirchner C, Kruse J, Knieps G (eds.) Telekommunikation im Wettbewerb: Eine Ordnungspolitische Konzeption nach erfolgreicher Marktöffnung. Verlag C.H. Beck, München

Kuznetsova OK, Draskova MA, Cherkasova AV (2006) HR management innovations in Russian telecom companies. Leningrad Research Institute in Telecommunications (LONIIS) presented in the 17th Regional ITS Conference in Berlin

Laffont J-J, Tirole J (1990) The regulation of multiproduct firms I and II. J Public Econ 43:1–66

Laffont J-J, Tirole J (1993) A theory of incentives in procurement and regulation. The MIT Press, Cambridge

Laffort J-J, Tirole J (2000) Competition in telecommunications. Munich Lectures in Economics. The MIT Press, Cambridge

Lee C, Chan-Olmsted SM (2004) Competitive advantage of broadband internet: a comparative study between South Korea and the United States. Telecommun Policy 28:649–677

Lee H, Choudrie J (2002) Investigating broadband technology deployment in South Korea. Report of Brunel- DTI International Technology Services Mission to South Korea, DISC, Brunel University, Uxbridge, UK

Lee Y-S, Bratton W, Shi WW (2005) The role of regulators in promoting broadband in developing countries. Global Symposium for Regulators, ITU, 5 December 2005, Tunisia

Liebowitz S, Margolis S (2002) Network effects. In: Cave M, Majumdar S, Vogelsang I (eds.) Handbook of telecommunications economics, vol. 1. Elsevier, Amsterdam, pp 75–96

Lipton D, Sachs J (1990) Creating a market economy in Eastern Europe: the case of Poland. Brookings Papers Econ Activity 1:75–147
Littlechild SC (1983) Regulation of british telecommunications' profitability. Department of Industry, London
Littlechild SC (2004) Mobile termination charges: calling party pays versus receiving party pays. Cambridge Working Paper in Economics, No. 0426, Cambridge University, Cambridge
Lopez-de-Silanes F (1997) Determinants of privatization prices. Q J Econ 112:965–1025
Lucas RE (1988) On the mechanics of economic development. J Monet Econ 22(1):3–42
Mankiw NG, Romer D, Weil DN (1992) A contribution to the empirics of economic growth. Q J Econ 107(2):407–437
Marder NC (2007) Regulierovanie telecommunicazii v svete smeni paradigmi in: Vestnik Svyazi, No. 2, 2007
Markova E, Ponder JK (2006) Bridging the Eastern European digital divide: significance of mobile telecommunications in Poland and Russia. Commun Strategies 58(2) quarter 2005
Masson T (2000) Third generation (3G) basics CDMA2000 & 3GPP W-CDMA. http://www.agilent.com/cm/wireless/pdf/3G-Seminar2001_02.pdf
McNary R (2000) The network penetration effects of telecommunications privatization and competition. http://home.uchicago.edu/~rmcnary/thesis.pdf
Megginson WL, Netter JM (2001) From state to market: a survey of empirical studies on privatization. J Econ Lit 39:321–389
Minsvyaz (2003a) Generalanaya Chema Razvitiija Obshei Transitnoi Seti dlja Federalnix Setei Sotovoi Podvishnoi Svyai na Period do 2010 goda/General Development Schema of the Transit Network for the Federal Mobile Operators until 2010. GKEC, 24 December 2003. http://www.minsvyaz.ru/ministry/documents/1077/1078/1079/1080.shtml
Minsvyaz (2003b) Ob Itogax Realizazii Federalnoi Zelevoi Programmi "Elektronnaja Rossija" v 2002 i Prioritetnix Napravlenijax i Aktualnix Zadachax Programmi na 2003 god. Postanovlenie Kollegii № 3-1, 25.02.2003, http://www.minsvyaz.ru/ministry/documents/967/984/1003.shtml
Minsvyaz (2004) Federalnja Zelevaja Programma "Electronnaja Rossia", Infokom 2004, http://www.e-rus.ru/upload/docs/20041215163020.ppt
Minsvyaz (2005) Statistika Otrasli 2000-05. http://www.minsvyaz.ru/industry/1193/1524/
Minsvyaz (2006) Statistika Otrasli 2006. http://www.minsvyaz.ru/industry/1193/2346/
Mitnick BM (1980) The political economy of regulation: creating, designing, and removing regulatory forms. Columbia University Press, New York
Motta M (2004) Competition policy: theory and practise. Cambridge University Press, Cambridge
Nellis J, Kireri S (1989) Public enterprise reform: privatization and the world bank. World Dev 17:659–672
Nellis J, Kireri S, Shirley MM (1992) Privatization: the lessons of experience. World Bank, Washington, DC
Noam EM (1997) Reforming universal service: a prerequisite to competition and interconnection. In: Noam EM, Wolfson AJ (eds.) Globalism and localism in telecommunications. Elsevier, Amsterdam
Noll RG (1999) Telecommunications reform in developing countries. AEI-Brookings Joint Center for Regulatory Studies, Working Paper 99–10
Norton SW (1992) Transaction costs, telecommunications, and the microeconomics of macroeconomic growth. Econ Dev Cultural Change 41(1):175–196
OECD (2000) Cellular mobile pricing structures and trends. OECD, Paris

OECD (2002) The telecommunications sector in Russia. OECD J Competition Law Policy 4(3):226–235

OECD (2004) Competition law and policy in Russia. OECD J Competition Law Policy 6(3):7–83

OECD (2005a) OECD communications outlook. OECD, Paris

OECD (2005b) ICT and economic growth: evidence from OECD countries, industries and firms. OECD, Paris

OECD (2005c) New GDP comparisons based on purchasing power parities for the year 2002. OECD, Paris

OECD (2006) OECD information technology outlook. OECD, Paris

OECD (2007a) OECD communications outlook. OECD, Paris

OECD (2007b) International investment perspectives 2007: freedom of investment in a changing world. OECD, Paris

Panzar JC, Willing RD (1977) Free entry and the sustainability of natural monopoly. Bell J Econ 8:1–22

Panzar JC, Willing RD (1981) Economies of scope. Am Econ Rev 71:268–272

Parfenov BA (2006) Ozhidanie shirokopolosnogo buma. Vestnik Svyazi, No 1, 2006

Peltzman S (1976) Toward a more general theory of regulation. J Law Econ 19:211–240

Petuhova S, Vronetz A (2000) Regulation of the telecommunication sector in Russia: direct foreign investments and options for competition. In: Welfens PJJ, Graack C, Grinberg R, Yarrow G (eds.) Towards competition in network industries. Springer, Heidelberg

Piatkowski M (2004) The impact of ICT on growth in transition economies. Tiger Working Paper Series, No. 59, Warsaw

Piazolo D (1999) Growth effects of institutional change and European integration. Econ Syst 23(4):305–330

Podpłońska M (2007) VoIP and its impact on competition in the telecommunications sector. Presentation at the ITU's Workshop "Future of Voice", Geneva, 15–16 January, 2007. http://www.itu.int/osg/spu/ni/voice/presentations/S5-4-UKE-Podplonska.ppt

Point Topic (2005) World broadband statistics 2Q 2005. September 2005, Point Topic http://point-topic.com/

Point Topic (2007) World broadband statistics 4Q 2006. March 2007, Point Topic http://point-topic.com/

Ponder JK (2005) Workable e-government from the perspective of new EU member states, Discussion Paper

Posner RA (1971) Taxation by regulation. Bell J Econ Manage Sci 2(1):22–50

Posner RA (1974) Theories of economic regulation. Bell J Econ Manage Sci 5(2):335–358

Ramsey F (1927) A contribution to the theory of taxation. Econ J 37:47–61

Riordan MH (2002) Universal residential telephone service. In: Cave M, Majumdar S, Vogelsang I (eds.) Handbook of telecommunications economics, vol. 1. Elsevier, Amsterdam, pp 477–485

Robles A, Feijóo C, Gómez JL (2005) Promoting broadband in developing countries: lessons from advanced countries experience. Presented at the 16th European Regional Conference of the International Telecommunications Society, Porto, Portugal

Roland G (1994) The role of political constraints in transition strategies. Econ Transit 2: 27–41

Röller L-H, Wavermann L (1996) The impact of telecommunications infrastructure on economic development. In: Howit P (ed.) The implications of knowledge-based growth for microeconomic policies. University of Calgary Press, Calgary, pp 363–387

Röller L-H, Wavermann L (2001) Telecommunications infrastructure and economic development: a simultaneous approach. Am Econ Rev 91(4):909–923

Romer PM (1990) Endogenous technological change. Journal of Political Economy 98(5): 71–102

Ros AJ (2003) The impact of the regulatory process and price-cap regulation in latin american telecommunications markets. Rev Netw Econ 2(3):270–286

Ros AJ, Banerjee A (2000) Telecommunications privatization and tariff rebalancing: evidence from Latin America. Telecommun Policy 24:233–252

Ros AJ, Banerjee A (2004) Patterns in global fixed and mobile telecommunications development: a cluster analysis. Telecommun Policy 28:107–132

Rovizzi L, Thompson D (1995) The regulation of product quality in public utilities. In: Bishop M, Kay J, Mayer C (eds.) The regulatory challenge. Oxford University Press, Oxford

Sappington D, Weisman D (1996) Designing incentive regulation for the telecommunication industry. The MIT Press, Cambridge

Saunders RJ, Warford JJ, Wellenius B (1994) Telecommunications and economic development, 2nd edn. The World Bank, Washington DC

Schenk K-E, Kruse J, Mueller J (eds.) (1997) Telecommunications take-off in transition countries. Avebury, Aldershot

Schipke A (2001) Why do governments divest? The Macroeconomics of Privatization. Springer, Heidelberg

Sedix VA, Fadin DU (2007) FMC: ocherednoi vitok consolidazii setei svyazi in: Vestnik Svyazi, No. 6

Sharkey WW (1982) The theory of natural monopoly. Cambridge University Press, Cambrige

Shaw R (2006) Networks in transition: emerging policy and regulatory challenges of next generation networks. ITU-T/ITU-D Workshop: "Standardization and development of next generation networks", Tanzania, 3–5 October 2006

Shy O (1999) The economics of network industries. Cambridge University Press, Cambridge

Small J, Aoki R (1999) The economics of number portability: switching costs and two-part tariffs. Working paper, University of Auckland, Auckland

Smith A (1973) An inquiry into the nature and causes of the wealth of nations. Penguin Books, Harmondsworth

Solow RM (1956) A contribution to the theory of economic growth. Q J Econ 70(1):65–94

Solow RM (1957) Technical change and the aggregate production function. Rev Econ Stat 39(3):312–320

Sotovik (2004) Konkurenzija na Rinke Sotovoi Svyazi RF. "Mif i Realnost". Sotovik, September 2004, http://www.sotovik.ru/analyt/index_172.html

Sotovik (2006a) Chislennost "aktivnix abonentov" sotovoi svyazi v RF na konez 2Q06 previsila 95 millionov. http://www.sotovik.ru/analyt/index_429.html?print=1 (05.05.2007)

Sotovik (2006b) Obzor rinka Sotovoi Svyazi PR. Itogi 4Q05 and 2005. http://www.sotovik.ru/analyt/index_348.html

Spence AM (1975) Monopoly, quality, and regulation. Bell J Econ 16:917–929

Stigler GJ (1968) Barriers to entry, economies of scale, and firm size. In: Stigler GJ (ed.): The organization of industry. Irwin, Homewood, pp 67–70

Stigler GJ (1971) The theory of economic regulation. Bell J Econ 2:3–21

Stock JH, Watson MW (2007) Introduction to econometrics. Addison-Wesley Series in Economics, Reading, MA

Taylor LD (1994) Telecommunications demand in theory and practice. Kluwer, Dorderecht

Telecom Policy Report (2006) Canada implements sweeping local deregulation. Telecom Policy Report, April 10, 2006. http://findarticles.com/p/articles/mi_m0PJR/is_15_4/ai_n16121106

The Global Competitiveness Report (2005) The global competitiveness report 2005–2006. In: Lopez-Claros A, Porter ME, Schwab K (eds.) Policies underspinning rising prosperity. World Economic Forum, Palgrave Macmillan, Hampshire

The Global Information Technology Report (2005) In: Dutta S, Lopez-Claros A (eds.) The global information technology report: efficiency in an increasingly connected world 2004–2005. World Economic Forum, Palgrave Macmillan, Hampshire

Thompson H, Renard O, Wright J (2005) Mobile termination. In: Dewenter R, Haucap J (eds.) Access pricing: theory, practice, empirical evidence. Elsevier, Amsterdam

Tjulpanow SI (1969) Ocherki po politicheskoi ekonomii. Misl', Moskva

Toivanen O (2004) Choosing standards. Discussion paper of Helsinki Center of Economic Research No. 28

Troika-Dialog (2004) Rostelecom Shunning the Last Mile? July 2004, Troika Dialog Research, Moscow

Troika-Dialog (2006) Fixed line sector: svyazinvest privatization insights. March 2006, Troika Dialog Research, Moscow

Ulset S (2002) Mobile virtual network operators: a strategic transaction cost analysis of preliminary experiences. Telecommun Policy 26:537–549

Vagliasindi M (2004) The role of investment and regulatory reforms in the development of infrastructure across transition economies. Utilities Policy, 12(4):303–314

Vagliasindi M, Taubman C (2004) Fixed and mobile competition in transition economies. http://userpage.fu-berlin.de/~jmueller/its/conf/berlin04/Papers/Taubman_Vagliasindi.pdf

Valleti TM (2003) Is mobile telephony a natural oligopoly? Rev Ind Org 22(1):47–65

Van Ark B (2001) The renewal of the old economy: an international comparative perspective. OECD STI Working Paper 5, Paris

Van Ark B, Piatkowski M (2004) Productivity, innovation and ICT in old and new Europe. Research Memorandum GD-69, March 2004

VNIICI (1982) Problemi Funktionirovanija i Razvitija Infrastructuri Narodnogo Xozjaistva. Institute for Systems Studies, Moskva

Vogelsang I (2003) The German telecommunications reform – where did it come from, where is it, and where is it going? Perspektiven der Wirtschaftspolitik 3(4):313–340

Vogelsang I, Mitchel BM (1991) Telecommunications pricing: theory and practice. University Press, Cambridge

Von Hirschausen C (1999) What infrastructure policies for post-socialist eastern europe? lesson from the public investment programs (PIP) in the Baltic countries. Eur Asia Stud 51(3):417–432

Von Hirschausen C (2002) Modernizing infrastructure in transformation economies: paving the way to European enlargement. Edward Elgar, Cheltenham, UK

Von Hirschausen C, Dodonov B, Opitz P, Sudulov P (2002) Efficient infrastructure supply for economic development in transition countries – the case of Ukraine. Post-Communist Econ 14(2):149–167

Von Hirschhausen C, Sugolov P, Dodonov B (2002) Infrastructure policies and economic development in east European transition countries: first evidence. Paper presented at the Workshop on Applied Infrastructure Research, 2002, Berlin

Wallsten SJ (1999) An empirical analysis of competition, privatization, and regulation in Africa and Latin America. World Bank Policy Research Working Paper, No. 2136

Wallsten SJ (2000) Telecommunications privatization in developing countries: the real effects of exclusivity periods. SIEPR Policy Paper No. 99–21

Wallsten SJ (2002) Does sequencing matter? regulation and privatization in telecommunications reforms. World Bank Policy Research Working Paper No. 2817

Waverman L, Meschi M, Fuss M (2005) The impact of telecoms on economic growth in developing countries. Africa: the impact of mobile phones. Vodafone Policy Paper Series No. 2, March 2005, Vodafone Group, pp 10–23

WDI (2003) World development indicators 2003 (CD-Rom). The International Bank for Reconstruction and Development, Washington DC

WDI (2005) World development indicators 2005 (CD-Rom). The International Bank for Reconstruction and Development, Washington DC

Welfens PJJ, Jungmittag A (2002) Internet, Telekomliberalisierung und Wirtschaftswachstum: 10 Gebote für ein digitales Wirtschaftswunder. Springer, Heidelberg

Welfens PJJ (1996) Telecommunications in systemic transformation: theoretical issues and policy options. In: Welfens PJJ, Yarrow G (eds.) Telecommunications and energy in systemic transformation. Springer, Heildelberg

Welfens PJJ (2000) Competition, privatization and foreign direct investment in network industries. In: Welfens PJJ, Graack C, Grinberg R, Yarrow G (eds.) Towards competition in network industries. Springer, Heidelberg

Welfens, PJJ (2006) Rational regulatory policy for the digital economy: theory and EU policy options. EIIW Discussion Paper 145, October 2006

Welfens PJJ et al (2005) Internetwitschaft 2010: Perspektiven und Auswirkungen. Physica, Heidelberg

Welfens PJJ, Graack C (1997) Telekommunikationsmärkte in Europa: Marktzutrittshemmnisse and Privatisierungsprobleme aus Sicht der Neuen Politischen Ökonomie. In: Schenk K-E, Schmidtchen D, Streit M (eds.) Neue Politische Ökonomie der Integration und Öffnung von Infrastrukturnetzen. Band 16, J.C.B. Mohr, Tübingen, pp 206–247

Welfens PJJ, Graack C (1996) Telekommunikationswirtschaft: Deregulierung, Privatisierung und Internationalisierung. Springer, Heidelberg

Wellenius B (2000) Extending telecommunications beyond the market: toward universal service in competitive environments. Note No. 206, The World Bank Group, Washington DC

Willing RD (1979) The theory of network access pricing. In: Trebing HM (ed.) Issues in public utility regulation. Public Utilities Papers, Michigan State University, Michigan

World Bank (2002) Building institutions for the markets. World Development Report, The World Bank, Washington DC

Wright J (1999) Competition and termination in cellular networks. Working paper, Centre for Research in Network Economics and Communications, University of Auckland, New Zealand

WTO (2004) World trade report 2004: exploring the linkages between the domestic policy environment and international trade. WTO, Geneva

Yarrow G (1986) Privatization in theory and practice. Econ Policy 2:323–364

Zajac EE (1970) A geometric treatment of averch-johnson's behavior of the firm model. Am Econ Rev 60:117–125

Index